SUPER HOROSCOPE
LIBRA

2009

SEPTEMBER 23 – OCTOBER 22

BERKLEY BOOKS, NEW YORK

THE BERKLEY PUBLISHING GROUP
Published by the Penguin Group
Penguin Group (USA) Inc.
375 Hudson Street, New York, New York 10014, USA
Penguin Group (Canada), 90 Eglinton Avenue East, Suite 700, Toronto, Ontario M4P 2Y3, Canada
(a division of Pearson Penguin Canada Inc.)
Penguin Books Ltd., 80 Strand, London WC2R 0RL, England
Penguin Group Ireland, 25 St. Stephen's Green, Dublin 2, Ireland (a division of Penguin Books Ltd.)
Penguin Group (Australia), 250 Camberwell Road, Camberwell, Victoria 3124, Australia
(a division of Pearson Australia Group Pty. Ltd.)
Penguin Books India Pvt. Ltd., 11 Community Centre, Panchsheel Park, New Delhi—110 017, India
Penguin Group (NZ), 67 Apollo Drive, Rosedale, North Shore 0632, New Zealand
(a division of Pearson New Zealand Ltd.)
Penguin Books (South Africa) (Pty.) Ltd., 24 Sturdee Avenue, Rosebank, Johannesburg 2196,
South Africa

Penguin Books Ltd., Registered Offices: 80 Strand, London WC2R 0RL, England

2009 SUPER HOROSCOPE LIBRA

The publishers regret that they cannot answer individual letters requesting personal horoscope information.

PRINTING HISTORY
Berkley trade paperback edition / July 2008

Berkley trade paperback ISBN: 978-0-425-22003-0

Library of Congress Cataloging-in-Publication Data

ISSN: 1535-8976

PRINTED IN THE UNITED STATES OF AMERICA

10 9 8 7 6 5 4 3 2 1

CONTENTS

THE CUSP-BORN LIBRA

Are you *really* a Libra? If your birthday falls around the fourth week in September, at the very beginning of Libra, will you still retain the traits of Virgo, the sign of the Zodiac before Libra? And what if you were born late in October—are you more Scorpio than Libra? Many people born at the edge, or cusp, of a sign have great difficulty in determining exactly what sign they are. If you are one of these people, here's how you can figure it out, once and for all.

Consult the cusp table on the facing page, then locate the year of your birth. The table will tell you the precise days on which the Sun entered and left your sign for the year of your birth. In that way you can determine if you are a true Libra—or whether you are a Virgo or Scorpio—according to the variations in cusp dates from year to year (see also page 17).

If you were born at the beginning or end of Libra, yours is a lifetime reflecting a process of subtle transformation. Your life on Earth will symbolize a significant change in consciousness, for you are either about to enter a whole new way of living or are leaving one behind.

If you were born at the beginning of Libra, you may want to read the horoscope book for Virgo as well as Libra, for Virgo holds the keys to much of the complexity of your spirit. Virgo reflects certain hidden weaknesses, uncertainties, and your secret wishes. You are eager to get involved with another person, yet you are pulled back often from total involvement by your sense of propriety or your wish to be pure and unspoiled. You hover between poetic romanticism and stiff mental analyzing.

At best, your powers of criticism serve you to develop your potentials and enhance the life of your partner. In that way, you are helpful and loving, considerate and faithful—a pure marriage of mind and body, head and heart.

If you were born at the end of Libra, you may want to read the horoscope book for Scorpio as well as Libra. Scorpio dominates your finances, money, assets, potentials, and your values in general. Although your sexual expectancies can be naive, unrealistic, and even adolescent, you are passionate, excitable, and highly seductive.

You may vacillate between a desire to please another and a fanatical determination to maintain control and survive on your own. You can love with a fatal obsession, where you will blind your eyes to keep peace in a relationship—then suddenly declare war. Although you could prolong the agony of a situation in order to avoid a confrontation, you are the personification of awakening passion and a spirit that longs for the joys of companionship and the simple harmonies of life.

THE CUSPS OF LIBRA

DATES SUN ENTERS LIBRA (LEAVES VIRGO)

September 23 every year from 1900 to 2010, except for the following:

September 22					September 24
1948	1968	1981	1992	2001	1903
52	72	84	93	2004	07
56	76	85	96	2005	
60	77	88	97	2008	
64	80	89	2000	2009	

DATES SUN LEAVES LIBRA (ENTERS SCORPIO)

October 23 every year from 1900 to 2010, except for the following:

October 22	October 24			
1992	1902	1911	1923	1943
1996	03	14	27	47
2000	06	15	31	51
2004	07	18	35	55
2008	10	19	39	59

THE ASCENDANT: LIBRA RISING

Could you be a "double" Libra? That is, could you have Libra as your Rising sign as well as your Sun sign? The tables on pages 8–9 will tell you Libras what your Rising sign happens to be. Just find the hour of your birth, then find the day of your birth, and you will see which sign of the Zodiac is your Ascendant, as the Rising sign is called. The Ascendant is called that because it is the sign rising on the eastern horizon at the time of your birth. For a more detailed discussion of the Rising sign and the twelve houses of the Zodiac, see pages 17–20.

The Ascendant, or Rising sign, is placed on the 1st house in a horoscope, of which there are twelve houses. The 1st house represents your response to the environment—your unique response. Call it identity, personality, ego, self-image, facade, come-on, body-mind-spirit—whatever term best conveys to you the meaning of the you that acts and reacts in the world. It is a you that is always changing, discovering a new you. Your identity started with birth and early environment, over which you had little conscious control, and continues to experience, to adjust, to express itself. The 1st house also represents how others see you. Has anyone ever guessed your sign to be your Rising sign? People may respond to that personality, that facade, that body type governed by your Rising sign.

Your Ascendant, or Rising sign, modifies your basic Sun sign personality, and it affects the way you act out the daily predictions for your Sun sign. If your Rising sign indeed is Libra, what follows is a description of its effects on your horoscope. If your Rising sign is not Libra but some other sign of the Zodiac, you may wish to read the horoscope book for that sign as well.

With Libra on the Ascendant, Venus—the planet that rules Libra—is rising in your 1st house. Venus here gives you the kindest disposition, genial and likable, and an elegant bearing, always graceful with just a touch of showiness. Your mind is well disposed to learning all that is subtle and fine, artistic subjects in general, and your body is attuned to refined, symmetrical rhythms. You could unselfishly put yourself in the service of noble causes, or you could get carried away with a life of sensual pleasure. A vain pursuit of brilliant company or an endless search for the perfect lover could waste your talents.

Your need for partnership underscores most of your activities, not only your love experiences. You have a highly developed social consciousness which acts as a spur to other people. Your insistence on fairness and honesty maintains the standards of any group of which you are a member. You bring a well balanced sense of social values to bear on group activity. The group dynamic is reciprocal, as you benefit by being needed, feeling that people appreciate and admire you. Though satisfying, your social and cultural participation is not sufficient. You must find a love partner with whom you can share everyday living as well as more exalted purposes.

You are well adapted for a life in tandem with another person. Like the Scales, the zodiacal symbol of Libra, you need that sensitive presence of another to achieve balance, to come to rest, both sides of the scales poised in perfect agreement. Alone, you may at times be indecisive, even idle. Seeing all sides of a question and being loathe to choose one side may cause an inability to act. When partnered, you gain a sponsorship that frees you. You can then weigh matters, make decisions, exercise judgments. As arbiter, judge, lawyer, you have no peer.

You put your individual stamp of beauty and harmony on your environment. Style-conscious, with an eye for line, color, and movement, you express your artistic sensibilities in all your surroundings. A blend of loveliness and liveliness is what you seek. Sometimes you can be fickle, a faddist. You can bewilder your close circle by endless experimentation with what pleases you and feels right. This vacillation is equally true in your love life; you may exhaust a round of admirers before you choose to settle down.

More sensitive than most people to nuances, perhaps underneath the surface activity you sense something awry; you will shy away from any situation or suggestion of tastelessness and vulgarity. Ever seeking harmony, you may need to select and discard until you find the right blend. Through this selection process you never really lose your intensity. You are deeply imbued with the belief that you can and will find equilibrium; this belief constantly nourishes, renews your spirit. But you can lose other things, such as opportunities to utilize your talents or a chance to negotiate in a personal relationship.

The key words for you with Libra Rising are balance and harmony. You may need to settle for less than your idealized conceptions so that you can deeply experience, rather than merely visualize, what life and love have actually to offer.

RISING SIGNS FOR LIBRA

Hour of Birth*	Day of Birth		
	September 22–26	September 27–30	October 1–6
Midnight	Cancer	Cancer	Cancer
1 AM	Leo	Leo	Leo
2 AM	Leo	Leo	Leo
3 AM	Leo	Leo	Virgo
4 AM	Virgo	Virgo	Virgo
5 AM	Virgo	Virgo	Virgo
6 AM	Libra	Libra	Libra
7 AM	Libra	Libra	Libra
8 AM	Libra	Scorpio	Scorpio
9 AM	Scorpio	Scorpio	Scorpio
10 AM	Scorpio	Scorpio	Scorpio; Sagittarius 10/6
11 AM	Sagittarius	Sagittarius	Sagittarius
Noon	Sagittarius	Sagittarius	Sagittarius
1 PM	Sagittarius	Capricorn	Capricorn
2 PM	Capricorn	Capricorn	Capricorn
3 PM	Capricorn	Aquarius	Aquarius
4 PM	Aquarius	Aquarius	Aquarius; Pisces 10/3
5 PM	Pisces	Pisces	Pisces; Aries 10/6
6 PM	Aries	Aries	Aries
7 PM	Aries	Aries	Taurus
8 PM	Taurus	Taurus	Taurus; Gemini 10/2
9 PM	Gemini	Gemini	Gemini
10 PM	Gemini	Gemini	Gemini; Cancer 10/2
11 PM	Cancer	Cancer	Cancer

*Hour of birth given here is for Standard Time in any time zone. If your hour of birth was recorded in Daylight Saving Time, subtract one hour from it and consult that hour in the table above. For example, if you were born at 6 AM D.S.T., see 5 AM above.

Hour of Birth*	Day of Birth		
	October 7–12	October 13–18	October 19–24
Midnight	Leo	Leo	Leo
1 AM	Leo	Leo	Leo
2 AM	Leo	Leo; Virgo 10/15	Virgo
3 AM	Virgo	Virgo	Virgo
4 AM	Virgo	Virgo	Virgo; Libra 10/22
5 AM	Libra	Libra	Libra
6 AM	Libra	Libra	Libra
7 AM	Libra	Libra; Scorpio 10/15	Scorpio
8 AM	Scorpio	Scorpio	Scorpio
9 AM	Scorpio	Scorpio	Scorpio; Sagittarius 10/22
10 AM	Sagittarius	Sagittarius	Sagittarius
11 AM	Sagittarius	Sagittarius	Sagittarius
Noon	Sagittarius; Capricorn 10/11	Capricorn	Capricorn
1 PM	Capricorn	Capricorn	Capricorn
2 PM	Capricorn; Aquarius 10/11	Aquarius	Aquarius
3 PM	Aquarius	Aquarius; Pisces 10/17	Pisces
4 PM	Pisces	Pisces	Pisces; Aries 10/21
5 PM	Aries	Aries	Aries
6 PM	Aries; Taurus 10/10	Taurus	Taurus
7 PM	Taurus	Taurus; Gemini 10/18	Gemini
8 PM	Gemini	Gemini	Gemini
9 PM	Gemini	Gemini; Cancer 10/17	Cancer
10 PM	Cancer	Cancer	Cancer
11 PM	Cancer	Cancer	Cancer; Leo 10/22

*See note on facing page.

THE PLACE OF ASTROLOGY IN TODAY'S WORLD

Does astrology have a place in the fast-moving, ultra-scientific world we live in today? Can it be justified in a sophisticated society whose outriders are already preparing to step off the moon into the deep space of the planets themselves? Or is it just a hangover of ancient superstition, a psychological dummy for neurotics and dreamers of every historical age?

These are the kind of questions that any inquiring person can be expected to ask when they approach a subject like astrology which goes beyond, but never excludes, the materialistic side of life.

The simple, single answer is that astrology works. It works for many millions of people in the western world alone. In the United States there are 10 million followers and in Europe, an estimated 25 million. America has more than 4000 practicing astrologers, Europe nearly three times as many. Even down-under Australia has its hundreds of thousands of adherents. In the eastern countries, astrology has enormous followings, again, because it has been proved to work. In India, for example, brides and grooms for centuries have been chosen on the basis of their astrological compatibility.

Astrology today is more vital than ever before, more practicable because all over the world the media devotes much space and time to it, more valid because science itself is confirming the precepts of astrological knowledge with every new exciting step. The ordinary person who daily applies astrology intelligently does not have to wonder whether it is true nor believe in it blindly. He can see it working for himself. And, if he can use it—and this book is designed to help the reader to do just that—he can make living a far richer experience, and become a more developed personality and a better person.

Astrology and Relationships

Astrology is the science of relationships. It is not just a study of planetary influences on man and his environment. It is the study of man himself.

We are at the center of our personal universe, of all our relationships. And our happiness or sadness depends on how we act, how we relate to the people and things that surround us. The emotions that we generate have a distinct effect—for better or worse—on the world around us. Our friends and our enemies will confirm this. Just look in the mirror the next time you are angry. In other words, each of us is a kind of sun or planet or star radiating our feelings on the environment around us. Our influence on our personal universe, whether loving, helpful, or destructive, varies with our changing moods, expressed through our individual character.

Our personal "radiations" are potent in the way they affect our moods and our ability to control them. But we usually are able to throw off our emotion in some sort of action—we have a good cry, walk it off, or tell someone our troubles—before it can build up too far and make us physically ill. Astrology helps us to understand the universal forces working on us, and through this understanding, we can become more properly adjusted to our surroundings so that we find ourselves coping where others may flounder.

The Challenge of Love

The challenge of love lies in recognizing the difference between infatuation, emotion, sex, and, sometimes, the intentional deceit of the other person. Mankind, with its record of broken marriages, despair, and disillusionment, is obviously not very good at making these distinctions.

Can astrology help?

Yes. In the same way that advance knowledge can usually help in any human situation. And there is probably no situation as human, as poignant, as pathetic and universal, as the failure of man's love.

Love, of course, is not just between man and woman. It involves love of children, parents, home, and friends. But the big problems usually involve the choice of partner.

Astrology has established degrees of compatibility that exist between people born under the various signs of the Zodiac. Because people are individuals, there are numerous variations and modifications. So the astrologer, when approached on mate and marriage matters, makes allowances for them. But the fact remains that some groups of people are suited for each other and some are not, and astrology has expressed this in terms of characteristics we all can study and use as a personal guide.

No matter how much enjoyment and pleasure we find in the different aspects of each other's character, if it is not an overall compatibility, the chances of our finding fulfillment or enduring happiness in each other are pretty hopeless. And astrology can help us to find someone compatible.

Astrology and Science

Closely related to our emotions is the "other side" of our personal universe, our physical welfare. Our body, of course, is largely influenced by things around us over which we have very little control. The phone rings, we hear it. The train runs late. We snag our stocking or cut our face shaving. Our body is under a constant bombardment of events that influence our daily lives to varying degrees.

The question that arises from all this is, what makes each of us act so that we have to involve other people and keep the ball of activity and evolution rolling? This is the question that both science and astrology are involved with. The scientists have attacked it from different angles: anthropology, the study of human evolution as body, mind and response to environment; anatomy, the study of bodily structure; psychology, the science of the human mind; and so on. These studies have produced very impressive classifications and valuable information, but because the approach to the problem is fragmented, so is the result. They remain "branches" of science. Science generally studies effects. It keeps turning up wonderful answers but no lasting solutions. Astrology, on the other hand, approaches the question from the broader viewpoint. Astrology began its inquiry with the totality of human experience and saw it as an effect. It then looked to find the cause, or at least the prime movers, and during thousands of years of observation of man and his *universal* environment came up with the extraordinary principle of planetary influence—or astrology, which, from the Greek, means the science of the stars.

Modern science, as we shall see, has confirmed much of astrology's foundations—most of it unintentionally, some of it reluctantly, but still, indisputably.

It is not difficult to imagine that there must be a connection between outer space and Earth. Even today, scientists are not too sure how our Earth was created, but it is generally agreed that it is only a tiny part of the universe. And as a part of the universe, people on Earth see and feel the influence of heavenly bodies in almost every aspect of our existence. There is no doubt that the Sun has the greatest influence on life on this planet. Without it there would be no life, for without it there would be no warmth, no division into day and night, no cycles of time or season at all. This is clear and easy to see. The influence of the Moon, on the other hand, is more subtle, though no less definite.

There are many ways in which the influence of the Moon manifests itself here on Earth, both on human and animal life. It is a well-known fact, for instance, that the large movements of water on our planet—that is the ebb and flow of the tides—are caused by the Moon's gravitational pull. Since this is so, it follows that these water movements do not occur only in the oceans, but that all bodies of water are affected, even down to the tiniest puddle.

The human body, too, which consists of about 70 percent water, falls within the scope of this lunar influence. For example the menstrual cycle of most women corresponds to the 28-day lunar month; the period of pregnancy in humans is 273 days, or equal to nine lunar months. Similarly, many illnesses reach a crisis at the change of the Moon, and statistics in many countries have shown that the crime rate is highest at the time of the Full Moon. Even human sexual desire has been associated with the phases of the Moon. But it is in the movement of the tides that we get the clearest demonstration of planetary influence, which leads to the irresistible correspondence between the so-called metaphysical and the physical.

Tide tables are prepared years in advance by calculating the future positions of the Moon. Science has known for a long time that the Moon is the main cause of tidal action. But only in the last few years has it begun to realize the possible extent of this influence on mankind. To begin with, the ocean tides do not rise and fall as we might imagine from our personal observations of them. The Moon as it orbits around Earth sets up a circular wave of attraction which pulls the oceans of the world after it, broadly in an east to west direction. This influence is like a phantom wave crest, a loop of power stretching from pole to pole which passes over and around the Earth like an invisible shadow. It travels with equal effect across the land masses and, as scientists were recently amazed to observe, caused oysters placed in the dark in the middle of the United States where there is no sea to open their shells to receive the nonexistent tide. If the land-locked oysters react to this invisible signal, what effect does it have on us who not so long ago in evolutionary time came out of the sea and still have its salt in our blood and sweat?

Less well known is the fact that the Moon is also the primary force behind the circulation of blood in human beings and animals, and the movement of sap in trees and plants. Agriculturists have established that the Moon has a distinct influence on crops, which explains why for centuries people have planted according to Moon cycles. The habits of many animals, too, are directed by the movement of the Moon. Migratory birds, for instance, depart only at or near the time of the Full Moon. And certain sea creatures, eels in particular, move only in accordance with certain phases of the Moon.

Know Thyself—Why?

In today's fast-changing world, everyone still longs to know what the future holds. It is the one thing that everyone has in common: rich and poor, famous and infamous, all are deeply concerned about tomorrow.

But the key to the future, as every historian knows, lies in the past. This is as true of individual people as it is of nations. You cannot understand your future without first understanding your past, which is simply another way of saying that you must first of all know yourself.

The motto "know thyself" seems obvious enough nowadays, but it was originally put forward as the foundation of wisdom by the ancient Greek philosophers. It was then adopted by the "mystery religions" of the ancient Middle East, Greece, Rome, and is still used in all genuine schools of mind training or mystical discipline, both in those of the East, based on yoga, and those of the West. So it is universally accepted now, and has been through the ages.

But how do you go about discovering what sort of person you are? The first step is usually classification into some sort of system of types. Astrology did this long before the birth of Christ. Psychology has also done it. So has modern medicine, in its way.

One system classifies people according to the source of the impulses they respond to most readily: the muscles, leading to direct bodily action; the digestive organs, resulting in emotion; or the brain and nerves, giving rise to thinking. Another such system says that character is determined by the endocrine glands, and gives us such labels as "pituitary," "thyroid," and "hyperthyroid" types. These different systems are neither contradictory nor mutually exclusive. In fact, they are very often different ways of saying the same thing.

Very popular, useful classifications were devised by Carl Jung, the eminent disciple of Freud. Jung observed among the different faculties of the mind, four which have a predominant influence on character. These four faculties exist in all of us without exception, but not in perfect balance. So when we say, for instance, that someone is a "thinking type," it means that in any situation he or she tries to be rational. Emotion, which may be the opposite of thinking, will be his or her weakest function. This thinking type can be sensible and reasonable, or calculating and unsympathetic. The emotional type, on the other hand, can often be recognized by exaggerated language—everything is either marvelous or terrible—and in extreme cases they even invent dramas and quarrels out of nothing just to make life more interesting.

The other two faculties are intuition and physical sensation. The sensation type does not only care for food and drink, nice clothes and furniture; he or she is also interested in all forms of physical experience. Many scientists are sensation types as are athletes and nature-lovers. Like sensation, intuition is a form of perception and we all possess it. But it works through that part of the mind which is not under conscious control—consequently it sees meanings and connections which are not obvious to thought or emotion. Inventors and original thinkers are always intuitive, but so, too, are superstitious people who see meanings where none exist.

Thus, sensation tells us what is going on in the world, feeling (that is, emotion) tells us how important it is to ourselves, thinking enables us to interpret it and work out what we should do about it, and intuition tells us what it means to ourselves and others. All four faculties are essential, and all are present in every one of us. But some people are guided chiefly by one, others by another. In addition, Jung also observed a division of the human personality into the extrovert and the introvert, which cuts across these four types.

A disadvantage of all these systems of classification is that one cannot tell very easily where to place oneself. Some people are reluctant to admit that they act to please their emotions. So they deceive themselves for years by trying to belong to whichever type they think is the "best." Of course, there is no best; each has its faults and each has its good points.

The advantage of the signs of the Zodiac is that they simplify classification. Not only that, but your date of birth is personal—

it is unarguably yours. What better way to know yourself than by going back as far as possible to the very moment of your birth? And this is precisely what your horoscope is all about, as we shall see in the next section.

WHAT IS A HOROSCOPE?

If you had been able to take a picture of the skies at the moment of your birth, that photograph would be your horoscope. Lacking such a snapshot, it is still possible to recreate the picture—and this is at the basis of the astrologer's art. In other words, your horoscope is a representation of the skies with the planets in the exact positions they occupied at the time you were born.

The year of birth tells an astrologer the positions of the distant, slow-moving planets Jupiter, Saturn, Uranus, Neptune, and Pluto. The month of birth indicates the Sun sign, or birth sign as it is commonly called, as well as indicating the positions of the rapidly moving planets Venus, Mercury, and Mars. The day and time of birth will locate the position of our Moon. And the moment—the exact hour and minute—of birth determines the houses through what is called the Ascendant, or Rising sign.

With this information the astrologer consults various tables to calculate the specific positions of the Sun, Moon, and other planets relative to your birthplace at the moment you were born. Then he or she locates them by means of the Zodiac.

The Zodiac

The Zodiac is a band of stars (constellations) in the skies, centered on the Sun's apparent path around the Earth, and is divided into twelve equal segments, or signs. What we are actually dividing up is the Earth's path around the Sun. But from our point of view here on Earth, it seems as if the Sun is making a great circle around our planet in the sky, so we say it is the Sun's apparent path. This twelvefold division, the Zodiac, is a reference system for the astrologer. At any given moment the planets—and in astrology both the Sun and Moon are considered to be planets—can all be located at a specific point along this path.

Now where in all this are you, the subject of the horoscope? Your character is largely determined by the sign the Sun is in. So that is where the astrologer looks first in your horoscope, at your Sun sign.

The Sun Sign and the Cusp

There are twelve signs in the Zodiac, and the Sun spends approximately one month in each sign. But because of the motion of the Earth around the Sun—the Sun's apparent motion—the dates when the Sun enters and leaves each sign may change from year to year. Some people born near the cusp, or edge, of a sign have difficulty determining which is their Sun sign. But in this book a Table of Cusps is provided for the years 1900 to 2010 (page 5) so you can find out what your true Sun sign is.

Here are the twelve signs of the Zodiac, their ancient zodiacal symbol, and the dates when the Sun enters and leaves each sign for the year 2009. Remember, these dates may change from year to year.

ARIES	Ram	March 20–April 19
TAURUS	Bull	April 19–May 20
GEMINI	Twins	May 20–June 21
CANCER	Crab	June 21–July 22
LEO	Lion	July 22–August 22
VIRGO	Virgin	August 22–September 22
LIBRA	Scales	September 22–October 23
SCORPIO	Scorpion	October 23–November 22
SAGITTARIUS	Archer	November 22–December 21
CAPRICORN	Sea Goat	December 21–January 19
AQUARIUS	Water Bearer	January 19–February 18
PISCES	Fish	February 18–March 20

It is possible to draw significant conclusions and make meaningful predictions based simply on the Sun sign of a person. There are many people who have been amazed at the accuracy of the description of their own character based only on the Sun sign. But an astrologer needs more information than just your Sun sign to interpret the photograph that is your horoscope.

The Rising Sign and the Zodiacal Houses

An astrologer needs the exact time and place of your birth in order to construct and interpret your horoscope. The illustration on the next page shows the flat chart, or natural wheel, an astrologer uses. Note the inner circle of the wheel labeled 1 through 12. These 12 divisions are known as the houses of the Zodiac.

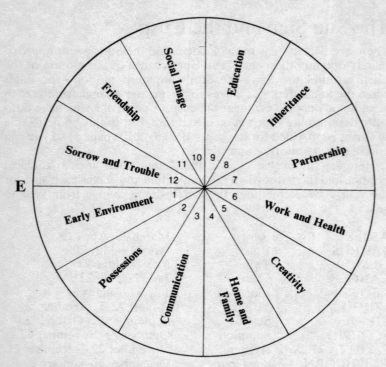

The 1st house always starts from the position marked E, which corresponds to the eastern horizon. The rest of the houses 2 through 12 follow around in a "counterclockwise" direction. The point where each house starts is known as a cusp, or edge.

The cusp, or edge, of the 1st house (point E) is where an astrologer would place your Rising sign, the Ascendant. And, as already noted, the exact time of your birth determines your Rising sign. Let's see how this works.

As the Earth rotates on its axis once every 24 hours, each one of the twelve signs of the Zodiac appears to be "rising" on the horizon, with a new one appearing about every 2 hours. Actually it is the turning of the Earth that exposes each sign to view, but in our astrological work we are discussing apparent motion. This Rising sign marks the Ascendant, and it colors the whole orientation of a horoscope. It indicates the sign governing the 1st house of the chart, and will thus determine which signs will govern all the other houses.

To visualize this idea, imagine two color wheels with twelve divisions superimposed upon each other. For just as the Zodiac is divided into twelve constellations that we identify as the signs, another twelvefold division is used to denote the houses. Now imagine one wheel (the signs) moving slowly while the other wheel (the houses) remains still. This analogy may help you see how the signs keep shifting the "color" of the houses as the Rising sign continues to change every two hours. To simplify things, a Table of Rising Signs has been provided (pages 8–9) for your specific Sun sign.

Once your Rising sign has been placed on the cusp of the 1st house, the signs that govern the rest of the 11 houses can be placed on the chart. In any individual's horoscope the signs do not necessarily correspond with the houses. For example, it could be that a sign covers part of two adjacent houses. It is the interpretation of such variations in an individual's horoscope that marks the professional astrologer.

But to gain a workable understanding of astrology, it is not necessary to go into great detail. In fact, we just need a description of the houses and their meanings, as is shown in the illustration above and in the table below.

THE 12 HOUSES OF THE ZODIAC

1st	Individuality, body appearance, general outlook on life	Personality house
2nd	Finance, possessions, ethical principles, gain or loss	Money house
3rd	Relatives, communication, short journeys, writing, education	Relatives house
4th	Family and home, parental ties, land and property, security	Home house
5th	Pleasure, children, creativity, entertainment, risk	Pleasure house
6th	Health, harvest, hygiene, work and service, employees	Health house
7th	Marriage and divorce, the law, partnerships and alliances	Marriage house
8th	Inheritance, secret deals, sex, death, regeneration	Inheritance house
9th	Travel, sports, study, philosophy Ω house	Travel house
10th	Career, social standing, success and honor	Business house
11th	Friendship, social life, hopes and wishes	Friends house
12th	Troubles, illness, secret enemies, hidden agendas	Trouble house

The Planets in the Houses

An astrologer, knowing the exact time and place of your birth, will use tables of planetary motion in order to locate the planets in your horoscope chart. He or she will determine which planet or planets are in which sign and in which house. It is not uncommon, in an individual's horoscope, for there to be two or more planets in the same sign and in the same house.

The characteristics of the planets modify the influence of the Sun according to their natures and strengths.

Sun: Source of life. Basic temperament according to the Sun sign. The conscious will. Human potential.

Moon: Emotions. Moods. Customs. Habits. Changeable. Adaptive. Nurturing.

Mercury: Communication. Intellect. Reasoning power. Curiosity. Short travels.

Venus: Love. Delight. Charm. Harmony. Balance. Art. Beautiful possessions.

Mars: Energy. Initiative. War. Anger. Adventure. Courage. Daring. Impulse.

Jupiter: Luck. Optimism. Generous. Expansive. Opportunities. Protection.

Saturn: Pessimism. Privation. Obstacles. Delay. Hard work. Research. Lasting rewards after long struggle.

Uranus: Fashion. Electricity. Revolution. Independence. Freedom. Sudden changes. Modern science.

Neptune: Sensationalism. Theater. Dreams. Inspiration. Illusion. Deception.

Pluto: Creation and destruction. Total transformation. Lust for power. Strong obsessions.

Superimpose the characteristics of the planets on the functions of the house in which they appear. Express the result through the character of the Sun sign, and you will get the basic idea.

Of course, many other considerations have been taken into account in producing the carefully worked out predictions in this book: the aspects of the planets to each other; their strength according to position and sign; whether they are in a house of exaltation or decline; whether they are natural enemies or not; whether a planet occupies its own sign; the position of a planet in relation to its own house or sign; whether the sign is male or female; whether the sign is a fire, earth, water, or air sign. These are only a few of the colors on the astrologer's pallet which he or she must mix with the inspiration of the artist and the accuracy of the mathematician.

How To Use These Predictions

A person reading the predictions in this book should understand that they are produced from the daily position of the planets for a group of people and are not, of course, individually specialized. To get the full benefit of them our readers should relate the predictions to their own character and circumstances, coordinate them, and draw their own conclusions from them.

If you are a serious observer of your own life, you should find a definite pattern emerging that will be a helpful and reliable guide.

The point is that we always retain our free will. The stars indicate certain directional tendencies but we are not compelled to follow. We can do or not do, and wisdom must make the choice.

We all have our good and bad days. Sometimes they extend into cycles of weeks. It is therefore advisable to study daily predictions in a span ranging from the day before to several days ahead.

Daily predictions should be taken very generally. The word "difficult" does not necessarily indicate a whole day of obstruction or inconvenience. It is a warning to you to be cautious. Your caution will often see you around the difficulty before you are involved. This is the correct use of astrology.

In another section (pages 78–84), detailed information is given about the influence of the Moon as it passes through each of the twelve signs of the Zodiac. There are instructions on how to use the Moon Tables (pages 85–92), which provide Moon Sign Dates throughout the year as well as the Moon's role in health and daily affairs. This information should be used in conjunction with the daily forecasts to give a fuller picture of the astrological trends.

HISTORY OF ASTROLOGY

The origins of astrology have been lost far back in history, but we do know that reference is made to it as far back as the first written records of the human race. It is not hard to see why. Even in primitive times, people must have looked for an explanation for the various happenings in their lives. They must have wanted to know why people were different from one another. And in their search they turned to the regular movements of the Sun, Moon, and stars to see if they could provide an answer.

It is interesting to note that as soon as man learned to use his tools in any type of design, or his mind in any kind of calculation, he turned his attention to the heavens. Ancient cave dwellings reveal dim crescents and circles representative of the Sun and Moon, rulers of day and night. Mesopotamia and the civilization of Chaldea, in itself the foundation of those of Babylonia and Assyria, show a complete picture of astronomical observation and well-developed astrological interpretation.

Humanity has a natural instinct for order. The study of anthropology reveals that primitive people—even as far back as prehistoric times—were striving to achieve a certain order in their lives. They tried to organize the apparent chaos of the universe. They had the desire to attach meaning to things. This demand for order has persisted throughout the history of man. So that observing the regularity of the heavenly bodies made it logical that primitive peoples should turn heavenward in their search for an understanding of the world in which they found themselves so random and alone.

And they did find a significance in the movements of the stars. Shepherds tending their flocks, for instance, observed that when the cluster of stars now known as the constellation Aries was in sight, it was the time of fertility and they associated it with the Ram. And they noticed that the growth of plants and plant life corresponded with different phases of the Moon, so that certain times were favorable for the planting of crops, and other times were not. In this way, there grew up a tradition of seasons and causes connected with the passage of the Sun through the twelve signs of the Zodiac.

Astrology was valued so highly that the king was kept informed of the daily and monthly changes in the heavenly bodies, and the results of astrological studies regarding events of the future. Head astrologers were clearly men of great rank and position, and the office was said to be a hereditary one.

Omens were taken, not only from eclipses and conjunctions of the Moon or Sun with one of the planets, but also from storms and earthquakes. In the eastern civilizations, particularly, the reverence inspired by astrology appears to have remained unbroken since the very earliest days. In ancient China, astrology, astronomy, and religion went hand in hand. The astrologer, who was also an astronomer, was part of the official government service and had his own corner in the Imperial Palace. The duties of the Imperial astrologer, whose office was one of the most important in the land, were clearly defined, as this extract from early records shows:

> This exalted gentleman must concern himself with the stars in the heavens, keeping a record of the changes and movements of the Planets, the Sun and the Moon, in order to examine the movements of the terrestrial world with the object of prognosticating good and bad fortune. He divides the territories of the nine regions of the empire in accordance with their dependence on particular celestial bodies. All the fiefs and principalities are connected with the stars and from this their prosperity or misfortune should be ascertained. He makes prognostications according to the twelve years of the Jupiter cycle of good and evil of the terrestrial world. From the colors of the five kinds of clouds, he determines the coming of floods or droughts, abundance or famine. From the twelve winds, he draws conclusions about the state of harmony of heaven and earth, and takes note of good and bad signs that result from their accord or disaccord. In general, he concerns himself with five kinds of phenomena so as to warn the Emperor to come to the aid of the government and to allow for variations in the ceremonies according to their circumstances.

The Chinese were also keen observers of the fixed stars, giving them such unusual names as Ghost Vehicle, Sun of Imperial Concubine, Imperial Prince, Pivot of Heaven, Twinkling Brilliance, Weaving Girl. But, great astrologers though they may have been, the Chinese lacked one aspect of mathematics that the Greeks applied to astrology—deductive geometry. Deductive geometry was the basis of much classical astrology in and after the time of the Greeks, and this explains the different methods of prognostication used in the East and West.

Down through the ages the astrologer's art has depended, not so much on the uncovering of new facts, though this is important, as on the interpretation of the facts already known. This is the essence of the astrologer's skill.

But why should the signs of the Zodiac have any effect at all on the formation of human character? It is easy to see why people thought they did, and even now we constantly use astrological expressions in our everyday speech. The thoughts of "lucky star," "ill-fated," "star-crossed," "mooning around," are interwoven into the very structure of our language.

Wherever the concept of the Zodiac is understood and used, it could well appear to have an influence on the human character. Does this mean, then, that the human race, in whose civilization the idea of the twelve signs of the Zodiac has long been embedded, is divided into only twelve types? Can we honestly believe that it is really as simple as that? If so, there must be pretty wide ranges of variation within each type. And if, to explain the variation, we call in heredity and environment, experiences in early childhood, the thyroid and other glands, and also the four functions of the mind together with extroversion and introversion, then one begins to wonder if the original classification was worth making at all. No sensible person believes that his favorite system explains everything. But even so, he will not find the system much use at all if it does not even save him the trouble of bothering with the others.

In the same way, if we were to put every person under only one sign of the Zodiac, the system becomes too rigid and unlike life. Besides, it was never intended to be used like that. It may be convenient to have only twelve types, but we know that in practice there is every possible gradation between aggressiveness and timidity, or between conscientiousness and laziness. How, then, do we account for this?

A person born under any given Sun sign can be mainly influenced by one or two of the other signs that appear in their individual horoscope. For instance, famous persons born under the sign of Gemini include Henry VIII, whom nothing and no one could have induced to abdicate, and Edward VIII, who did just that. Obviously, then, the sign Gemini does not fully explain the complete character of either of them.

Again, under the opposite sign, Sagittarius, were both Stalin, who was totally consumed with the notion of power, and Charles V, who freely gave up an empire because he preferred to go into a monastery. And we find under Scorpio many uncompromising characters such as Luther, de Gaulle, Indira Gandhi, and Montgomery, but also Petain, a successful commander whose name later became synonymous with collaboration.

A single sign is therefore obviously inadequate to explain the differences between people; it can only explain resemblances, such as the combativeness of the Scorpio group, or the far-reaching devotion of Charles V and Stalin to their respective ideals—the Christian heaven and the Communist utopia.

But very few people have only one sign in their horoscope chart.

In addition to the month of birth, the day and, even more, the hour to the nearest minute if possible, ought to be considered. Without this, it is impossible to have an actual horoscope, for the word horoscope literally means "a consideration of the hour."

The month of birth tells you only which sign of the Zodiac was occupied by the Sun. The day and hour tell you what sign was occupied by the Moon. And the minute tells you which sign was rising on the eastern horizon. This is called the Ascendant, and, as some astrologers believe, it is supposed to be the most important thing in the whole horoscope.

The Sun is said to signify one's heart, that is to say, one's deepest desires and inmost nature. This is quite different from the Moon, which signifies one's superficial way of behaving. When the ancient Romans referred to the Emperor Augustus as a Capricorn, they meant that he had the Moon in Capricorn. Or, to take another example, a modern astrologer would call Disraeli a Scorpion because he had Scorpio Rising, but most people would call him Sagittarius because he had the Sun there. The Romans would have called him Leo because his Moon was in Leo.

So if one does not seem to fit one's birth month, it is always worthwhile reading the other signs, for one may have been born at a time when any of them were rising or occupied by the Moon. It also seems to be the case that the influence of the Sun develops as life goes on, so that the month of birth is easier to guess in people over the age of forty. The young are supposed to be influenced mainly by their Ascendant, the Rising sign, which characterizes the body and physical personality as a whole.

It is nonsense to assume that all people born at a certain time will exhibit the same characteristics, or that they will even behave in the same manner. It is quite obvious that, from the very moment of its birth, a child is subject to the effects of its environment, and that this in turn will influence its character and heritage to a decisive extent. Also to be taken into account are education and economic conditions, which play a very important part in the formation of one's character as well.

People have, in general, certain character traits and qualities which, according to their environment, develop in either a positive or a negative manner. Therefore, selfishness (inherent selfishness, that is) might emerge as unselfishness; kindness and consideration as cruelty and lack of consideration toward others. In the same way, a naturally constructive person may, through frustration, become destructive, and so on. The latent characteristics with which people are born can, therefore, through environment and good or bad training, become something that would appear to be its opposite, and so give the lie to the astrologer's description of their character.

But this is not the case. The true character is still there, but it is buried deep beneath these external superficialities.

Careful study of the character traits of various signs of the Zodiac are of immeasurable help, and can render beneficial service to the intelligent person. Undoubtedly, the reader will already have discovered that, while he is able to get on very well with some people, he just "cannot stand" others. The causes sometimes seem inexplicable. At times there is intense dislike, at other times immediate sympathy. And there is, too, the phenomenon of love at first sight, which is also apparently inexplicable. People appear to be either sympathetic or unsympathetic toward each other for no apparent reason.

Now if we look at this in the light of the Zodiac, we find that people born under different signs are either compatible or incompatible with each other. In other words, there are good and bad interrelating factors among the various signs. This does not, of course, mean that humanity can be divided into groups of hostile camps. It would be quite wrong to be hostile or indifferent toward people who happen to be born under an incompatible sign. There is no reason why everybody should not, or cannot, learn to control and adjust their feelings and actions, especially after they are aware of the positive qualities of other people by studying their character analyses, among other things.

Every person born under a certain sign has both positive and negative qualities, which are developed more or less according to our free will. Nobody is entirely good or entirely bad, and it is up to each of us to learn to control ourselves on the one hand and at the same time to endeavor to learn about ourselves and others.

It cannot be emphasized often enough that it is free will that determines whether we will make really good use of our talents and abilities. Using our free will, we can either overcome our failings or allow them to rule us. Our free will enables us to exert sufficient willpower to control our failings so that they do not harm ourselves or others.

Astrology can reveal our inclinations and tendencies. Astrology can tell us about ourselves so that we are able to use our free will to overcome our shortcomings. In this way astrology helps us do our best to become needed and valuable members of society as well as helpmates to our family and our friends. Astrology also can save us a great deal of unhappiness and remorse.

Yet it may seem absurd that an ancient philosophy could be a prop to modern men and women. But below the materialistic surface of modern life, there are hidden streams of feeling and thought. Symbology is reappearing as a study worthy of the scholar; the psychosomatic factor in illness has passed from the writings of the crank to those of the specialist; spiritual healing in all its forms is no longer a pious hope but an accepted phenomenon. And it is into this context that we consider astrology, in the sense that it is an analysis of human types.

Astrology and medicine had a long journey together, and only parted company a couple of centuries ago. There still remain in medical language such astrological terms as "saturnine," "choleric," and "mercurial," used in the diagnosis of physical tendencies. The herbalist, for long the handyman of the medical profession, has been dominated by astrology since the days of the Greeks. Certain herbs traditionally respond to certain planetary influences, and diseases must therefore be treated to ensure harmony between the medicine and the disease.

But the stars are expected to foretell and not only to diagnose.

Astrological forecasting has been remarkably accurate, but often it is wide of the mark. The brave person who cares to predict world events takes dangerous chances. Individual forecasting is less clear cut; it can be a help or a disillusionment. Then we come to the nagging question: if it is possible to foreknow, is it right to foretell? This is a point of ethics on which it is hard to pronounce judgment. The doctor faces the same dilemma if he finds that symptoms of a mortal disease are present in his patient and that he can only prognosticate a steady decline. How much to tell an individual in a crisis is a problem that has perplexed many distinguished scholars. Honest and conscientious astrologers in this modern world, where so many people are seeking guidance, face the same problem.

Five hundred years ago it was customary to call in a learned man who was an astrologer who was probably also a doctor and a philosopher. By his knowledge of astrology, his study of planetary influences, he felt himself qualified to guide those in distress. The world has moved forward at a fantastic rate since then, and yet people are still uncertain of themselves. At first sight it seems fantastic in the light of modern thinking that they turn to the most ancient of all studies, and get someone to calculate a horoscope for them. But is it really so fantastic if you take a second look? For astrology is concerned with tomorrow, with survival. And in a world such as ours, tomorrow and survival are the keywords for the twenty-first century.

ASTROLOGICAL BRIDGE TO THE 21st CENTURY

Themes connecting past, present, and future are in play as the first decade reveals hidden paths and personal hints for achieving your potential. Make the most of the messages from the planets.

With the dawning of the twenty-first century look first to Jupiter, the planet of good fortune. Each new yearly Jupiter cycle follows the natural progression of the Zodiac. First is Jupiter in Aries and in Taurus through spring 2000, next Jupiter is in Gemini to summer 2001, then in Cancer to midsummer 2002, in Leo to late summer 2003, in Virgo to early autumn 2004, in Libra to midautumn 2005, and so on through Jupiter in Pisces through June 2010. The beneficent planet Jupiter promotes your professional and educational goals while urging informed choice and deliberation, providing a rich medium for creativity. Planet Jupiter's influence is protective, the generous helper that comes to the rescue just in the nick of time. And while safeguarding good luck, Jupiter can turn unusual risks into achievable aims.

In order to take advantage of luck and opportunity, to gain wisdom from experience, to persevere against adversity, look to beautiful planet Saturn. Saturn, planet of reason and responsibility, began a new cycle in earthy Taurus at the turn of the century. Saturn in Taurus until spring 2001 inspires industry and affection, blends practicality and imagination, all the while inviting caution and care. Saturn in Taurus lends beauty, order, and structure to your life. Then Saturn is in Gemini, the sign of mind and communication, until June 2003. Saturn in Gemini gives a lively intellectual capacity, so the limits of creativity can be stretched and boundaries broken. Saturn in Gemini holds the promise of fruitful endeavor through sustained study, learning, and application. Saturn in Cancer from early June 2003 to mid-July 2005 poses issues of long-term security versus immediate gratification. Rely on deliberation and choice to make sense out of diversity and change. Saturn in Cancer can be a revealing cycle, leading to the desired outcomes of growth and maturity. Saturn in Leo from mid-July 2005 to early September 2007 can be a test of boldness versus caution. Here every challenge must be met with benevolent authority, matched by a caring and generous outlook. Saturn in Virgo early September 2007 into October 2009 sharpens and deepens the mind. Saturn in Virgo presents chances to excel, to gain prominence through good words and good works. Saturn in Libra end of October 2009 into November 2012 promotes artistry, balance, goodwill, and peace.

Uranus, planet of innovation and surprise, started an important new cycle in January of 1996. At that time Uranus entered its natural home in airy Aquarius. Uranus in Aquarius into the year 2003 has a profound effect on your personality and the lens through which you see the world. A basic change in the way you project yourself is just one impact of Uranus in Aquarius. More significantly, a whole new consciousness is evolving. Winds of change blowing your way emphasize movement and freedom. Uranus in Aquarius poses involvement in the larger community beyond self, family, friends, lovers, associates. Radical ideas and progressive thought signal a journey of liberation. As the new century begins, follow Uranus on the path of humanitarianism. A new Uranus cycle begins March 2003 when Uranus visits Pisces, briefly revisits Aquarius, then returns late in 2003 to Pisces where it will stay into May 2010. Uranus in Pisces, a strongly intuitive force, urges work and service for the good of humankind to make the world a better place for all people.

Neptune, planet of vision and mystery, is enjoying a long cycle that excites creativity and imaginative thinking. Neptune is in airy Aquarius from November 1998 to February of 2012. Neptune in Aquarius, the sign of the Water Bearer, represents two sides of the coin of wisdom: inspiration and reason. Here Neptune stirs powerful currents bearing a rich and varied harvest, the fertile breeding ground for idealistic aims and practical considerations. Neptune's fine intuition tunes in to your dreams, your imagination, your spirituality. You can never turn your back on the mysteries of life. Uranus and Neptune, the planets of enlightenment and idealism, give you glimpses into the future, letting you peek through secret doorways into the twenty-first century.

Pluto, dwarf planet of beginnings and endings, started a new cycle of transformative power in the year 2008. Pluto entered the earthy sign of Capricorn and journeys there for sixteen years until 2024. Pluto in Capricorn over the course of this extensive journey has the capacity to change the landscape as well as the human-scape. The transforming energy of Pluto combines with the persevering power of Capricorn to give depth and character to potential change. Pluto in Capricorn can bring focus and cohesion to disparate, diverse creativities. As new forms arise and take root, Pluto in Capricorn organizes the rebuilding process. Freedom versus limitation, freedom versus authority is part of the picture. Reasonableness struggles with recklessness to solve divisive issues. Pluto in Capricorn can teach important lessons about adversity, and the lessons will be learned.

THE SIGNS OF THE ZODIAC

Dominant Characteristics

Aries: March 21–April 20

The Positive Side of Aries

The Aries has many positive points to his character. People born under this first sign of the Zodiac are often quite strong and enthusiastic. On the whole, they are forward-looking people who are not easily discouraged by temporary setbacks. They know what they want out of life and they go out after it. Their personalities are strong. Others are usually quite impressed by the Ram's way of doing things. Quite often they are sources of inspiration for others traveling the same route. Aries men and women have a special zest for life that can be contagious; for others, they are a fine example of how life should be lived.

The Aries person usually has a quick and active mind. He is imaginative and inventive. He enjoys keeping busy and active. He generally gets along well with all kinds of people. He is interested in mankind, as a whole. He likes to be challenged. Some would say he thrives on opposition, for it is when he is set against that he often does his best. Getting over or around obstacles is a challenge he generally enjoys. All in all, Aries is quite positive and young-thinking. He likes to keep abreast of new things that are happening in the world. Aries are often fond of speed. They like things to be done quickly, and this sometimes aggravates their slower colleagues and associates.

The Aries man or woman always seems to remain young. Their whole approach to life is youthful and optimistic. They never say die, no matter what the odds. They may have an occasional setback, but it is not long before they are back on their feet again.

The Negative Side of Aries

Everybody has his less positive qualities—and Aries is no exception. Sometimes the Aries man or woman is not very tactful in communicating with others; in his hurry to get things done he is apt to be a little callous or inconsiderate. Sensitive people are likely to find him somewhat sharp-tongued in some situations. Often in his eagerness to get the show on the road, he misses the mark altogether and cannot achieve his aims.

At times Aries can be too impulsive. He can occasionally be stubborn and refuse to listen to reason. If things do not move quickly enough to suit the Aries man or woman, he or she is apt to become rather nervous or irritable. The uncultivated Aries is not unfamiliar with moments of doubt and fear. He is capable of being destructive if he does not get his way. He can overcome some of his emotional problems by steadily trying to express himself as he really is, but this requires effort.

Taurus: April 21–May 20

The Positive Side of Taurus

The Taurus person is known for his ability to concentrate and for his tenacity. These are perhaps his strongest qualities. The Taurus man or woman generally has very little trouble in getting along with others; it's his nature to be helpful toward people in need. He can always be depended on by his friends, especially those in trouble.

Taurus generally achieves what he wants through his ability to persevere. He never leaves anything unfinished but works on something until it has been completed. People can usually take him at his word; he is honest and forthright in most of his dealings. The Taurus person has a good chance to make a success of his life because of his many positive qualities. The Taurus who aims high seldom falls short of his mark. He learns well by experience. He is thorough and does not believe in shortcuts of any kind. The Bull's thoroughness pays off in the end, for through his deliberateness he learns how to rely on himself and what he has learned. The Taurus person tries to get along with others, as a rule. He is not overly critical and likes people to be themselves. He is a tolerant person and enjoys peace and harmony—especially in his home life.

Taurus is usually cautious in all that he does. He is not a person

who believes in taking unnecessary risks. Before adopting any one line of action, he will weigh all of the pros and cons. The Taurus person is steadfast. Once his mind is made up it seldom changes. The person born under this sign usually is a good family person— reliable and loving.

The Negative Side of Taurus

Sometimes the Taurus man or woman is a bit too stubborn. He won't listen to other points of view if his mind is set on something. To others, this can be quite annoying. Taurus also does not like to be told what to do. He becomes rather angry if others think him not too bright. He does not like to be told he is wrong, even when he is. He dislikes being contradicted.

Some people who are born under this sign are very suspicious of others—even of those persons close to them. They find it difficult to trust people fully. They are often afraid of being deceived or taken advantage of. The Bull often finds it difficult to forget or forgive. His love of material things sometimes makes him rather avaricious and petty.

Gemini: May 21–June 20

The Positive Side of Gemini

The person born under this sign of the Heavenly Twins is usually quite bright and quick-witted. Some of them are capable of doing many different things. The Gemini person very often has many different interests. He keeps an open mind and is always anxious to learn new things.

Gemini is often an analytical person. He is a person who enjoys making use of his intellect. He is governed more by his mind than by his emotions. He is a person who is not confined to one view; he can often understand both sides to a problem or question. He knows how to reason, how to make rapid decisions if need be.

He is an adaptable person and can make himself at home almost anywhere. There are all kinds of situations he can adapt to. He is a person who seldom doubts himself; he is sure of his talents and his ability to think and reason. Gemini is generally most satisfied when he is in a situation where he can make use of his intellect. Never

short of imagination, he often has strong talents for invention. He is rather a modern person when it comes to life; Gemini almost always moves along with the times—perhaps that is why he remains so youthful throughout most of his life.

Literature and art appeal to the person born under this sign. Creativity in almost any form will interest and intrigue the Gemini man or woman.

The Gemini is often quite charming. A good talker, he often is the center of attraction at any gathering. People find it easy to like a person born under this sign because he can appear easygoing and usually has a good sense of humor.

The Negative Side of Gemini

Sometimes the Gemini person tries to do too many things at one time—and as a result, winds up finishing nothing. Some Twins are easily distracted and find it rather difficult to concentrate on one thing for too long a time. Sometimes they give in to trifling fancies and find it rather boring to become too serious about any one thing. Some of them are never dependable, no matter what they promise.

Although the Gemini man or woman often appears to be well-versed on many subjects, this is sometimes just a veneer. His knowledge may be only superficial, but because he speaks so well he gives people the impression of erudition. Some Geminis are sharp-tongued and inconsiderate; they think only of themselves and their own pleasure.

Cancer: June 21–July 20

The Positive Side of Cancer

The Moon Child's most positive point is his understanding nature. On the whole, he is a loving and sympathetic person. He would never go out of his way to hurt anyone. The Cancer man or woman is often very kind and tender; they give what they can to others. They hate to see others suffering and will do what they can to help someone in less fortunate circumstances than themselves. They are often very concerned about the world. Their interest in people generally goes beyond that of just their own families and close friends; they have a deep sense of community and respect humanitarian values. The Moon Child means what he says, as a rule; he is honest about his feelings.

The Cancer man or woman is a person who knows the art of patience. When something seems difficult, he is willing to wait until the situation becomes manageable again. He is a person who knows how to bide his time. Cancer knows how to concentrate on one thing at a time. When he has made his mind up he generally sticks with what he does, seeing it through to the end.

Cancer is a person who loves his home. He enjoys being surrounded by familiar things and the people he loves. Of all the signs, Cancer is the most maternal. Even the men born under this sign often have a motherly or protective quality about them. They like to take care of people in their family—to see that they are well loved and well provided for. They are usually loyal and faithful. Family ties mean a lot to the Cancer man or woman. Parents and in-laws are respected and loved. Young Cancer responds very well to adults who show faith in him. The Moon Child has a strong sense of tradition. He is very sensitive to the moods of others.

The Negative Side of Cancer

Sometimes Cancer finds it rather hard to face life. It becomes too much for him. He can be a little timid and retiring, when things don't go too well. When unfortunate things happen, he is apt to just shrug and say, "Whatever will be will be." He can be fatalistic to a fault. The uncultivated Cancer is a bit lazy. He doesn't have very much ambition. Anything that seems a bit difficult he'll gladly leave to others. He may be lacking in initiative. Too sensitive, when he feels he's been injured, he'll crawl back into his shell and nurse his imaginary wounds. The immature Moon Child often is given to crying when the smallest thing goes wrong.

Some Cancers find it difficult to enjoy themselves in environments outside their homes. They make heavy demands on others, and need to be constantly reassured that they are loved. Lacking such reassurance, they may resort to sulking in silence.

Leo: July 21–August 21

The Positive Side of Leo

Often Leos make good leaders. They seem to be good organizers and administrators. Usually they are quite popular with others. Whatever group it is that they belong to, the Leo man or woman is almost sure to be or become the leader. Loyalty, one of the Lion's noblest traits, enables him or her to maintain this leadership position.

Leo is generous most of the time. It is his best characteristic. He or she likes to give gifts and presents. In making others happy, the Leo person becomes happy himself. He likes to splurge when spending money on others. In some instances it may seem that the Lion's generosity knows no boundaries. A hospitable person, the Leo man or woman is very fond of welcoming people to his house and entertaining them. He is never short of company.

Leo has plenty of energy and drive. He enjoys working toward some specific goal. When he applies himself correctly, he gets what he wants most often. The Leo person is almost never unsure of himself. He has plenty of confidence and aplomb. He is a person who is direct in almost everything he does. He has a quick mind and can make a decision in a very short time.

He usually sets a good example for others because of his ambitious manner and positive ways. He knows how to stick to something once he's started. Although Leo may be good at making a joke, he is not superficial or glib. He is a loving person, kind and thoughtful.

There is generally nothing small or petty about the Leo man or woman. He does what he can for those who are deserving. He is a person others can rely upon at all times. He means what he says. An honest person, generally speaking, he is a friend who is valued and sought out.

The Negative Side of Leo

Leo, however, does have his faults. At times, he can be just a bit too arrogant. He thinks that no one deserves a leadership position except him. Only he is capable of doing things well. His opinion of himself is often much too high. Because of his conceit, he is

sometimes rather unpopular with a good many people. Some Leos are too materialistic; they can only think in terms of money and profit.

Some Leos enjoy lording it over others—at home or at their place of business. What is more, they feel they have the right to. Egocentric to an impossible degree, this sort of Leo cares little about how others think or feel. He can be rude and cutting.

Virgo: August 22–September 22

The Positive Side of Virgo

The person born under the sign of Virgo is generally a busy person. He knows how to arrange and organize things. He is a good planner. Above all, he is practical and is not afraid of hard work.

Often called the sign of the Harvester, Virgo knows how to attain what he desires. He sticks with something until it is finished. He never shirks his duties, and can always be depended upon. The Virgo person can be thoroughly trusted at all times.

The man or woman born under this sign tries to do everything to perfection. He doesn't believe in doing anything halfway. He always aims for the top. He is the sort of a person who is always learning and constantly striving to better himself—not because he wants more money or glory, but because it gives him a feeling of accomplishment.

The Virgo man or woman is a very observant person. He is sensitive to how others feel, and can see things below the surface of a situation. He usually puts this talent to constructive use.

It is not difficult for the Virgo to be open and earnest. He believes in putting his cards on the table. He is never secretive or underhanded. He's as good as his word. The Virgo person is generally plainspoken and down to earth. He has no trouble in expressing himself.

The Virgo person likes to keep up to date on new developments in his particular field. Well-informed, generally, he sometimes has a keen interest in the arts or literature. What he knows, he knows well. His ability to use his critical faculties is well-developed and sometimes startles others because of its accuracy.

Virgos adhere to a moderate way of life; they avoid excesses. Virgo is a responsible person and enjoys being of service.

The Negative Side of Virgo

Sometimes a Virgo person is too critical. He thinks that only he can do something the way it should be done. Whatever anyone else does is inferior. He can be rather annoying in the way he quibbles over insignificant details. In telling others how things should be done, he can be rather tactless and mean.

Some Virgos seem rather emotionless and cool. They feel emotional involvement is beneath them. They are sometimes too tidy, too neat. With money they can be rather miserly. Some Virgos try to force their opinions and ideas on others.

Libra: September 23–October 22

The Positive Side of Libra

Libras love harmony. It is one of their most outstanding character traits. They are interested in achieving balance; they admire beauty and grace in things as well as in people. Generally speaking, they are kind and considerate people. Libras are usually very sympathetic. They go out of their way not to hurt another person's feelings. They are outgoing and do what they can to help those in need.

People born under the sign of Libra almost always make good friends. They are loyal and amiable. They enjoy the company of others. Many of them are rather moderate in their views; they believe in keeping an open mind, however, and weighing both sides of an issue fairly before making a decision.

Alert and intelligent, Libra, often known as the Lawgiver, is always fair-minded and tries to put himself in the position of the other person. They are against injustice; quite often they take up for the underdog. In most of their social dealings, they try to be tactful and kind. They dislike discord and bickering, and most Libras strive for peace and harmony in all their relationships.

The Libra man or woman has a keen sense of beauty. They appreciate handsome furnishings and clothes. Many of them are artistically inclined. Their taste is usually impeccable. They know how to use color. Their homes are almost always attractively arranged and inviting. They enjoy entertaining people and see to it that their guests always feel at home and welcome.

Libra gets along with almost everyone. He is well-liked and socially much in demand.

The Negative Side of Libra

Some people born under this sign tend to be rather insincere. So eager are they to achieve harmony in all relationships that they will even go so far as to lie. Many of them are escapists. They find facing the truth an ordeal and prefer living in a world of make-believe.

In a serious argument, some Libras give in rather easily even when they know they are right. Arguing, even about something they believe in, is too unsettling for some of them.

Libras sometimes care too much for material things. They enjoy possessions and luxuries. Some are vain and tend to be jealous.

Scorpio: October 23–November 22

The Positive Side of Scorpio

The Scorpio man or woman generally knows what he or she wants out of life. He is a determined person. He sees something through to the end. Scorpio is quite sincere, and seldom says anything he doesn't mean. When he sets a goal for himself he tries to go about achieving it in a very direct way.

The Scorpion is brave and courageous. They are not afraid of hard work. Obstacles do not frighten them. They forge ahead until they achieve what they set out for. The Scorpio man or woman has a strong will.

Although Scorpio may seem rather fixed and determined, inside he is often quite tender and loving. He can care very much for others. He believes in sincerity in all relationships. His feelings about someone tend to last; they are profound and not superficial.

The Scorpio person is someone who adheres to his principles no matter what happens. He will not be deterred from a path he believes to be right.

Because of his many positive strengths, the Scorpion can often achieve happiness for himself and for those that he loves.

He is a constructive person by nature. He often has a deep understanding of people and of life, in general. He is perceptive and unafraid. Obstacles often seem to spur him on. He is a positive person who enjoys winning. He has many strengths and resources; challenge of any sort often brings out the best in him.

The Negative Side of Scorpio

The Scorpio person is sometimes hypersensitive. Often he imagines injury when there is none. He feels that others do not bother to recognize him for his true worth. Sometimes he is given to excessive boasting in order to compensate for what he feels is neglect.

Scorpio can be proud, arrogant, and competitive. They can be sly when they put their minds to it and they enjoy outwitting persons or institutions noted for their cleverness.

Their tactics for getting what they want are sometimes devious and ruthless. They don't care too much about what others may think. If they feel others have done them an injustice, they will do their best to seek revenge. The Scorpion often has a sudden, violent temper; and this person's interest in sex is sometimes quite unbalanced or excessive.

Sagittarius: November 23–December 20

The Positive Side of Sagittarius

People born under this sign are honest and forthright. Their approach to life is earnest and open. Sagittarius is often quite adult in his way of seeing things. They are broad-minded and tolerant people. When dealing with others the person born under the sign of the Archer is almost always open and forthright. He doesn't believe in deceit or pretension. His standards are high. People who associate with Sagittarius generally admire and respect his tolerant viewpoint.

The Archer trusts others easily and expects them to trust him. He is never suspicious or envious and almost always thinks well of others. People always enjoy his company because he is so friendly and easygoing. The Sagittarius man or woman is often good-humored. He can always be depended upon by his friends, family, and co-workers.

The person born under this sign of the Zodiac likes a good joke every now and then. Sagittarius is eager for fun and laughs, which makes him very popular with others.

A lively person, he enjoys sports and outdoor life. The Archer is fond of animals. Intelligent and interesting, he can begin an ani-

mated conversation with ease. He likes exchanging ideas and discussing various views.

He is not selfish or proud. If someone proposes an idea or plan that is better than his, he will immediately adopt it. Imaginative yet practical, he knows how to put ideas into practice.

The Archer enjoys sport and games, and it doesn't matter if he wins or loses. He is a forgiving person, and never sulks over something that has not worked out in his favor.

He is seldom critical, and is almost always generous.

The Negative Side of Sagittarius

Some Sagittarius are restless. They take foolish risks and seldom learn from the mistakes they make. They don't have heads for money and are often mismanaging their finances. Some of them devote much of their time to gambling.

Some are too outspoken and tactless, always putting their feet in their mouths. They hurt others carelessly by being honest at the wrong time. Sometimes they make promises which they don't keep. They don't stick close enough to their plans and go from one failure to another. They are undisciplined and waste a lot of energy.

Capricorn: December 21–January 19

The Positive Side of Capricorn

The person born under the sign of Capricorn, known variously as the Mountain Goat or Sea Goat, is usually very stable and patient. He sticks to whatever tasks he has and sees them through. He can always be relied upon and he is not averse to work.

An honest person, Capricorn is generally serious about whatever he does. He does not take his duties lightly. He is a practical person and believes in keeping his feet on the ground.

Quite often the person born under this sign is ambitious and knows how to get what he wants out of life. The Goat forges ahead and never gives up his goal. When he is determined about something, he almost always wins. He is a good worker—a hard worker. Although things may not come easy to him, he will not complain, but continue working until his chores are finished.

He is usually good at business matters and knows the value of money. He is not a spendthrift and knows how to put something away for a rainy day; he dislikes waste and unnecessary loss.

Capricorn knows how to make use of his self-control. He can apply himself to almost anything once he puts his mind to it. His ability to concentrate sometimes astounds others. He is diligent and does well when involved in detail work.

The Capricorn man or woman is charitable, generally speaking, and will do what is possible to help others less fortunate. As a friend, he is loyal and trustworthy. He never shirks his duties or responsibilities. He is self-reliant and never expects too much of the other fellow. He does what he can on his own. If someone does him a good turn, then he will do his best to return the favor.

The Negative Side of Capricorn

Like everyone, Capricorn, too, has faults. At times, the Goat can be overcritical of others. He expects others to live up to his own high standards. He thinks highly of himself and tends to look down on others.

His interest in material things may be exaggerated. The Capricorn man or woman thinks too much about getting on in the world and having something to show for it. He may even be a little greedy.

He sometimes thinks he knows what's best for everyone. He is too bossy. He is always trying to organize and correct others. He may be a little narrow in his thinking.

Aquarius: January 20–February 18

The Positive Side of Aquarius

The Aquarius man or woman is usually very honest and forthright. These are his two greatest qualities. His standards for himself are generally very high. He can always be relied upon by others. His word is his bond.

Aquarius is perhaps the most tolerant of all the Zodiac personalities. He respects other people's beliefs and feels that everyone is entitled to his own approach to life.

He would never do anything to injure another's feelings. He is never unkind or cruel. Always considerate of others, the Water

Bearer is always willing to help a person in need. He feels a very strong tie between himself and all the other members of mankind.

The person born under this sign, called the Water Bearer, is almost always an individualist. He does not believe in teaming up with the masses, but prefers going his own way. His ideas about life and mankind are often quite advanced. There is a saying to the effect that the average Aquarius is fifty years ahead of his time.

Aquarius is community-minded. The problems of the world concern him greatly. He is interested in helping others no matter what part of the globe they live in. He is truly a humanitarian sort. He likes to be of service to others.

Giving, considerate, and without prejudice, Aquarius have no trouble getting along with others.

The Negative Side of Aquarius

Aquarius may be too much of a dreamer. He makes plans but seldom carries them out. He is rather unrealistic. His imagination has a tendency to run away with him. Because many of his plans are impractical, he is always in some sort of a dither.

Others may not approve of him at all times because of his unconventional behavior. He may be a bit eccentric. Sometimes he is so busy with his own thoughts that he loses touch with the realities of existence.

Some Aquarius feel they are more clever and intelligent than others. They seldom admit to their own faults, even when they are quite apparent. Some become rather fanatic in their views. Their criticism of others is sometimes destructive and negative.

Pisces: February 19–March 20

The Positive Side of Pisces

Known as the sign of the Fishes, Pisces has a sympathetic nature. Kindly, he is often dedicated in the way he goes about helping others. The sick and the troubled often turn to him for advice and assistance. Possessing keen intuition, Pisces can easily understand people's deepest problems.

He is very broad-minded and does not criticize others for their faults. He knows how to accept people for what they are. On the whole, he is a trustworthy and earnest person. He is loyal to his friends and will do what he can to help them in time of need. Generous and good-natured, he is a lover of peace; he is often willing to help others solve their differences. People who have taken a wrong turn in life often interest him and he will do what he can to persuade them to rehabilitate themselves.

He has a strong intuitive sense and most of the time he knows how to make it work for him. Pisces is unusually perceptive and often knows what is bothering someone before that person, himself, is aware of it. The Pisces man or woman is an idealistic person, basically, and is interested in making the world a better place in which to live. Pisces believes that everyone should help each other. He is willing to do more than his share in order to achieve cooperation with others.

The person born under this sign often is talented in music or art. He is a receptive person; he is able to take the ups and downs of life with philosophic calm.

The Negative Side of Pisces

Some Pisces are often depressed; their outlook on life is rather glum. They may feel that they have been given a bad deal in life and that others are always taking unfair advantage of them. Pisces sometimes feel that the world is a cold and cruel place. The Fishes can be easily discouraged. The Pisces man or woman may even withdraw from the harshness of reality into a secret shell of his own where he dreams and idles away a good deal of his time.

Pisces can be lazy. He lets things happen without giving the least bit of resistance. He drifts along, whether on the high road or on the low. He can be lacking in willpower.

Some Pisces people seek escape through drugs or alcohol. When temptation comes along they find it hard to resist. In matters of sex, they can be rather permissive.

Sun Sign Personalities

ARIES: Hans Christian Andersen, Pearl Bailey, Marlon Brando, Wernher Von Braun, Charlie Chaplin, Joan Crawford, Da Vinci, Bette Davis, Doris Day, W.C. Fields, Alec Guinness, Adolf Hitler, William Holden, Thomas Jefferson, Nikita Khrushchev, Elton John, Arturo Toscanini, J.P. Morgan, Paul Robeson, Gloria Steinem, Sarah Vaughn, Vincent van Gogh, Tennessee Williams

TAURUS: Fred Astaire, Charlotte Brontë, Carol Burnett, Irving Berlin, Bing Crosby, Salvador Dali, Tchaikovsky, Queen Elizabeth II, Duke Ellington, Ella Fitzgerald, Henry Fonda, Sigmund Freud, Orson Welles, Joe Louis, Lenin, Karl Marx, Golda Meir, Eva Peron, Bertrand Russell, Shakespeare, Kate Smith, Benjamin Spock, Barbra Streisand, Shirley Temple, Harry Truman

GEMINI: Ruth Benedict, Josephine Baker, Rachel Carson, Carlos Chavez, Walt Whitman, Bob Dylan, Ralph Waldo Emerson, Judy Garland, Paul Gauguin, Allen Ginsberg, Benny Goodman, Bob Hope, Burl Ives, John F. Kennedy, Peggy Lee, Marilyn Monroe, Joe Namath, Cole Porter, Laurence Olivier, Harriet Beecher Stowe, Queen Victoria, John Wayne, Frank Lloyd Wright

CANCER: "Dear Abby," Lizzie Borden, David Brinkley, Yul Brynner, Pearl Buck, Marc Chagall, Princess Diana, Babe Didrikson, Mary Baker Eddy, Henry VIII, John Glenn, Ernest Hemingway, Lena Horne, Oscar Hammerstein, Helen Keller, Ann Landers, George Orwell, Nancy Reagan, Rembrandt, Richard Rodgers, Ginger Rogers, Rubens, Jean-Paul Sartre, O.J. Simpson

LEO: Neil Armstrong, James Baldwin, Lucille Ball, Emily Brontë, Wilt Chamberlain, Julia Child, William J. Clinton, Cecil B. De Mille, Ogden Nash, Amelia Earhart, Edna Ferber, Arthur Goldberg, Alfred Hitchcock, Mick Jagger, George Meany, Annie Oakley, George Bernard Shaw, Napoleon, Jacqueline Onassis, Henry Ford, Francis Scott Key, Andy Warhol, Mae West, Orville Wright

VIRGO: Ingrid Bergman, Warren Burger, Maurice Chevalier, Agatha Christie, Sean Connery, Lafayette, Peter Falk, Greta Garbo, Althea Gibson, Arthur Godfrey, Goethe, Buddy Hackett, Michael Jackson, Lyndon Johnson, D.H. Lawrence, Sophia Loren, Grandma Moses, Arnold Palmer, Queen Elizabeth I, Walter Reuther, Peter Sellers, Lily Tomlin, George Wallace

LIBRA: Brigitte Bardot, Art Buchwald, Truman Capote, Dwight D. Eisenhower, William Faulkner, F. Scott Fitzgerald, Gandhi, George Gershwin, Micky Mantle, Helen Hayes, Vladimir Horowitz, Doris Lessing, Martina Navratalova, Eugene O'Neill, Luciano Pavarotti, Emily Post, Eleanor Roosevelt, Bruce Springsteen, Margaret Thatcher, Gore Vidal, Barbara Walters, Oscar Wilde

SCORPIO: Vivien Leigh, Richard Burton, Art Carney, Johnny Carson, Billy Graham, Grace Kelly, Walter Cronkite, Marie Curie, Charles de Gaulle, Linda Evans, Indira Gandhi, Theodore Roosevelt, Rock Hudson, Katherine Hepburn, Robert F. Kennedy, Billie Jean King, Martin Luther, Georgia O'Keeffe, Pablo Picasso, Jonas Salk, Alan Shepard, Robert Louis Stevenson

SAGITTARIUS: Jane Austen, Louisa May Alcott, Woody Allen, Beethoven, Willy Brandt, Mary Martin, William F. Buckley, Maria Callas, Winston Churchill, Noel Coward, Emily Dickinson, Walt Disney, Benjamin Disraeli, James Doolittle, Kirk Douglas, Chet Huntley, Jane Fonda, Chris Evert Lloyd, Margaret Mead, Charles Schulz, John Milton, Frank Sinatra, Steven Spielberg

CAPRICORN: Muhammad Ali, Isaac Asimov, Pablo Casals, Dizzy Dean, Marlene Dietrich, James Farmer, Ava Gardner, Barry Goldwater, Cary Grant, J. Edgar Hoover, Howard Hughes, Joan of Arc, Gypsy Rose Lee, Martin Luther King, Jr., Rudyard Kipling, Mao Tse-tung, Richard Nixon, Gamal Nasser, Louis Pasteur, Albert Schweitzer, Stalin, Benjamin Franklin, Elvis Presley

AQUARIUS: Marian Anderson, Susan B. Anthony, Jack Benny, John Barrymore, Mikhail Baryshnikov, Charles Darwin, Charles Dickens, Thomas Edison, Clark Gable, Jascha Heifetz, Abraham Lincoln, Yehudi Menuhin, Mozart, Jack Nicklaus, Ronald Reagan, Jackie Robinson, Norman Rockwell, Franklin D. Roosevelt, Gertrude Stein, Charles Lindbergh, Margaret Truman

PISCES: Edward Albee, Harry Belafonte, Alexander Graham Bell, Chopin, Adelle Davis, Albert Einstein, Golda Meir, Jackie Gleason, Winslow Homer, Edward M. Kennedy, Victor Hugo, Mike Mansfield, Michelangelo, Edna St. Vincent Millay, Liza Minelli, John Steinbeck, Linus Pauling, Ravel, Renoir, Diana Ross, William Shirer, Elizabeth Taylor, George Washington

The Signs and Their Key Words

		POSITIVE	NEGATIVE
ARIES	self	courage, initiative, pioneer instinct	brash rudeness, selfish impetuosity
TAURUS	money	endurance, loyalty, wealth	obstinacy, gluttony
GEMINI	mind	versatility	capriciousness, unreliability
CANCER	family	sympathy, homing instinct	clannishness, childishness
LEO	children	love, authority, integrity	egotism, force
VIRGO	work	purity, industry, analysis	faultfinding, cynicism
LIBRA	marriage	harmony, justice	vacillation, superficiality
SCORPIO	sex	survival, regeneration	vengeance, discord
SAGITTARIUS	travel	optimism, higher learning	lawlessness
CAPRICORN	career	depth	narrowness, gloom
AQUARIUS	friends	human fellowship, genius	perverse unpredictability
PISCES	confine-ment	spiritual love, universality	diffusion, escapism

The Elements and Qualities of The Signs

Every sign has both an *element* and a *quality* associated with it. The element indicates the basic makeup of the sign, and the quality describes the kind of activity associated with each.

Element	Sign	Quality	Sign
FIRE .....ARIES	LEO	CARDINAL ...ARIES	LIBRA
	SAGITTARIUS		CANCER
			CAPRICORN
EARTH ...TAURUS	VIRGO		
	CAPRICORN	FIXED ....TAURUS	LEO
			SCORPIO
AIR ......GEMINI	LIBRA		AQUARIUS
	AQUARIUS		
		MUTABLE ....GEMINI	VIRGO
WATER ...CANCER	SCORPIO		SAGITTARIUS
	PISCES		PISCES

Signs can be grouped together according to their element and quality. Signs of the same element share many basic traits in common. They tend to form stable configurations and ultimately harmonious relationships. Signs of the same quality are often less harmonious, but they share many dynamic potentials for growth as well as profound fulfillment.

Further discussion of each of these sign groupings is provided on the following pages.

The Fire Signs

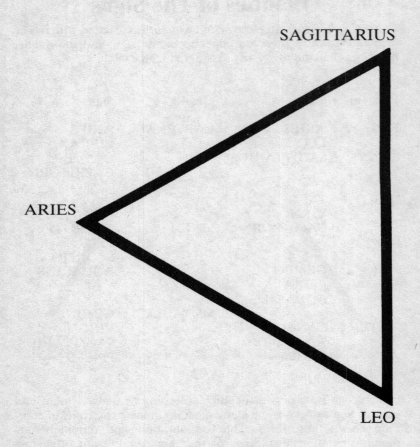

This is the fire group. On the whole these are emotional, volatile types, quick to anger, quick to forgive. They are adventurous, powerful people and act as a source of inspiration for everyone. They spark into action with immediate exuberant impulses. They are intelligent, self-involved, creative, and idealistic. They all share a certain vibrancy and glow that outwardly reflects an inner flame and passion for living.

The Earth Signs

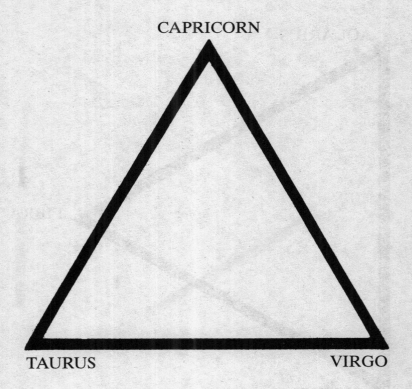

CAPRICORN

TAURUS

VIRGO

This is the earth group. They are in constant touch with the material world and tend to be conservative. Although they are all capable of spartan self-discipline, they are earthy, sensual people who are stimulated by the tangible, elegant, and luxurious. The thread of their lives is always practical, but they do fantasize and are often attracted to dark, mysterious, emotional people. They are like great cliffs overhanging the sea, forever married to the ocean but always resisting erosion from the dark, emotional forces that thunder at their feet.

The Air Signs

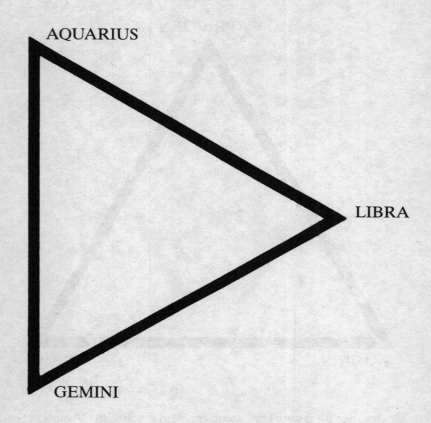

AQUARIUS

LIBRA

GEMINI

This is the air group. They are light, mental creatures desirous of contact, communication, and relationship. They are involved with people and the forming of ties on many levels. Original thinkers, they are the bearers of human news. Their language is their sense of word, color, style, and beauty. They provide an atmosphere suitable and pleasant for living. They add change and versatility to the scene, and it is through them that we can explore new territory of human intelligence and experience.

The Water Signs

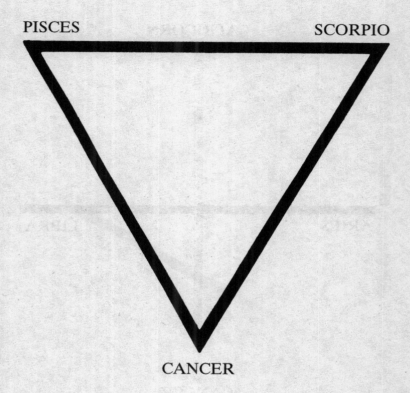

PISCES   SCORPIO

CANCER

This is the water group. Through the water people, we are all joined together on emotional, nonverbal levels. They are silent, mysterious types whose magic hypnotizes even the most determined realist. They have uncanny perceptions about people and are as rich as the oceans when it comes to feeling, emotion, or imagination. They are sensitive, mystical creatures with memories that go back beyond time. Through water, life is sustained. These people have the potential for the depths of darkness or the heights of mysticism and art.

The Cardinal Signs

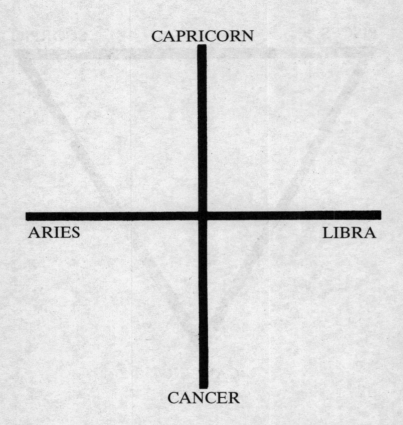

Put together, this is a clear-cut picture of dynamism, activity, tremendous stress, and remarkable achievement. These people know the meaning of great change since their lives are often characterized by significant crises and major successes. This combination is like a simultaneous storm of summer, fall, winter, and spring. The danger is chaotic diffusion of energy; the potential is irrepressible growth and victory.

The Fixed Signs

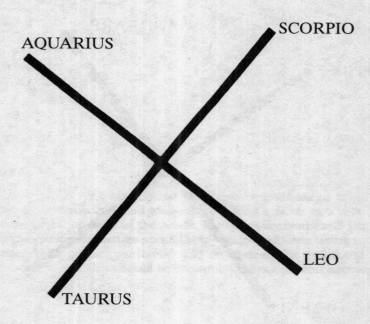

Fixed signs are always establishing themselves in a given place or area of experience. Like explorers who arrive and plant a flag, these people claim a position from which they do not enjoy being deposed. They are staunch, stalwart, upright, trusty, honorable people, although their obstinacy is well-known. Their contribution is fixity, and they are the angels who support our visible world.

The Mutable Signs

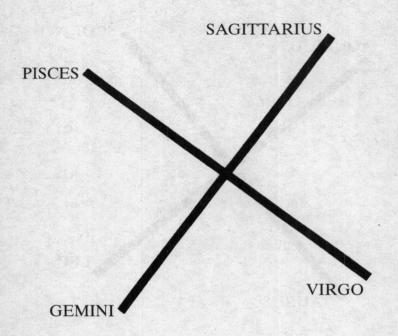

Mutable people are versatile, sensitive, intelligent, nervous, and deeply curious about life. They are the translators of all energy. They often carry out or complete tasks initiated by others. Combinations of these signs have highly developed minds; they are imaginative and jumpy and think and talk a lot. At worst their lives are a Tower of Babel. At best they are adaptable and ready creatures who can assimilate one kind of experience and enjoy it while anticipating coming changes.

THE PLANETS
OF THE SOLAR SYSTEM

This section describes the planets of the solar system. In astrology, both the Sun and the Moon are considered to be planets. Because of the Moon's influence in our day-to-day lives, the Moon is described in a separate section following this one.

The Planets and the Signs They Rule

The signs of the Zodiac are linked to the planets in the following way. Each sign is governed or ruled by one or more planets. No matter where the planets are located in the sky at any given moment, they still rule their respective signs, and when they travel through the signs they rule, they have special dignity and their effects are stronger.

Following is a list of the planets and the signs they rule. After looking at the list, read the definitions of the planets and see if you can determine how the planet ruling *your* Sun sign has affected your life.

SIGNS	RULING PLANETS
Aries	Mars, Pluto
Taurus	Venus
Gemini	Mercury
Cancer	Moon
Leo	Sun
Virgo	Mercury
Libra	Venus
Scorpio	Mars, Pluto
Sagittarius	Jupiter
Capricorn	Saturn
Aquarius	Saturn, Uranus
Pisces	Jupiter, Neptune

Characteristics of the Planets

The following pages give the meaning and characteristics of the planets of the solar system. They all travel around the Sun at different speeds and different distances. Taken with the Sun, they all distribute individual intelligence and ability throughout the entire chart.

The planets modify the influence of the Sun in a chart according to their own particular natures, strengths, and positions. Their positions must be calculated for each year and day, and their function and expression in a horoscope will change as they move from one area of the Zodiac to another.

We start with a description of the sun.

THE SUN

SUN

This is the center of existence. Around this flaming sphere all the planets revolve in endless orbits. Our star is constantly sending out its beams of light and energy without which no life on Earth would be possible. In astrology it symbolizes everything we are trying to become, the center around which all of our activity in life will always revolve. It is the symbol of our basic nature and describes the natural and constant thread that runs through everything that we do from birth to death on this planet.

To early astrologers, the Sun seemed to be another planet because it crossed the heavens every day, just like the rest of the bodies in the sky.

It is the only star near enough to be seen well—it is, in fact, a dwarf star. Approximately 860,000 miles in diameter, it is about ten times as wide as the giant planet Jupiter. The next nearest star is nearly 300,000 times as far away, and if the Sun were located as far away as most of the bright stars, it would be too faint to be seen without a telescope.

Everything in the horoscope ultimately revolves around this singular body. Although other forces may be prominent in the charts of some individuals, still the Sun is the total nucleus of being and symbolizes the complete potential of every human being alive. It is vitality and the life force. Your whole essence comes from the position of the Sun.

You are always trying to express the Sun according to its position by house and sign. Possibility for all development is found in the Sun, and it marks the fundamental character of your personal radiations all around you.

It is the symbol of strength, vigor, wisdom, dignity, ardor, and generosity, and the ability for a person to function as a mature individual. It is also a creative force in society. It is consciousness of the gift of life.

The underdeveloped solar nature is arrogant, pushy, undependable, and proud, and is constantly using force.

MERCURY

Mercury is the planet closest to the Sun. It races around our star, gathering information and translating it to the rest of the system. Mercury represents your capacity to understand the desires of your own will and to translate those desires into action.

In other words it is the planet of mind and the power of communication. Through Mercury we develop an ability to think, write, speak, and observe—to become aware of the world around us. It colors our attitudes and vision of the world, as well as our capacity to communicate our inner responses to the outside world. Some people who have serious disabilities in their power of verbal communication have often wrongly been described as people lacking intelligence.

Although this planet (and its position in the horoscope) indicates your power to communicate your thoughts and perceptions to the world, intelligence is something deeper. Intelligence is distributed throughout all the planets. It is the relationship of the planets to each other that truly describes what we call intelligence. Mercury rules speaking, language, mathematics, draft and design, students, messengers, young people, offices, teachers, and any pursuits where the mind of man has wings.

VENUS

Venus is beauty. It symbolizes the harmony and radiance of a rare and elusive quality: beauty itself. It is refinement and delicacy, softness and charm. In astrology it indicates grace, balance, and the aesthetic sense. Where Venus is we see beauty, a gentle drawing in of energy and the need for satisfaction and completion. It is a special touch that finishes off rough edges. It is sensitivity, and affection, and it is always the place for that other elusive phenomenon: love. Venus describes our sense of what is beautiful and loving. Poorly developed, it is vulgar, tasteless, and self-indulgent. But its ideal is the flame of spiritual love—Aphrodite, goddess of love, and the sweetness and power of personal beauty.

MARS

Mars is raw, crude energy. The planet next to Earth but outward from the Sun is a fiery red sphere that charges through the horoscope with force and fury. It represents the way you reach out for new adventure and new experience. It is energy and drive, initiative, courage, and daring. It is the power to start something and see it through. It can be thoughtless, cruel and wild, angry and hostile, causing cuts, burns, scalds, and wounds. It can stab its way through a chart, or it can be the symbol of healthy spirited adventure, well-channeled constructive power to begin and keep up the drive. If you have trouble starting things, if you lack the get-up-and-go to start the ball rolling, if you lack aggressiveness and self-confidence, chances are there's another planet influencing your Mars. Mars rules soldiers, butchers, surgeons, salesmen—any field that requires daring, bold skill, operational technique, or self-promotion.

JUPITER

This is the largest planet of the solar system. Scientists have recently learned that Jupiter reflects more light than it receives from the Sun. In a sense it is like a star itself. In astrology it rules good luck and good cheer, health, wealth, optimism, happiness, success, and joy. It is the symbol of opportunity and always opens the way for new possibilities in your life. It rules exuberance, enthusiasm, wisdom, knowledge, generosity, and all forms of expansion in general. It rules actors, statesmen, clerics, professional people, religion, publishing, and the distribution of many people over large areas.

Sometimes Jupiter makes you think you deserve everything, and you become sloppy, wasteful, careless and rude, prodigal and lawless, in the illusion that nothing can ever go wrong. Then there is the danger of overconfidence, exaggeration, undependability, and overindulgence.

Jupiter is the minimization of limitation and the emphasis on spirituality and potential. It is the thirst for knowledge and higher learning.

SATURN

Saturn circles our system in dark splendor with its mysterious rings, forcing us to be awakened to whatever we have neglected in the past. It will present real puzzles and problems to be solved, causing delays, obstacles, and hindrances. By doing so, Saturn stirs our own sensitivity to those areas where we are laziest.

Here we must patiently develop *method*, and only through painstaking effort can our ends be achieved. It brings order to a horoscope and imposes reason just where we are feeling least reasonable. By creating limitations and boundary, Saturn shows the consequences of being human and demands that we accept the changing cycles inevitable in human life. Saturn rules time, old age, and sobriety. It can bring depression, gloom, jealousy, and greed, or serious acceptance of responsibilities out of which success will develop. With Saturn there is nothing to do but face facts. It rules laborers, stones, granite, rocks, and crystals of all kinds.

THE OUTER PLANETS:
URANUS, NEPTUNE, PLUTO

Uranus, Neptune, Pluto are the outer planets. They liberate human beings from cultural conditioning, and in that sense are the law-breakers. In early times it was thought that Saturn was the last planet of the system—the outer limit beyond which we could never go. The discovery of the next three planets ushered in new phases of human history, revolution, and technology.

URANUS

Uranus rules unexpected change, upheaval, revolution. It is the symbol of total independence and asserts the freedom of an individual from all restriction and restraint. It is a breakthrough planet and indicates talent, originality, and genius in a horoscope. It usually causes last-minute reversals and changes of plan, unwanted separations, accidents, catastrophes, and eccentric behavior. It can add irrational rebelliousness and perverse bohemianism to a personality or a streak of unaffected brilliance in science and art. It rules technology, aviation, and all forms of electrical and electronic advancement. It governs great leaps forward and topsy-turvy situations, and *always* turns things around at the last minute. Its effects are difficult to predict, since it rules sudden last-minute decisions and events that come like lightning out of the blue.

NEPTUNE

Neptune dissolves existing reality the way the sea erodes the cliffs beside it. Its effects are subtle like the ringing of a buoy's bell in the fog. It suggests a reality higher than definition can usually describe. It awakens a sense of higher responsibility often causing guilt, worry, anxieties, or delusions. Neptune is associated with all forms of escape and can make things seem a certain way so convincingly that you are absolutely sure of something that eventually turns out to be quite different.

It is the planet of illusion and therefore governs the invisible realms that lie beyond our ordinary minds, beyond our simple factual ability to prove what is "real." Treachery, deceit, disillusionment, and disappointment are linked to Neptune. It describes a vague reality that promises eternity and the divine, yet in a manner so complex that we cannot really fathom it at all. At its worst Neptune is a cheap intoxicant; at its best it is the poetry, music, and inspiration of the higher planes of spiritual love. It has dominion over movies, photographs, and much of the arts.

PLUTO

Pluto lies at the outpost of our system and therefore rules finality in a horoscope—the final closing of chapters in your life, the passing of major milestones and points of development from which there is no return. It is a final wipeout, a closeout, an evacuation. It is a distant, subtle but powerful catalyst in all transformations that occur. It creates, destroys, then recreates. Sometimes Pluto starts its influence with a minor event or insignificant incident that might even go unnoticed. Slowly but surely, little by little, everything changes, until at last there has been a total transformation in the area of your life where Pluto has been operating. It rules mass thinking and the trends that society first rejects, then adopts, and finally outgrows.

Pluto rules the dead and the underworld—all the powerful forces of creation and destruction that go on all the time beneath, around, and above us. It can bring a lust for power with strong obsessions.

It is the planet that rules the metamorphosis of the caterpillar into a butterfly, for it symbolizes the capacity to change totally and forever a person's lifestyle, way of thought, and behavior.

THE MOON IN EACH SIGN

The Moon is the nearest planet to the Earth. It exerts more observable influence on us from day to day than any other planet. The effect is very personal, very intimate, and if we are not aware of how it works it can make us quite unstable in our ideas. And the annoying thing is that at these times we often see our own instability but can do nothing about it. A knowledge of what can be expected may help considerably. We can then be prepared to stand strong against the Moon's negative influences and use its positive ones to help us to get ahead. Who has not heard of going with the tide?

The Moon reflects, has no light of its own. It reflects the Sun—the life giver—in the form of vital movement. The Moon controls the tides, the blood rhythm, the movement of sap in trees and plants. Its nature is inconstancy and change so it signifies our moods, our superficial behavior—walking, talking, and especially thinking. Being a true reflector of other forces, the Moon is cold, watery like the surface of a still lake, brilliant and scintillating at times, but easily ruffled and disturbed by the winds of change.

The Moon takes about 27⅓ days to make a complete transit of the Zodiac. It spends just over 2¼ days in each sign. During that time it reflects the qualities, energies, and characteristics of the sign and, to a degree, the planet which rules the sign. When the Moon in its transit occupies a sign incompatible with our own birth sign, we can expect to feel a vague uneasiness, perhaps a touch of irritableness. We should not be discouraged nor let the feeling get us down, or, worse still, allow ourselves to take the discomfort out on others. Try to remember that the Moon has to change signs within 55 hours and, provided you are not physically ill, your mood will probably change with it. It is amazing how frequently depression lifts with the shift in the Moon's position. And, of course, when the Moon is transiting a sign compatible or sympathetic to yours, you will probably feel some sort of stimulation or just be plain happy to be alive.

In the horoscope, the Moon is such a powerful indicator that competent astrologers often use the sign it occupied at birth as the birth sign of the person. This is done particularly when the Sun is on the cusp, or edge, of two signs. Most experienced astrologers, however, coordinate both Sun and Moon signs by reading and confirming from one to the other and secure a far more accurate and personalized analysis.

For these reasons, the Moon tables which follow this section (see pages 86–92) are of great importance to the individual. They show the days and the exact times the Moon will enter each sign of the Zodiac for the year. Remember, you have to adjust the indicated times to local time. The corrections, already calculated for most of the main cities, are at the beginning of the tables. What follows now is a guide to the influences that will be reflected to the Earth by the Moon while it transits each of the twelve signs. The influence is at its peak about 26 hours after the Moon enters a sign. As you read the daily forecast, check the Moon sign for any given day and glance back at this guide.

MOON IN ARIES

This is a time for action, for reaching out beyond the usual self-imposed limitations and faint-hearted cautions. If you have plans in your head or on your desk, put them into practice. New ventures, applications, new jobs, new starts of any kind—all have a good chance of success. This is the period when original and dynamic impulses are being reflected onto Earth. Such energies are extremely vital and favor the pursuit of pleasure and adventure in practically every form. Sick people should feel an improvement. Those who are well will probably find themselves exuding confidence and optimism. People fond of physical exercise should find their bodies growing with tone and well-being. Boldness, strength, determination should characterize most of your activities with a readiness to face up to old challenges. Yesterday's problems may seem petty and exaggerated—so deal with them. Strike out alone. Self-reliance will attract others to you. This is a good time for making friends. Business and marriage partners are more likely to be impressed with the man and woman of action. Opposition will be overcome or thrown aside with much less effort than usual. CAUTION: Be dominant but not domineering.

MOON IN TAURUS

The spontaneous, action-packed person of yesterday gives way to the cautious, diligent, hardworking "thinker." In this period ideas will probably be concentrated on ways of improving finances. A great deal of time may be spent figuring out and going over schemes and plans. It is the right time to be careful with detail. People will find themselves working longer than usual at their desks. Or devoting more time to serious thought about the future. A strong desire to put order into business and financial arrangements may cause extra work. Loved ones may complain of being neglected and may fail to appreciate that your efforts are for their ultimate benefit. Your desire for system may extend to criticism of arrangements in the home and lead to minor upsets. Health may be affected through overwork. Try to secure a reasonable amount of rest and relaxation, although the tendency will be to "keep going" despite good advice. Work done conscientiously in this period should result in a solid contribution to your future security. CAUTION: Try not to be as serious with people as the work you are engaged in.

MOON IN GEMINI

The humdrum of routine and too much work should suddenly end. You are likely to find yourself in an expansive, quicksilver world of change and self-expression. Urges to write, to paint, to experience the freedom of some sort of artistic outpouring, may be very strong. Take full advantage of them. You may find yourself finishing something you began and put aside long ago. Or embarking on something new which could easily be prompted by a chance meeting, a new acquaintance, or even an advertisement. There may be a yearning for a change of scenery, the feeling to visit another country (not too far away), or at least to get away for a few days. This may result in short, quick journeys. Or, if you are planning a single visit, there may be some unexpected changes or detours on the way. Familiar activities will seem to give little satisfaction unless they contain a fresh element of excitement or expectation. The inclination will be toward untried pursuits, particularly those that allow you to express your inner nature. The accent is on new faces, new places. CAUTION: Do not be too quick to commit yourself emotionally.

MOON IN CANCER

Feelings of uncertainty and vague insecurity are likely to cause problems while the Moon is in Cancer. Thoughts may turn frequently to the warmth of the home and the comfort of loved ones. Nostalgic impulses could cause you to bring out old photographs and letters and reflect on the days when your life seemed to be much more rewarding and less demanding. The love and understanding of parents and family may be important, and, if it is not forthcoming, you may have to fight against bouts of self-pity. The cordiality of friends and the thought of good times with them that are sure to be repeated will help to restore you to a happier frame of mind. The desire to be alone may follow minor setbacks or rebuffs at this time, but solitude is unlikely to help. Better to get on the telephone or visit someone. This period often causes peculiar dreams and upsurges of imaginative thinking which can be helpful to authors of occult and mystical works. Preoccupation with the personal world of simple human needs can overshadow any material strivings. CAUTION: Do not spend too much time thinking— seek the company of loved ones or close friends.

MOON IN LEO
New horizons of exciting and rather extravagant activity open up. This is the time for exhilarating entertainment, glamorous and lavish parties, and expensive shopping sprees. Any merrymaking that relies upon your generosity as a host has every chance of being a spectacular success. You should find yourself right in the center of the fun, either as the life of the party or simply as a person whom happy people like to be with. Romance thrives in this heady atmosphere and friendships are likely to explode unexpectedly into serious attachments. Children and younger people should be attracted to you and you may find yourself organizing a picnic or a visit to a fun-fair, the movies, or the beach. The sunny company and vitality of youthful companions should help you to find some unsuspected energy. In career, you could find an opening for promotion or advancement. This should be the time to make a direct approach. The period favors those engaged in original research. CAUTION: Bask in popularity, not in flattery.

MOON IN VIRGO
Off comes the party cap and out steps the busy, practical worker. He wants to get his personal affairs straight, to rearrange them, if necessary, for more efficiency, so he will have more time for more work. He clears up his correspondence, pays outstanding bills, makes numerous phone calls. He is likely to make inquiries, or sign up for some new insurance and put money into gilt-edged investment. Thoughts probably revolve around the need for future security—to tie up loose ends and clear the decks. There may be a tendency to be "finicky," to interfere in the routine of others, particularly friends and family members. The motive may be a genuine desire to help with suggestions for updating or streamlining their affairs, but these will probably not be welcomed. Sympathy may be felt for less fortunate sections of the community and a flurry of some sort of voluntary service is likely. This may be accompanied by strong feelings of responsibility on several fronts and health may suffer from extra efforts made. CAUTION: Everyone may not want your help or advice.

MOON IN LIBRA

These are days of harmony and agreement and you should find yourself at peace with most others. Relationships tend to be smooth and sweet-flowing. Friends may become closer and bonds deepen in mutual understanding. Hopes will be shared. Progress by cooperation could be the secret of success in every sphere. In business, established partnerships may flourish and new ones get off to a good start. Acquaintances could discover similar interests that lead to congenial discussions and rewarding exchanges of some sort. Love, as a unifying force, reaches its optimum. Marriage partners should find accord. Those who wed at this time face the prospect of a happy union. Cooperation and tolerance are felt to be stronger than dissension and impatience. The argumentative are not quite so loud in their bellowings, nor as inflexible in their attitudes. In the home, there should be a greater recognition of the other point of view and a readiness to put the wishes of the group before selfish insistence. This is a favorable time to join an art group. CAUTION: Do not be too independent—let others help you if they want to.

MOON IN SCORPIO

Driving impulses to make money and to economize are likely to cause upsets all around. No area of expenditure is likely to be spared the ax, including the household budget. This is a time when the desire to cut down on extravagance can become near fanatical. Care must be exercised to try to keep the aim in reasonable perspective. Others may not feel the same urgent need to save and may retaliate. There is a danger that possessions of sentimental value will be sold to realize cash for investment. Buying and selling of stock for quick profit is also likely. The attention turns to organizing, reorganizing, tidying up at home and at work. Neglected jobs could suddenly be done with great bursts of energy. The desire for solitude may intervene. Self-searching thoughts could disturb. The sense of invisible and mysterious energies in play could cause some excitability. The reassurance of loves ones may help. CAUTION: Be kind to the people you love.

MOON IN SAGITTARIUS

These are days when you are likely to be stirred and elevated by discussions and reflections of a religious and philosophical nature. Ideas of faraway places may cause unusual response and excitement. A decision may be made to visit someone overseas, perhaps a person whose influence was important to your earlier character development. There could be a strong resolution to get away from present intellectual patterns, to learn new subjects, and to meet more interesting people. The superficial may be rejected in all its forms. An impatience with old ideas and unimaginative contacts could lead to a change of companions and interests. There may be an upsurge of religious feeling and metaphysical inquiry. Even a new insight into the significance of astrology and other occult studies is likely under the curious stimulus of the Moon in Sagittarius. Physically, you may express this need for fundamental change by spending more time outdoors: sports, gardening, long walks appeal. CAUTION: Try to channel any restlessness into worthwhile study.

MOON IN CAPRICORN

Life in these hours may seem to pivot around the importance of gaining prestige and honor in the career, as well as maintaining a spotless reputation. Ambitious urges may be excessive and could be accompanied by quite acquisitive drives for money. Effort should be directed along strictly ethical lines where there is no possibility of reproach or scandal. All endeavors are likely to be characterized by great earnestness, and an air of authority and purpose which should impress those who are looking for leadership or reliability. The desire to conform to accepted standards may extend to sharp criticism of family members. Frivolity and unconventional actions are unlikely to amuse while the Moon is in Capricorn. Moderation and seriousness are the orders of the day. Achievement and recognition in this period could come through community work or organizing for the benefit of some amateur group. CAUTION: Dignity and esteem are not always self-awarded.

MOON IN AQUARIUS

Moon in Aquarius is in the second last sign of the Zodiac where ideas can become disturbingly fine and subtle. The result is often a mental "no-man's land" where imagination cannot be trusted with the same certitude as other times. The dangers for the individual are the extremes of optimism and pessimism. Unless the imagination is held in check, situations are likely to be misread, and rosy conclusions drawn where they do not exist. Consequences for the unwary can be costly in career and business. Best to think twice and not speak or act until you think again. Pessimism can be a cruel self-inflicted penalty for delusion at this time. Between the two extremes are strange areas of self-deception which, for example, can make the selfish person think he is actually being generous. Eerie dreams which resemble the reality and even seem to continue into the waking state are also possible. CAUTION: Look for the fact and not just for the image in your mind.

MOON IN PISCES

Everything seems to come to the surface now. Memory may be crystal clear, throwing up long-forgotten information which could be valuable in the career or business. Flashes of clairvoyance and intuition are possible along with sudden realizations of one's own nature, which may be used for self-improvement. A talent, never before suspected, may be discovered. Qualities not evident before in friends and marriage partners are likely to be noticed. As this is a period in which the truth seems to emerge, the discovery of false characteristics is likely to lead to disenchantment or a shift in attachments. However, when qualities are accepted, it should lead to happiness and deeper feeling. Surprise solutions could bob up for old problems. There may be a public announcement of the solving of a crime or mystery. People with secrets may find someone has "guessed" correctly. The secrets of the soul or the inner self also tend to reveal themselves. Religious and philosophical groups may make some interesting discoveries. CAUTION: Not a time for activities that depend on secrecy.

NOTE: When you read your daily forecasts, use the Moon Sign Dates that are provided in the following section of Moon Tables. Then you may want to glance back here for the Moon's influence in a given sign.

MOON TABLES

CORRECTION FOR NEW YORK TIME, FIVE HOURS WEST OF GREENWICH

Atlanta, Boston, Detroit, Miami, Washington, Montreal,
Ottawa, Quebec, Bogota,Havana, Lima, Santiago ... Same time
Chicago, New Orleans, Houston, Winnipeg, Churchill,
Mexico City .... Deduct 1 hour
Albuquerque, Denver, Phoenix, El Paso, Edmonton,
Helena .... Deduct 2 hours
Los Angeles, San Francisco, Reno, Portland,
Seattle, Vancouver .... Deduct 3 hours
Honolulu, Anchorage, Fairbanks, Kodiak .... Deduct 5 hours
Nome, Samoa, Tonga, Midway .... Deduct 6 hours
Halifax, Bermuda, San Juan, Caracas, La Paz,
Barbados .... Add 1 hour
St. John's, Brasilia, Rio de Janeiro, Sao Paulo,
Buenos Aires, Montevideo .... Add 2 hours
Azores, Cape Verde Islands .... Add 3 hours
Canary Islands, Madeira, Reykjavik .... Add 4 hours
London, Paris, Amsterdam, Madrid, Lisbon,
Gibraltar, Belfast, Raba .... Add 5 hours
Frankfurt, Rome, Oslo, Stockholm, Prague,
Belgrade .... Add 6 hours
Bucharest, Beirut, Tel Aviv, Athens, Istanbul, Cairo,
Alexandria, Cape Town, Johannesburg .... Add 7 hours
Moscow, Leningrad, Baghdad, Dhahran,
Addis Ababa, Nairobi, Teheran, Zanzibar .... Add 8 hours
Bombay, Calcutta, Sri Lanka .... Add 10$\frac{1}{2}$
Hong Kong, Shanghai, Manila, Peking, Perth ...... Add 13 hours
Tokyo, Okinawa, Darwin, Pusan .... Add 14 hours
Sydney, Melbourne, Port Moresby, Guam .... Add 15 hours
Auckland, Wellington, Suva, Wake .... Add 17 hours

2009 MOON SIGN DATES—
NEW YORK TIME

JANUARY Day Moon Enters		FEBRUARY Day Moon Enters		MARCH Day Moon Enters	
1. Pisces		1. Taurus	5:10 pm	1. Taurus	
2. Pisces		2. Taurus		2. Taurus	
3. Aries	4:51 am	3. Gemini	9:16 pm	3. Gemini	3:00 pm
4. Aries		4. Gemini		4. Gemini	
5. Taurus	10:47 am	5. Cancer	11:07 pm	5. Cancer	6:08 am
6. Taurus		6. Cancer		6. Cancer	
7. Gemini	1:13 pm	7. Leo	11:44 pm	7. Leo	8:25 am
8. Gemini		8. Leo		8. Leo	
9. Cancer	1:15 pm	9. Leo		9. Virgo	10:35 am
10. Cancer		10. Virgo	12:39 am	10. Virgo	
11. Leo	12:42 pm	11. Virgo		11. Libra	1:47 pm
12. Leo		12. Libra	3:34 am	12. Libra	
13. Virgo	1:34 pm	13. Libra		13. Scorp.	7:24 pm
14. Virgo		14. Scorp.	9:52 am	14. Scorp.	
15. Libra	5:31 pm	15. Scorp.		15. Scorp.	
16. Libra		16. Sagitt.	7:54 pm	16. Sagitt.	4:23 am
17. Libra		17. Sagitt.		17. Sagitt.	
18. Scorp.	1:21 am	18. Sagitt.		18. Capric.	4:20 pm
19. Scorp.		19. Capric.	8:26 am	19. Capric.	
20. Sagitt.	12:31 pm	20. Capric.		20. Capric.	
21. Sagitt.		21. Aquar.	9:07 pm	21. Aquar.	5:08 am
22. Sagitt.		22. Aquar.		22. Aquar.	
23. Capric.	1:19 am	23. Aquar.		23. Pisces	4:09 pm
24. Capric.		24. Pisces	8:01 am	24. Pisces	
25. Aquar.	1:58 pm	25. Pisces		25. Pisces	
26. Aquar.		26. Aries	4:25 pm	26. Aries	12:04 am
27. Aquar.		27. Aries		27. Aries	
28. Pisces	1:13 am	28. Taurus	10:34 pm	28. Taurus	10:10 am
29. Pisces				29. Taurus	
30. Aries	10:26 am			30. Gemini	8:37 am
31. Aries				31. Gemini	

Daylight saving time to be considered where applicable.

2009 MOON SIGN DATES—
NEW YORK TIME

APRIL Day Moon Enters		MAY Day Moon Enters		JUNE Day Moon Enters	
1. Cancer	11:31 am	1. Leo		1. Libra	10:18 am
2. Cancer		2. Virgo	11:38 pm	2. Libra	
3. Leo	2:34 pm	3. Virgo		3. Scorp.	5:45 pm
4. Leo		4. Virgo		4. Scorp.	
5. Virgo	6:02 pm	5. Libra	4:52 am	5. Scorp.	
6. Virgo		6. Libra		6. Sagitt.	3:25 am
7. Libra	10:23 pm	7. Scorp.	11:49 am	7. Sagitt.	
8. Libra		8. Scorp.		8. Capric.	3:01 pm
9. Libra		9. Sagitt.	8:50 pm	9. Capric.	
10. Scorp.	4:24 am	10. Sagitt.		10. Capric.	
11. Scorp.		11. Sagitt.		11. Aquar.	3:54 am
12. Sagitt.	1:02 pm	12. Capric.	8:10 am	12. Aquar.	
13. Sagitt.		13. Capric.		13. Pisces	4:33 pm
14. Sagitt.		14. Aquar.	9:02 pm	14. Pisces	
15. Capric.	12:28 am	15. Aquar.		15. Pisces	
16. Capric.		16. Aquar.		16. Aries	2:53 am
17. Aquar.	1:20 pm	17. Pisces	9:18 am	17. Aries	
18. Aquar.		18. Pisces		18. Taurus	9:21 am
19. Aquar.		19. Aries	6:31 pm	19. Taurus	
20. Pisces	12:56 am	20. Aries		20. Gemini	12:01 pm
21. Pisces		21. Taurus	11:41 pm	21. Gemini	
22. Aries	9:10 am	22. Taurus		22. Cancer	12:13 pm
23. Aries		23. Taurus		23. Cancer	
24. Taurus	1:47 pm	24. Gemini	1:35 am	24. Leo	11:51 pm
25. Taurus		25. Gemini		25. Leo	
26. Gemini	4:03 pm	26. Cancer	1:59 am	26. Virgo	12:48 pm
27. Gemini		27. Cancer		27. Virgo	
28. Cancer	5:39 pm	28. Leo	2:45 am	28. Libra	4:26 pm
29. Cancer		29. Leo		29. Libra	
30. Leo	7:57 pm	30. Virgo	5:19 am	30. Scorp.	11:20 pm
		31. Virgo			

Daylight saving time to be considered where applicable.

2009 MOON SIGN DATES—
NEW YORK TIME

JULY Day Moon Enters		AUGUST Day Moon Enters		SEPTEMBER Day Moon Enters	
1. Scorp.		1. Sagitt.		1. Aquar.	
2. Scorp.		2. Capric.	3:09 am	2. Aquar.	
3. Sagitt.	9:12 am	3. Capric.		3. Pisces	10:59 am
4. Sagitt.		4. Aquar.	5:09 pm	4. Pisces	
5. Capric.	9:09 pm	5. Aquar.		5. Aries	9:15 pm
6. Capric.		6. Aquar.		6. Aries	
7. Capric.		7. Pisces	4:35 pm	7. Aries	
8. Aquar.	10:04 am	8. Pisces		8. Taurus	5:19 am
9. Aquar.		9. Aries	3:24 pm	9. Taurus	
10. Pisces	10:45 pm	10. Aries		10. Gemini	11:18 am
11. Pisces		11. Taurus	11:51 pm	11. Gemini	
12. Pisces		12. Taurus		12. Cancer	3:21 pm
13. Aries	9:41 am	13. Taurus		13. Cancer	
14. Aries		14. Gemini	5:27 am	14. Leo	5:40 pm
15. Taurus	5:31 pm	15. Gemini		15. Leo	
16. Taurus		16. Cancer	8:14 am	16. Virgo	6:57 pm
17. Gemini	9:42 pm	17. Cancer		17. Virgo	
18. Gemini		18. Leo	8:58 am	18. Libra	8:27 pm
19. Cancer	10:52 pm	19. Leo		19. Libra	
20. Cancer		20. Virgo	9:02 am	20. Scorp.	11:53 pm
21. Leo	10:29 pm	21. Virgo		21. Scorp.	
22. Leo		22. Libra	10:13 am	22. Scorp.	
23. Virgo	10:24 pm	23. Libra		23. Sagitt.	6:44 am
24. Virgo		24. Scorp.	2:17 pm	24. Sagitt.	
25. Virgo		25. Scorp.		25. Capric.	5:20 pm
26. Libra	12:27 am	26. Sagitt.	10:17 pm	26. Capric.	
27. Libra		27. Sagitt.		27. Capric.	
28. Scorp.	5:57 am	28. Sagitt.		28. Aquar.	6:08 am
29. Scorp.		29. Capric.	9:45 am	29. Aquar.	
30. Sagitt.	3:11 pm	30. Capric.		30. Pisces	6:27 pm
31. Sagitt.		31. Aquar.	10:44 pm		

Daylight saving time to be considered where applicable.

2009 MOON SIGN DATES—
NEW YORK TIME

OCTOBER Day Moon Enters		NOVEMBER Day Moon Enters		DECEMBER Day Moon Enters	
1. Pisces		1. Taurus	7:46 pm	1. Gemini	9:25 am
2. Pisces		2. Taurus		2. Gemini	
3. Aries	4:22 am	3. Gemini	11:54 pm	3. Cancer	11:02 am
4. Aries		4. Gemini		4. Cancer	
5. Taurus	11:34 am	5. Gemini		5. Leo	12:06 pm
6. Taurus		6. Cancer	2:44 am	6. Leo	
7. Gemini	4:48 pm	7. Cancer		7. Virgo	2:07 pm
8. Gemini		8. Leo	5:24 am	8. Virgo	
9. Cancer	8:49 pm	9. Leo		9. Libra	5:48 pm
10. Cancer		10. Virgo	8:31 am	10. Libra	
11. Cancer		11. Virgo		11. Scorp.	11:33 pm
12. Leo	12:04 am	12. Libra	12:23 pm	12. Scorp.	
13. Leo		13. Libra		13. Scorp.	
14. Virgo	2:46 am	14. Scorp.	5:25 pm	14. Sagitt.	7:26 am
15. Virgo		15. Scorp.		15. Sagitt.	
16. Libra	5:31 am	16. Scorp.		16. Capric.	5:33 pm
17. Libra		17. Sagitt.	12:23 am	17. Capric.	
18. Scorp.	9:24 am	18. Sagitt.		18. Capric.	
19. Scorp.		19. Capric.	10:02 am	19. Aquar.	5:40 am
20. Sagitt.	3:50 pm	20. Capric.		20. Aquar.	
21. Sagitt.		21. Aquar.	10:12 pm	21. Pisces	6:43 pm
22. Sagitt.		22. Aquar.		22. Pisces	
23. Capric.	1:40 am	23. Aquar.		23. Pisces	
24. Capric.		24. Pisces	11:09 am	24. Aries	6:41 am
25. Aquar.	2:09 pm	25. Pisces		25. Aries	
26. Aquar.		26. Aries	10:12 pm	26. Taurus	3:27 pm
27. Aquar.		27. Aries		27. Taurus	
28. Pisces	2:46 am	28. Aries		28. Gemini	8:14 pm
29. Pisces		29. Taurus	5:35 am	29. Gemini	
30. Aries	12:58 pm	30. Taurus		30. Cancer	9:46 pm
31. Aries				31. Cancer	

Daylight saving time to be considered where applicable.

2009 PHASES OF THE MOON—
NEW YORK TIME

New Moon	First Quarter	Full Moon	Last Quarter
Dec. 27 ('08)	Jan. 4	Jan. 10	Jan. 17
Jan. 26	Feb. 2	Feb. 9	Feb. 16
Feb. 24	March 4	March 10	March 18
March 26	April 2	April 9	April 17
April 24	May 1	May 9	May 17
May 24	May 30	June 7	June 15
June 22	June 29	July 7	July 15
July 21	July 28	August 5	August 13
August 20	August 27	Sept. 4	Sept. 11
Sept. 18	Sept. 26	Oct. 4	Oct. 11
Oct. 18	Oct. 25	Nov. 2	Nov. 9
Nov. 16	Nov. 24	Dec. 2	Dec. 8
Dec. 15	Dec. 24	Dec. 31	Jan. 7 ('10)

Each phase of the Moon lasts approximately seven to eight days, during which the Moon's shape gradually changes as it comes out of one phase and goes into the next.

There will be a solar eclipse during the New Moon phase on January 26 and July 21.

There will be a lunar eclipse during the Full Moon phase on February 9, July 7, August 5, and December 31.

2009 FISHING GUIDE

	Good	Best
January	4-8-9-11-12-13-14-26	10-18
February	8-9-10-11-17	2-6-7-25
March	4-9-10-11-19-26	12-13-14-15
April	7-8-13-17-18	2-8-9-10-11-25
May	1-10-11-17-24-31	5-6-7-8-9
June	6-7-8-16-22	4-5-9-10-29
July	4-5-8-9-10-15-21	6-7-28
August	4-5-6-20-27	2-3-7-8-13
September	2-3-6-7-8-11	4-5-19-26
October	1-3-4-5-7-26-31	2-6-11-18-29
November	1-4-5-9-16-29	2-3-25-30
December	1-2-3-5-9-16-25-29-30	4-27-31

2009 PLANTING GUIDE

	Aboveground Crops	Root Crops
January	1-2-6-10-29	16-17-18-19-23-24
February	2-3-6-7-24-25	12-13-14-15-20-21
March	1-2-5-6-29	13-14-15-16-19-20-24-25
April	2-8-9-25-29-30	10-11-15-16-21
May	5-6-7-8-26-27	13-14-18-19-22-23
June	2-3-4-5-23-29-30	9-10-14-15-19
July	1-2-6-27-28-29	7-11-16-17-20-21
August	2-3-23-24-25-26-30	7-8-12-13-17
September	4-19-20-21-22-26-27	5-9-13
October	2-18-19-23-24-28-29	6-10-11-17
November	2-19-20-25-30	3-6-7-13-14-15-16
December	17-18-22-23-27-28	4-10-11-12-13

	Pruning	Weeds and Pests
January	18-10	12-13-14-15-21-22
February	14-15	1-11-17-18-22
March	14-15-24-25	16-17-21-22
April	10-11-21	13-14-18-23
May	17-18	10-11-15-16-20-21
June	14-15	11-12-17-21
July	12-20-21	9-10-13-14-18-19
August	8-9-17	10-11-14-15-19
September	4-13	6-7-11-15-16-17
October	10-11	8-12-13-14-15
November	6-7-15-16	4-5-8-9-10-11
December	4-12-13	1-5-6-7-8-14-15

MOON'S INFLUENCE OVER PLANTS

Centuries ago it was established that seeds planted when the Moon is in signs and phases called Fruitful will produce more growth than seeds planted when the Moon is in a Barren sign.

Fruitful Signs: Taurus, Cancer, Libra, Scorpio, Capricorn, Pisces
Barren Signs: Aries, Gemini, Leo, Virgo, Sagittarius, Aquarius
Dry Signs: Aries, Gemini, Sagittarius, Aquarius

Activity	Moon In
Mow lawn, trim plants	**Fruitful sign:** 1st & 2nd quarter
Plant flowers	**Fruitful sign:** 2nd quarter; best in Cancer and Libra
Prune	**Fruitful sign:** 3rd & 4th quarter
Destroy pests; spray	**Barren sign:** 4th quarter
Harvest potatoes, root crops	**Dry sign:** 3rd & 4th quarter; Taurus, Leo, and Aquarius

MOON'S INFLUENCE OVER YOUR HEALTH

ARIES   Head, brain, face, upper jaw
TAURUS   Throat, neck, lower jaw
GEMINI   Hands, arms, lungs, shoulders, nervous system
CANCER   Esophagus, stomach, breasts, womb, liver
LEO   Heart, spine
VIRGO   Intestines, liver
LIBRA   Kidneys, lower back
SCORPIO   Sex and eliminative organs
SAGITTARIUS   Hips, thighs, liver
CAPRICORN   Skin, bones, teeth, knees
AQUARIUS   Circulatory system, lower legs
PISCES   Feet, tone of being

Try to avoid work being done on that part of the body when the Moon is in the sign governing that part.

MOON'S INFLUENCE OVER DAILY AFFAIRS

The Moon makes a complete transit of the Zodiac every 27 days 7 hours and 43 minutes. In making this transit the Moon forms different aspects with the planets and consequently has favorable or unfavorable bearings on affairs and events for persons according to the sign of the Zodiac under which they were born.

When the Moon is in conjunction with the Sun it is called a New Moon; when the Moon and Sun are in opposition it is called a Full Moon. From New Moon to Full Moon, first and second quarter— which takes about two weeks—the Moon is increasing or waxing. From Full Moon to New Moon, third and fourth quarter, the Moon is decreasing or waning.

Activity	Moon In
Business: buying and selling new, requiring public support	Sagittarius, Aries, Gemini, Virgo 1st and 2nd quarter
meant to be kept quiet	3rd and 4th quarter
Investigation	3rd and 4th quarter
Signing documents	1st & 2nd quarter, Cancer, Scorpio, Pisces
Advertising	2nd quarter, Sagittarius
Journeys and trips	1st & 2nd quarter, Gemini, Virgo
Renting offices, etc.	Taurus, Leo, Scorpio, Aquarius
Painting of house/apartment	3rd & 4th quarter, Taurus, Scorpio, Aquarius
Decorating	Gemini, Libra, Aquarius
Buying clothes and accessories	Taurus, Virgo
Beauty salon or barber shop visit	1st & 2nd quarter, Taurus, Leo, Libra, Scorpio, Aquarius
Weddings	1st & 2nd quarter

Libra

LIBRA

Character Analysis

People born under the sign of Libra are generally quite kind and sympathetic. They dislike seeing others suffer and do what they can to help those in dire straits. Another outstanding characteristic of a Libra is love of harmony and beauty. They generally have a deep appreciation for all forms of art. Libra only feels comfortable in places that radiate harmony and beauty. They are often willing to sacrifice to make their environment suit their tastes.

Libras like people. They are often afraid of being alone. They love company. Others like them for their charm and gentle ways. They are happiest when with others. A Libra alone is likely to fall into a depressed state easily. Being with others helps them to keep their spirits up even during difficult moments. A Libra rarely goes through life alone. They need permanent and reliable relationships. Often they marry early in life.

Libra has a kind and gentle nature. They would never go out of their way to hurt someone. Libra is considerate of others feelings. They will always keep up their end of a bargain. He or she is cooperative and courteous—sometimes to a fault.

The Libra man or woman is someone who is constantly weighing both sides of a problem. This characteristic is represented by the Scales, which is the zodiacal symbol for Libra. Libras are difficult people to satisfy. They want to make sure they are right in all the decisions they make. They may take a long time before coming to a decision. They may even change their minds several times in the process of weighing the pros and cons.

Balance is central to the Libra man or woman, just as balance typifies the function of the Scales. Outwardly Libra remains calm and intelligent in order to present the face of harmony, while inwardly he or she is mulling over the consequences of a proposed action. Libra's interest in harmony extends to social and business relationships. These individuals seldom hold a grudge. They put unpleasant things out of mind. Libra easily forgives and forgets.

Both men and women born under this sign are a bit soft in their dispositions. Sometimes others take advantage of this. The Libra person searches for a world where all things are beautiful and well-balanced—a place where harmony reigns. Because such a search would be useless in the real world, Libra takes refuge in daydreaming and flights of fancy. The harshness they might meet in life makes them unhappy. They may have an intricate fantasy world where they retreat when the going gets too rough.

Libra is gentle and easygoing. They seldom go where they know they are not wanted. Their interest in beauty and art leads them along the less troublesome and conflicting roads of life.

Libra can often achieve what he wants through friendly persuasion. Because of his calm, others often find him a port in a storm. He will tell people what he knows they want to hear in order to bolster their confidence and to avoid unpleasantness. He is tactful and knows how to use his gentleness to his own advantage. People may try to take advantage of him, but when he has his wits about him, this is rather difficult. Even when others think they see through him, they find him a difficult nut to crack. He is so strong in his ways of persuasion that he is almost never undermined.

The Libra man or woman is even-tempered generally, but can flare up when cornered. Still and all, they cool off quite rapidly and are willing to let bygones be bygones. Libra understands others quite deeply because of his sympathetic nature; it is quite easy for him to put himself in another's place. He is considerate of other people's opinions no matter how wrong they may seem.

Libra is fair-minded. He dislikes it when someone is mistreated or cheated out of a chance that is rightfully his. Injustice infuriates him. In all matters, he tries to make the right decision. He may take his time about coming to a conclusion.

In most social affairs, Libra is quite popular and charming. People like Libras because of their pleasant, easygoing ways. Most Libras have a lot of friends. All kinds of people attract Libra. They seldom make preferences on a superficial basis.

Harmony plays an important part in the life of every Libra. He or she will try to preserve it at all costs. Harsh realities disturb the Libra man or woman so at times they are given to lying in order to preserve peace and harmony.

Health

Libras are generally well-groomed and graceful. Their features, for the most part, are small. They are interested in maintaining good health and would never do anything that might encourage illness—even in a slight way. Quite often the man or woman born under this sign is not terribly vigorous and may require lots of rest in order to feel fit. Although they may never say no to a social obligation, Libra often tires quickly as a result of socializing. If they do not have proper rest, they are easily irritated.

Still, Libra is built well and strongly. In spite of this, they are not what you could really call strong. Their resistance is not always what it should be; they can catch colds easily. Still, they have remarkable powers of recovery and do not stay out of commission for very long. In spite of the fact that Libra is delicate, they are surprisingly resilient.

The weakest points of a Libra's body are the kidneys, spine, and loins. When they do fall ill, one of these three points is often affected.

Libra women are often remarkably beautiful. They seldom have problems attracting the opposite sex. Their voices are generally soft and their eyes lively.

Even though the Libra man may not look terribly strong, he is often capable of handling work that would exhaust someone who is bigger or seemingly more vigorous.

Libras become somewhat out of sorts when ill. Being sick tends to make them finicky and ill-humored. They like sympathy when in this condition. When their whims are not satisfied, they may complain about being neglected or unloved.

Occupation

The Libra man or woman is usually pleasant to work with. They like to cooperate with others. They will not oppose authority unless they feel it is unjust. Libra is flexible. It is not difficult for them to shift from one phase of an operation to another.

Environment may have an uncommonly strong influence on Libra. It may spur him or her on to greater heights or slow them down. Sometimes Libra needs to be inspired by the activities of those working in the immediate vicinity. They will sometimes look at the other fellow to see how he is working before they begin on their own.

Libra likes to work in pleasant surroundings. They abhor filth and disorder. They do what they can to bring about the working conditions best suited to their nature. Libra people are not attracted to work that is likely to be strenuous or untidy.

Libra people make good business partners. They are quite good at making the proper decisions at the right time. The person born under this sign knows how to weigh the pros and cons of an argument or problem. People often turn to Libra to make the right decision. Others find it easy to believe in Libra's powers of reasoning. They seldom make a wrong move. Libra can always be relied upon to do what is proper.

On the whole Libra is rather moderate or conservative in most things. This stems from their desire to avoid extremes—especially if they are apt to bring about controversy. Secrets are safe with Libra, especially if they might do someone some harm.

The person born under this sign is often quite intelligent. They have the ability to reason well and to analyze. Philosophical argument does not frighten them, and they can hold their own in almost any intellectual debate. They have a talent for objectivity, putting themselves in another's shoes quite easily. As a mediator Libra is excellent. People born under the sign of the Scales also make good diplomats.

Often called the Lawgiver, the Libra man or woman plays a powerful role as a mediator. In law, Libra can be of service to many, maintaining the peacekeeping and arbitration functions of society. These men and woman make competent judges and lawyers.

Libra can view things calmly and rationally. He or she is not easily swayed by emotions if truth or justice is at stake. Libra wants what is good for everybody concerned. They tend to look at things the way they are. They are not prone to make a mountain out of a molehill. In moments of confusion, Libra's mind is as clear as a bell.

Because of their natural objectivity, many Libras turn out to be admirable scientists and mathematicians. Also, Libra knows how to criticize without hurting. So these men and women could do well as reviewers of books, plays, films, and art in general.

Most Libras are good in creative matters. Anything to do with art or aesthetics appeals to them most of the time. Some of them make good painters, writers, or musicians. The person under this sign sometimes ignores surges of inspiration when they overcome him for fear of being too self-indulgent. The strong Libra knows how to seize these moments to further creative aims and interests. Some of the greatest painters in the world were born under the sign of Libra.

Because Libra is so good at persuasion, they make invaluable salespeople. They possess so much charm that their customers often buy more than they originally intended. Because of their rare beauty, Libra men and women often do well in the field of modeling or acting.

Libra is capable of spending more money than they actually have. During their lifetime, great sums are apt to come into their hands. They do not care too much about money, though. They are generous to a fault, and find it hard to refuse people who claim they are in need.

Libra usually has expensive tastes. They find it hard to save money. Because they like people and a busy social life, the person born under this sign often spends considerable sums in entertainment. Luxuries are as important to Libra at times as necessities are to someone else.

In spite of their light ways with money, Libra is no fool. They know well how to discourage someone who is only interested in them for their finances.

Home and Family

Home is important to the average Libra. It must be a place where they can relax and feel comfortable. It must radiate charm, beauty, and harmony. A popular person, the Libra man or woman loves to entertain. Nothing excites them more than company of good friends and acquaintances. Libra usually makes a good host. They know how to put guests at ease. People like to visit Libra because of their charming and easygoing ways.

The furnishings in a Libra's home are usually of excellent taste. They like ornamental furnishings, things that are often a bit ostentatious. No Libra home is without its paintings or pieces of sculpture. The Libra woman or man is often excellent at interior decorating. They may have a habit of changing the interior of their house quite often.

The Libra person is refined in nature and is not fond of getting their hands soiled. They would rather leave the rough tasks for others to do. If they have enough money, they'll see to it that someone comes to the house several times a week to clean up. There are always flowers and plants in the Libra home. In general, they are fond of light gardening.

There is usually a definite relationship between the Libra woman and her home. It usually complements or supplements her charm and personality.

The person born under Libra is generally a good parent. He or she does what they can to bring up youngsters properly. Libra never tries to influence the children unnecessarily. Libra lets them develop along natural lines, never forcing them into a mold he or she has designed. One thing a Libra respects in a child is originality and individuality.

The Libra parent is far from strict, yet the children seldom turn out spoiled. The Libra mother or father will correct or punish whenever it is absolutely necessary. Most of the time, the children listen to them because of their calm sure way. Kids have faith in their Libra parent and usually respect their judgment. Children like being with Libra adults because in them they have a sympathetic friend—someone who can understand their point of view.

Libras as children are often happy and friendly. Parents find them ideal because they are so agreeable and cooperative. They never challenge their parents' authority and do what is expected of them most of the time. Libra children are often creative. Whenever they show signs of artistic ability, they should be encouraged. Some of them are great daydreamers at school and have to be encouraged and inspired in order to do their best.

Social Relationships

The Libra man or woman usually makes a good friend because of their even disposition and easygoing ways. Others turn to Libra in time of need. He or she always is able to advise someone in a helpful manner. Generally, Libra is honest and sincere in their dealings with associates and friends. However, he or she may feel a bit envious if friends have nicer things.

Libras do not enjoy being alone and perhaps this is the reason they are so friendly. They enjoy being popular and well-liked. They seldom disappoint people who believe in them. All in all, they are quite cooperative and easy to get along with. They can be counted on to do the right thing at all times.

The person born under this sign usually becomes angry rather quickly. However, he quickly gets over it and is willing to kiss and make up within a short time after his explosion. Whatever he does he will try to avoid hurting someone else's feelings. He is not cruel or petty. That is not his nature.

The Libra person is a good conversationalist. Often at parties they are the center of attention. People generally have the impression that Libra is well-informed and rather aristocratic. Whenever Libra is upset or disturbed—off balance, so to speak—they try not to let it show.

Love and Marriage

In matters of love and romance, Libra is without equal. They are well-informed on everything that has to do with romance. Love is essential to Libras because they are born under the love planet Venus. As sons and daughters of Venus, Libras are affectionate and gentle, truly considerate of their mate or lover.

At times, the Libra man or woman may be uncertain of their feelings. They may go through a series of love affairs before they really know what they are looking for in a mate. Libra is fickle. He or she can be quite passionate in a love affair, then some days later break it off or lose interest for no apparent reason. It is just one of Libra's ways—difficult as it may be to understand.

Libra is easily attracted to members of the opposite sex and enjoys their company immensely. People find the Libra charm difficult to resist. Some people born under this seventh sign of the Zodiac are somewhat sentimental and are easily moved. This quality often appeals to their lovers or admirers. When Libras desire to transfer their affection, they usually do so with much tact and consideration.

Libras are often passionate lovers in spite of their calm and gentle ways. Their calm fronts often hide a hot temperament. When in love, they'll forsake their usual lamb-like ways for those of a ram.

The Libra woman expects to be handled with kid gloves by the man who professes to love her. She enjoys small courtesies and enjoys having things done for her.

Libra people are generally quite well suited for marriage or permanent love relationships. Although they may go from one romance to the other quite easily, what they are always in search of is permanent union. They are quite domestic by nature and enjoy setting up house and attending to family affairs. Some of them marry quite young. Although they may not be faithful at all times, they are honest in their intention of being steadfast.

The Libra person enjoys home life. A place for entertaining and sharing the company of loved ones, the home is something special. Libra is usually a very considerate partner. A mate may find it a difficult task keeping up. Libra's ease in social relationships is a quality that is rare to come by.

In spite of an occasional post-marital fling that they may find difficult to pass up from time to time, Libras shun all thoughts of divorce or separation. They do what they can to keep the marriage together and will try to keep serious faults under wraps. Libra is not likely to be open about indiscretions for fear of upsetting a mate and the relationship.

Romance and the Libra Woman

Libra women are quite passionate and affectionate. Most of them possess a mysterious charm which makes them much in demand with the opposite sex. The Libra woman is never short of admirers. She may have a difficult time trying to make up her mind about which one to settle down with, but she does what she can to enjoy herself during her state of indecision. She may go from one affair to the other without any regrets or misgivings. Others may accuse her of being a great flirt, but in all love relationships she is quite sincere. She is changeable and impulsive, though, which makes it hard for her to be consistent in her affections at times.

The Libra woman adjusts to married life very well. When she has found the right man, she is willing to do all she can to keep their life a peaceful and harmonious one. In spite of her inclination to flirt, the Libra woman usually remains faithful after she has married. At times, she may find herself strongly attracted to another man. But she knows how to control herself and would do nothing that might jeopardize her marriage.

The Libra woman is usually poised and charming in a standoff-ish way. Underneath, however, she may be very passionate and loving. Her husband may find her more romantic than he expected. She is the kind of woman most men adore. There is something helpless yet seductive about her. She is not the sort of woman who would like to wear the pants in the family. She is only too glad to let someone else manage everything. She likes being taken care of.

Although she may seem terribly dependent and clinging, when the situation calls for her to take things over, she can do this quite ably. She's the kind of a woman who generally gets things her own way. Her charm and beauty are indeed irresistible.

The Libra woman makes an ideal wife. She knows how to arrange things in a home so that they radiate peace, harmony, and beauty. When guests arrive, she knows how to make them feel comfortable immediately. She makes an excellent hostess. Her husband is apt to find her an invaluable companion. He can discuss things with her at his ease. The Libra woman is quite intelligent and has no difficulty in discussing matters that many women fail to understand or master.

She is a lover of a busy social life. However, she would be willing to give up all the glitter and laughter of party going if it interfered with her duties as a wife or mother.

Her tastes are rather expensive. She may run up bills without giving it much thought. If her husband can afford her extravagance, chances are he won't complain. He is apt to feel that his charming wife is worth the extra expense.

The Libra woman makes an understanding mother. It is important to her that her children get a chance to develop their real personalities. She is quite persuasive in a gentle way.

Romance and the Libra Man

Libra men have no trouble at all in attracting members of the opposite sex. Women find them charming and handsome. They are usually quite considerate of their women friends and know how to make them feel important and loved. The Libra man is quite a lover. He is not at a loss when it comes to romancing, for he finds love one of the most important things there is about life.

One fault, however, is the Libra man's ability to change from one love to another with appalling ease. He is always sincere in his love interests, but sometimes he finds it difficult to remain in love with the same person for a long period of time.

Women like him because he seems to know what is right; he never does the wrong thing, no matter what the occasion. His interest in the arts and such matters impress women. His sensitivity is another quality they often admire. The Libra man does not stint when it comes to demonstrating his affection for the woman he believes he loves. However, he is quite crestfallen if the woman should indicate that she is not ready to reciprocate.

Once he settles down, the Libra man makes a good husband and father. He is well suited to family life. Home is important to him. He likes to entertain close friends and relatives frequently. He is generally a very considerate and lively host. It is important that the Libra man find the right woman for his married life. If he has selected someone who finds it difficult to show the same interest in him that he shows in her, he will begin to look elsewhere for companionship. However, he is interested in having stability in his home and will do what he can to keep things in order.

He may be difficult to please at times, particularly if his wife does not share his refined tastes. If his wife has a practical mind, so much the better. Generally, Libra has a poor head for financial matters and is apt to let money slip through his fingers like water.

As a father he is quite considerate and encouraging. He is anxious to see his children express themselves as they desire. Yet he will not tolerate spoiled behavior. Children respect his gentle ways, and they do what they can to please him.

Woman—Man

LIBRA WOMAN
ARIES MAN

In some ways, the Aries man resembles his zodiacal symbol the Ram, roaming the meadow in search of good grazing land. He has an insatiable thirst for knowledge. He's ambitious and is apt to have his finger in many pies. He can do with a woman like you—someone attractive, quick-witted, and smart.

He is not interested in a clinging vine for a mate. He wants someone who is there when he needs her, someone who listens and understands what he says, someone who can give advice if he should ever need it—which is not likely to be often. The Aries man wants a woman who will look good on his arm without hanging on it too heavily.

He is looking for a woman who has both feet on the ground and yet is mysterious and enticing—a kind of domestic Helen of Troy whose face or fine dinner can launch a thousand business deals if need be. That woman he's in search of sounds a little like you, doesn't she? If the shoe fits, put it on. You won't regret it.

The Aries man makes a good husband. He is faithful and attentive. He is an affectionate kind of man. He'll make you feel needed and loved. Love is a serious matter for the Aries man. He does not believe in flirting or playing the field—especially after he's found the woman of his dreams. He'll expect you to be as constant in your affection as he is in his. He'll expect you to be one hundred percent his; he won't put up with any nonsense while romancing you.

The Aries man may be fairly progressive and modern about many things. However, when it comes to pants wearing, he's downright conventional: it's strictly male attire. The best role you can take in the relationship is a supporting one. He's the boss and that's that. Once you have learned to accept the role playing, you'll find the going easy.

The Aries man, with his endless energy and drive, likes to relax in the comfort of his home at the end of the day. The good homemaker can be sure of holding his love. He's keen on watching the news from a comfortable armchair. If you see to it that everything in the house is where he expects to find it, you'll have no difficulty keeping the relationship on an even keel.

Life and love with an Aries man may be just the medicine you need. He'll be a good provider. He'll spoil you if he's financially able to do so.

Aries is your zodiacal mate, as well as your zodiacal opposite, so the Aries-Libra couple will make wonderful parents together. Kids take to Aries like ducks to water. His quick mind and energetic behavior appeal to the young. His ability to jump from one thing to another will delight the kids and keep them active. The Aries father is young at heart and will spoil children every chance he gets. You will set standards for their growing up and see to it that they observe social etiquette and good manners.

LIBRA WOMAN
TAURUS MAN

If you've got your heart set on a man born under the sign of Taurus, you'll have to learn the art of being patient. Taurus take their time about everything—even love.

The steady and deliberate Taurus man is a little slow on the draw. It may take him quite a while before he gets around to popping that question. For the woman who doesn't mind twiddling her thumbs, the waiting and anticipating will almost always pay off in the end. Taurus men want to make sure that every step they take is a good one—particularly if they feel that the path they're on is one that leads to the altar.

If you are in the mood for a whirlwind romance, you had better cast your net in shallower waters. Moreover, most Taurus prefer to do the angling themselves. They are not keen on women taking the lead. If she does, he might drop her like a dead fish. If you let yourself get caught on his terms, you'll find that he's fallen for you—hook, line, and sinker.

The Taurus man is fond of a comfortable home life. It is very important to him. If you keep those home fires burning you will have no trouble keeping that flame in your Bull's heart aglow. You have a talent for homemaking; use it. Your taste in furnishings is excellent. You know how to make a house come to life with colors and decorations.

Taurus, the strong, steady, and protective Bull, may not be your idea of a man on the move. Still, he's reliable. Perhaps he could be the anchor for your dreams and plans. He could help you to acquire a more balanced outlook and approach to your life. If you're given to impulsiveness, he could help you to curb it. He's the man who is always there when you need him.

When you tie the knot with a man born under Taurus, you can put away fears about creditors pounding on the front door. Taurus are practical about everything including bill paying. When he carries you over that threshold, you can be certain that the entire house is paid for, not only the doorsill.

As a wife, you won't have to worry about putting aside your many interests for the sake of back-breaking house chores. Your Taurus hubby will see to it that you have all the latest time-saving appliances and comforts.

Taurus, born under the planet Venus just as you are, has much affection for the children, and he has no trouble demonstrating his love and warmth. Yet the Taurus father does not believe in spoiling the kids. He believes that children have a place, and that place is mainly to be seen but not heard. He is an excellent disciplinarian. With your cooperation, he will see to it that the youngsters grow up to be polite, obedient, and respectful.

LIBRA WOMAN
GEMINI MAN

The Gemini man is quite a catch. Many a woman has set her cap for him and failed to bag him. Generally, Gemini men are intelligent, witty, and outgoing. Many of them tend to be versatile and multitalented. The Gemini man could easily wind up being your better half.

One thing that causes a Twin's mind and affection to wander is a bore. But it is unlikely that a socially chic woman like Libra would ever allow herself to be accused of being that. The Gemini man who has caught your heart will admire you for your ideas and intellect—perhaps even more than for your homemaking talents and good looks.

The woman who hitches up with a Twin needn't feel that once she's made her marriage vows she'll have to store her interests and ambition in the attic somewhere. The Gemini man will admire you for your zeal and liveliness. He's the kind of guy who won't scowl if you let him shift for himself in the kitchen once in a while. In fact, he'll enjoy the challenge of wrestling with pots and pans himself for a change. Chances are, too, that he might turn out to be a better cook than you—that is, if he isn't already.

The man born under the sign of the Twins is a very active person. There aren't many women who have enough pep to keep up with him, but this should be no problem for the airy Libra female.

The Gemini man is a dreamer, planner, and idealist. A woman with a strong personality could easily fill the role of rudder for her Gemini's ship-without-a-sail. If you are a cultivated, purposeful woman, he won't mind it too much. The intelligent Twin is often aware of his shortcomings and doesn't resent it if someone with better bearings than himself gives him a shove in the right direction—when it's needed. The average Gemini does not have serious ego hang-ups and will even accept a well-deserved chewing out from his mate quite good-naturedly.

When you team up with a Gemini man, you'll probably always have a houseful of people to entertain—interesting people, too, which suits your Libra sociability. Geminis find it hard to tolerate antisocial characters who have little to say.

People born under Gemini generally have two sides to their natures, as different as night and day. It's very easy for them to be happy-go-lucky one minute, then down in the dumps the next. They hate to be bored and will generally do anything to make their lives interesting, vivid, and action-packed.

Gemini men are always attractive to the opposite sex. He'll flirt occasionally, but it will never amount to anything serious.

The Gemini father and the Libra mother combine the airy qualities basic to both your zodiacal signs, and as a result the children will grow up in a very open, tolerant environment. The Gemini father is a pushover for the kids. He loves them so much, he generally lets them do what they want. His sense of humor is infectious, so the youngsters will naturally come to see the fun and funny sides of life. You will have to introduce a few rules and regulations.

LIBRA WOMAN
CANCER MAN

Chances are you won't hit it off too well with the man born under Cancer if your plans are love. But then, Cupid has been known to do some pretty unlikely things. The Cancer man is very sensitive— thin-skinned and occasionally moody. You've got to keep on your toes—and not step on his—if you're determined to make a go of the relationship.

The Cancer man may be lacking in some of the qualities you seek in a man. But when it comes to being faithful and being a good provider, he's hard to beat.

The perceptive woman will not mistake the Crab's quietness for sullenness or his thriftiness for penny-pinching. In some respects, he is like that wise old owl out on a limb; he may look like he's dozing but actually he hasn't missed a thing.

Cancer people often possess a well of knowledge about human behavior. They can come across with some pretty helpful advice to those in trouble or in need. He can certainly guide you in making investments both in time and money. He may not say much, but he's always got his wits about him.

The Crab may not be the match or catch for the sociable Libra woman. At times, you are likely to find him downright dull. True to his sign, he can be fairly cranky and crabby when handled the wrong way. He is perhaps more sensitive than he should be.

If you're smarter than your Cancer friend, be smart enough not to let him know. Never give him the idea that you think he's a little short on brainpower. It would send him scurrying back into his shell—and all that ground lost in the relationship will perhaps never be recovered.

The Crab is most himself at home. Once settled down for the night or the weekend, wild horses couldn't drag him farther than the gatepost—that is, unless those wild horses were dispatched by his mother. The Crab is sometimes a Momma's boy. If his mate does not put her foot down, he will see to it that his mother always comes first. No self-respecting wife would ever allow herself to play second fiddle to her mother-in-law. With a little bit of tact, however, she'll find that slipping into that number-one position is as easy as pie (that legendary one his mother used to bake).

If you pamper your Cancer man, you'll find that Mother turns up less and less, at the front door as well as in conversations.

Cancers make proud, patient, and protective fathers. But they can be a little too protective. Their sheltering instincts can interfere with a youngster's natural inclination to test the waters outside the home. Still, the Cancer father doesn't want to see his kids learning about life the hard way from the streets. Your qualities of grace and refinement, fairness and tolerance will help the youngsters cope with a variety of life situations.

LIBRA WOMAN
LEO MAN

For the woman who enjoys being swept off her feet in a romantic whirlwind fashion, Leo is the sign of love. When the Lion puts his mind to romancing, he doesn't stint. It's all wining and dining and dancing till the wee hours of the morning.

Leo is all heart and knows how to make his woman feel like a woman. The girl in constant search of a man she can look up to need go no farther: Leo is ten-feet tall—in spirit if not in stature. He's a man not only in full control of his faculties but in full control of just about any situation he finds himself in. He's a winner.

The Leo man may not look like Tarzan, but he knows how to roar and beat his chest if he has to. The woman who has had her fill of weak-kneed men finds in a Leo someone she can at last lean upon. He can support you not only physically but spiritually as well. He's good at giving advice that pays off.

Leos are direct people. They don't believe in wasting time or effort. They almost never make unwise investments.

Many Leos rise to the top of their profession. Through example, they often prove to be a source of great inspiration to others.

Although he's a ladies' man, the Leo man is very particular about his ladies. His standards are high when it comes to love interests. The idealistic and cultivated Libra should have no trouble keeping her balance on the pedestal the Lion sets her on. Leo believes that romance should be played on a fair give-and-take basis. He won't stand for any monkey business in a love relationship. It's all or nothing.

You'll find him a frank, off-the-shoulder person. He generally says what is on his mind.

If you decide upon a Leo man for a mate, you must be prepared to stand behind him full force. He expects it—and usually deserves it. He's the head of the house and can handle that position without a hitch. He knows how to go about breadwinning. If he has his way, and most Leos do have their own way, he'll see to it that you'll have all the luxuries you crave and the comforts you need.

It's unlikely that the romance in your marriage will ever die out. Lions need love like flowers need sunshine. They're ever-amorous and generally expect full attention and affection from their mates. Leos are fond of going out on the town. They love to give parties, as well as go to them.

Leo fathers have a tendency to spoil the children—up to a point. That point is reached when the children become the center of attention, and Leo feels neglected. Then the Leo father becomes strict and insists that his rules be followed. You will have your hands full pampering both your Leo mate and the children. As long as he comes first in your affections, the family will be happy and loving.

LIBRA WOMAN
VIRGO MAN

The Virgo man is all business—at least he may seem so to you. He is usually very cool, calm, and collected. He's perhaps too much of a fussbudget to wake up deep romantic interests in the Venus-born Libra woman.

Torrid romancing to Virgo is just so much sentimental mush. He can do without it and can make that quite evident in short order. He's keen on chastity and, if necessary, he can lead a sedentary, sexless life without caring too much about the fun others think he's missing.

In short, you might find the Virgo man a first-class dud. He doesn't have much of an imagination; flights of fancy don't interest him. He is always correct and likes to be handled correctly. Almost everything about him is orderly, with a place for everything and everything in its place.

He does have an honest-to-goodness heart, believe it or not. The woman who finds herself strangely attracted to his cool, feet-flat-on-the-ground ways will discover that his is a constant heart, not one that goes in for flings or sordid affairs. Virgos take an awfully long time to warm up to someone. A practical man, even in matters of the heart, he wants to know just what kind of person you are before he takes a chance on you.

The impulsive date had better not make the mistake of kissing her Virgo friend on the street—even if it's only a peck on the cheek. He's not at all demonstrative and hates public displays of affection. Love, according to him, should be kept within the confines of one's home—with the curtains drawn.

Once he believes that you are on the level with him as far as your love is concerned, you'll see how fast he can lose his cool. Virgos are considerate, gentle lovers. He'll spend a long time, though, getting to know you. He'll like you before he loves you.

A romance with a Virgo man can be a sometime—or, rather, a one-time—thing. If the bottom ever falls out, don't bother reaching for the adhesive tape. Nine times out of ten he won't care about patching up. He's a once-burnt-twice-shy guy. When he crosses your telephone number out of his address book, he's crossing you out of his life—for good.

Neat as a pin, he's thumbs-down on what he considers sloppy housekeeping. An ashtray with just one stubbed out cigarette in it can annoy him even if it's only two seconds old. Glassware should always sparkle and shine if you want to keep him happy.

If you marry him, keep your sunny-side up.

The Virgo father appreciates courtesy, good manners, and proper etiquette as much, if not more, than you do. He will instill a sense of order in the household, and he expects the children to respect his wishes. He is very concerned about the kids' health and hygiene, so he may try to restrict their freedom. You'll have to step in and let the youngsters break a few rules now and then.

LIBRA WOMAN
LIBRA MAN

If there's a Libra man in your life, you may have found the male complement to your side of the Libra equation for balance and harmony. Men born under this sign have a way with women. You'll always feel at ease in a Libra's company. You can be yourself when you're with him.

The Libra man can be moody at times. His moodiness is often puzzling. One moment he comes on hard and strong with declarations of his love, the next moment you find that he's left you like yesterday's mashed potatoes. He'll come back, though; don't worry. Libras are like that. Deep down inside he really knows what he wants even though he may not appear to.

You'll appreciate his admiration of beauty and harmony. If you're dressed to the teeth and never looked lovelier, you'll get a ready compliment—and one that's really deserved. Libras don't indulge in idle flattery. If they don't like something, they are tactful enough to remain silent.

Libras will go to great lengths to preserve peace and harmony—even tell a fat lie if necessary. They don't like showdowns or disagreeable confrontations. The frank woman is all for getting whatever is bothering her off her chest and out into the open, even if it comes out all wrong. To the Libra man, making a clean breast of everything seems like sheer folly sometimes.

One of you Libras may lose your patience while waiting for the other to make up your mind. It takes ages sometimes for Libra to make a decision. You both weigh all sides carefully before committing to anything. You both dillydally—at least about small things—and often find it difficult to come to a decision.

All in all, the Libra man is kind, considerate, and fair. He is interested in the real truth. He'll try to balance everything out until he has all the correct answers. It's not difficult for him to see both sides of a story.

Libras are not show-offs. Generally, they are well-balanced, modest people. Honest, wholesome, and affectionate, they are serious about every love encounter they have. If he should find that the woman he's dating is not really suited to him, he will end the relationship in such a tactful manner that no hard feelings will come about.

The Libra father is patient and fair. He can be firm without exercising undue strictness or discipline. Although he can be a harsh judge at times, with the kids he will radiate sweetness and light in the hope that they will grow up imitating his gentle manner. Together, the Libra couple will set a sterling example of graciousness and charm for the youngsters to follow.

LIBRA WOMAN
SCORPIO MAN

Many find the Scorpio's sting a fate worse than death. When his anger breaks loose, you had better clear out of the vicinity.

The average Scorpio may strike you as a brute. He'll stick pins into the balloons of your plans and dreams if they don't line up with what he thinks is right. If you do anything to irritate him—just anything—you'll wish you hadn't. He'll give you a sounding out that would make you pack your bags and go back to mother—if you were that kind of woman.

The Scorpio man hates being tied down to home life. He would rather be out on the battlefield of life, belting away at whatever he feels is a just and worthy cause, instead of staying home nestled in a comfortable armchair with the evening paper. If you are a woman who has a homemaking streak, don't keep those home fires burning too brightly, too long; you may run out of firewood.

As passionate as he is in business affairs and politics, the Scorpio man still has plenty of pepper and ginger stored away for lovemaking.

Most women are easily attracted to him—perhaps you are no exception. Those who allow a man born under this sign to sweep them off their feet soon find that they are dealing with a cauldron of seething excitement. The Scorpio is passionate with a capital P, you can be sure of that. But he's capable of dishing out as much pain as pleasure.

Scorpios are blunt. An insult is likely to whiz out of his mouth quicker than a compliment.

If you're the kind of woman who can keep a stiff upper lip, take it on the chin, turn a deaf ear, and all that, because you feel you are still under his love spell in spite of everything—lots of luck.

If you have decided to take the bitter with the sweet, prepare yourself for a lot of ups and downs. Chances are you won't have as much time for your own affairs and interests as you'd like. The Scorpio's love of power may cause you to be at his constant beck and call.

Scorpios like fathering large families. He is proud of his children, but often he fails to live up to his responsibilities as a parent. In spite of the extremes in his personality, the Scorpio man is able to transform the conflicting characteristics within himself when he becomes a father. When he takes his fatherly duties seriously, he is a powerful teacher. He believes in preparing his children for the hard knocks life sometimes delivers. He is adept with difficult youngsters because he knows how to tap the best in each child.

LIBRA WOMAN
SAGITTARIUS MAN

If you've set your cap for a man born under the sign of Sagittarius, you may have to apply an awful lot of strategy before you can persuade him to get down on bended knee. Although some Sagittarius may be marriage-shy, they're not ones to skitter away from romance. You'll find a love relationship with an Archer—whether a fling or the real thing—a very enjoyable experience.

As a rule, Sagittarius are bright, happy, healthy people. They have a strong sense of fair play. Often they are a source of inspiration to others. They are full of drive and ideas.

You'll be taken by the Archer's infectious grin and his light-hearted friendly nature. If you do wind up being the woman in his life, you'll find that he's apt to treat you more like a buddy than the love of his life. It's just his way. Sagittarius is often more chummy than romantic.

You'll admire his broad-mindedness in most matters—including those of the heart. If, while dating you, he claims that he still wants to play the field, he'll expect you to enjoy the same liberty. Once he's promised to love, honor, and obey, however, he does just that. Marriage for him, once he's taken that big step, is very serious business.

The Sagittarius man is quick-witted. He has a genuine interest in equality. He hates prejudice and injustice. Generally, Archers are good at sports. They love the great outdoors and respect wildlife and wilderness in all its forms.

He's not much of a homebody. Quite often he's occupied with faraway places either in his daydreams or in reality. He enjoys being on the move. He's got ants in his pants and refuses to sit still for long stretches at a time. Humdrum routine—especially at home—bores him.

He likes to surprise people. At the drop of a hat, he may ask you to hop on a plane and dine in some foreign port—most likely down the road and not too far from home by car. He also likes to tease.

He'll take great pride in showing you off to his friends. He'll always be considerate of your feelings. He will never embarrass or disappoint you intentionally.

His friendly, sunshiny nature is capable of attracting many people. Like you, he's very tolerant when it comes to friends. You will most likely spend a great deal of time helping him entertain people and being the gracious Libra hostess for his big parties.

The Sagittarius father can be all thumbs when it comes to tiny tots. He will dote on any son or daughter dutifully, but he may be bewildered by the newborn. The Archer usually becomes comfortable with youngsters once they have passed through the baby stage. As soon as the children are old enough to walk and talk, the Sagittarius dad encourages each and every visible sign of talent and skill in his kids.

LIBRA WOMAN
CAPRICORN MAN

A with-it Libra woman like you is likely to find the average Capricorn man a bit of a drag. The man born under the sign of the Goat is often a closed person and difficult to get to know. Even if you do get to know him, you may not find him very interesting.

In romance, Capricorn men are a little on the rusty side. You'll probably have to make all the passes.

You may find his plodding manner irritating and his conservative, traditional ways downright maddening. He's not one to take chances on anything. If it was good enough for his father, it's good enough for him. He follows a way that is tried and true.

The Capricorn man is habit-bound. Whenever adventure rears its tantalizing head, the Goat will turn the other way.

He may be just as ambitious as you are—perhaps even more so—but his ways of accomplishing his aims are more subterranean or, at least, seem so. He operates from the background a good deal of the time. At a gathering you may never even notice him, but he's there, taking in everything, sizing everyone up—planning his next careful move.

Although Capricorns may be intellectual to a degree, it is not generally the kind of intelligence you appreciate. He may not be as quick or as bright as you; it may take him ages to understand a simple joke.

If you do decide to take up with a man born under this sign, you ought to be pretty good in the cheering up department. The Capricorn man often acts as though he's constantly being followed by a cloud of gloom.

The Capricorn man is most himself when in the comfort and privacy of his own home. The security possible within four walls can make him a happy man. He'll spend as much time as he can at home. If he is loaded down with extra work, he'll bring it home instead of working overtime at the office.

You'll most likely find yourself frequently confronted by his relatives. Family is very important to the Capricorn—his family, that is. They had better take a pretty important place in your life, too, if you want to keep your home a happy one.

Although his caution in most matters may all but drive the luxury-loving Libra woman up the wall, you'll find that his concerned way with money is justified most of the time. He'll plan everything right down to the last penny.

The Capricorn father is a dutiful parent and takes a lifelong interest in seeing that his children make something of themselves. He may not understand their hopes and dreams because he often tries to put his head on their shoulders. The Capricorn father believes that there are certain goals to be achieved, and there is a traditional path to achieving them. He can be quite a scold if the youngsters break the rules. You will have to balance his sometimes rigid approach and smooth things over for the kids.

LIBRA WOMAN
AQUARIUS MAN

Aquarius individuals love everybody—even their worst enemies sometimes. Through your love relationship with an Aquarius you'll find yourself running into all sorts of people, ranging from near-genius to downright insane—and they're all friends of his.

As a rule, Aquarius are extremely friendly and open. Of all the signs, they are perhaps the most tolerant. In the thinking department, they are often miles ahead of others.

You'll most likely find your relationship with this man a challenging one. Your high respect for intelligence and imagination may be reason enough for you to set your heart on a Water Bearer. You'll find that you can learn a lot from him.

In the holding-hands phase of your romance, you may find that your Water Bearer friend has cold feet. Aquarius take quite a bit of warming up before they are ready to come across with that first goodnight kiss. More than likely, he'll just want to be your pal in the beginning. For him, that's an important first step in any relationship—love included.

The poetry and flowers stage—if it ever comes—will come later. Aquarius is all heart. Still, when it comes to tying himself down to one person and for keeps, he is almost always sure to hesitate. He may even try to get out of it if you breathe down his neck too heavily.

The Aquarius man is no Valentino and wouldn't want to be. The kind of love life he's looking for is one that's made up mainly of companionship. Although he may not be very romantic, the memory of his first romance will always hold an important position in his heart. Some Aquarius wind up marrying their childhood sweethearts.

You won't find it difficult to look up to a man born under the sign of the Water Bearer, but you may find the challenge of trying to keep up with him dizzying. He can pierce through the most complicated problem as if it were simple math. You may find him a little too lofty and high-minded, but don't judge him too harshly if that's the case. He's way ahead of his time—your time, too, most likely.

If you marry this man, he'll stay true to you. Don't think that once the honeymoon is over, you'll be chained to the kitchen sink forever. Your Aquarius husband will encourage you to keep active in your own interests and affairs. You'll most likely have a minor tiff now and again but never anything serious.

The Aquarius father has an almost intuitive understanding of children. He sees them as individuals in their own right, not as extensions of himself or as beings who are supposed to take a certain place in the world. He can talk to the kids on a variety of subjects, and his knowledge can be awe-inspiring. You will sometimes have to bring the youngsters back down to earth, but you will appreciate the lessons of tolerance and fairness your Aquarius mate has transmitted to the children.

LIBRA WOMAN
PISCES MAN

The man born under Pisces is quite a dreamer. Sometimes he's so wrapped up in his dreams that he's difficult to reach. To the average, ambitious woman, he may seem a little passive.

He's easygoing most of the time. He seems to take things in his stride. He'll entertain all kinds of views and opinions from just about anyone, nodding or smiling vaguely, giving the impression that he's with them 100 percent while that may not be the case at all. His attitude may be why bother when he is confronted with someone wrong who thinks he's right. The Pisces man will seldom speak his mind if he thinks he'll be rigidly opposed.

The Pisces man is oversensitive at times—he's afraid of getting his feelings hurt. He'll sometimes imagine a personal affront when none's been made. Chances are you'll find this complex of his maddening. At times, you may feel like giving him a swift kick where it hurts the most. It won't do any good, though. It would just add fuel to the fire of his complex.

One thing you will admire about this man is his concern for people who are sickly or troubled. He'll make his shoulder available to anyone in the mood for a good cry. He can listen to one hard-luck story after another without seeming to tire. When his advice is asked, he is capable of coming across with some pretty important words of wisdom. He often knows what's bothering someone before that person is aware of it. It's almost intuitive with Pisces, it seems.

Still, at the end of the day, your Pisces lover looks forward to some peace and quiet. If you've got a problem on your mind, don't dump it into his lap. If you do, you're apt to find him short-tempered. He's a good listener, but he can only take so much.

Pisces men are not aimless although they may seem so at times. The positive sort of Pisces man is quite often successful in his profession and is likely to wind up rich and influential. Material gain, however, is not a direct goal for a man born under the sign of the Fishes.

The weaker Pisces is usually content to stay put on the level where he happens to find himself. He won't complain too much if the roof leaks or the fence is in need of repair. He'll just shrug it off as a minor inconvenience. He's got more important things to think about, he'll say.

Because of their seemingly laissez-faire manner, Pisces fathers and Pisces men in general are immensely popular with children. For tots, Pisces plays the double role of confidant and playmate. It will never enter his mind to discipline a child, no matter how spoiled or incorrigible that child becomes.

Man—Woman

LIBRA MAN
ARIES WOMAN

Aries and Libra are zodiacal mates or zodiacal opposites, depending how individuals of these signs link up in love. For many a mild Libra man, the Aries woman may be a little too bossy and busy. Aries women are ambitious creatures. They tend to lose their patience with thorough and deliberate people, like Libra, who take a lot of time to complete something.

The Aries woman is a fast worker. Sometimes she's so fast she forgets to look where she's going. When she stumbles or falls, it would be nice if you were there to grab her. But Aries women are very proud. They don't like to be criticized when they err. Tongue-wagging can turn them into blocks of ice.

However, don't think that the Aries woman frequently gets tripped up in her plans. Quite often they are capable of taking aim and hitting the bull's-eye. You'll be flabbergasted at times by their accuracy as well as by their ambition.

You are perhaps somewhat slower than the Aries woman in attaining your goals. Still, you are not apt to make mistakes along the way. Libra is seldom ill-prepared.

The Aries woman is sensitive at times. She likes to be handled with gentleness and respect. Let her know that you love her for her brains as well as for her good looks. Never give her cause to become jealous. When your Aries woman sees green, you'd better forget about sharing a rosy future together. Handle her with tender love and care and she's yours.

The Aries woman can be giving if she feels her partner is deserving. She is no iceberg; she responds to the proper masculine flame. She needs a man she can look up to and feel proud of. If the shoe fits, put it on. If not, better put your sneakers back on and quietly tiptoe out of her sight.

She can cause you plenty of heartache if you've made up your mind about her and she hasn't made up hers about you. Aries women are very demanding at times. Some of them tend to be high-strung. They can be difficult if they feel their independence is being hampered.

The cultivated Aries woman makes a wonderful homemaker and hostess. You'll find that she's very clever in decorating; she knows how to use colors. Your house will be tastefully furnished. Both of you see to it that it radiates harmony. Friends and acquaintances will love your Aries wife. She knows how to make everyone feel at home and welcome.

Although the Aries woman may not be keen on burdensome responsibilities, she is fond of children and the joy they bring. She is skilled at juggling both career and motherhood, so her kids will never feel that she is an absentee parent. In fact, as the youngsters grow older, they might want a little more of the liberation that is so important to her.

LIBRA MAN
TAURUS WOMAN

The woman born under the sign of Taurus may lack a little of the sparkle and bubble you often like to find in a woman. The Taurus woman is generally down to earth and never flighty. It's important to her that she keep both feet flat on the ground. She is not fond of bounding all over the place, especially if she's under the impression that there's no profit in it.

On the other hand, if you hit it off with a Taurus woman, you won't be disappointed in the romance area. The Taurus woman is all woman and proud of it, too. She can be very devoted and loving once she decides that her relationship with you is no fly-by-night romance. Basically, she's a passionate person. In sex, she's direct and to the point. If she really loves you, she'll let you know she's yours—and without reservations.

Better not flirt with other women once you've committed yourself to her. She's capable of being very jealous and possessive.

She'll stick by you through thick and thin. It's almost certain that if the going ever gets rough, she won't go running home to her mother. She can adjust to the hard times just as graciously as she can to the good times.

Taurus are, on the whole, even-tempered. They like to be treated with kindness. Luxurious things and artistic objects win their hearts.

You may find her a little cautious and deliberate. She likes to be safe and sure about everything. Let her plod along if she likes. Don't coax her, but just let her take her own sweet time. Everything she does is done thoroughly and, generally, without mistakes.

Don't deride her caution or shyness. It could lead to an explosive scene. The Taurus woman doesn't anger readily but when prodded often enough, she's capable of letting loose with a cyclone of ill will. If you treat her with kindness and consideration, you'll have no cause for complaint.

The Taurus woman loves doing things for her man. She's a whiz in the kitchen and can whip up feasts fit for a king if she thinks they'll be royally appreciated. She may not fully understand you, but she'll adore you and be faithful to you if she feels you're worthy of it.

The Taurus woman, ruled by lovely planet Venus as you are, will share with you the joys and burdens of parenthood. But the Taurus mother seldom puts up with any nonsense from the youngsters. It is not that she is strict, she is just concerned. She likes the children to be well behaved. She can wield an iron fist in a velvet glove.

Nothing pleases a Taurus mother more than a compliment from a neighbor or teacher about her child's behavior. She may have some difficult times with them when they reach adolescence. And some teenagers may inwardly resent their Taurus mother's tutelage. But in later life they are often thankful they were brought up in such a conscientious fashion.

LIBRA MAN
GEMINI WOMAN

You may find a romance with a woman born under the sign of the Twins a many-splendored thing. In her you can find the intellectual companionship you often look for in a friend or mate. A Gemini partner can appreciate your aims and desires because she travels pretty much the same road as you do intellectually—that is, at least part of the way. She may share your interest, but she will lack your tenacity.

She suffers from itchy feet. She can be here, there, all over the place and at the same time, or so it would seem. Her eagerness to move about may make you dizzy, still you'll enjoy and appreciate her liveliness and mental agility.

Geminis often have sparkling personalities. You'll be attracted by her warmth and grace. While she's on your arm you'll probably notice that many male eyes are drawn to her. She may even return a gaze or two, but don't let that worry you. All women born under this sign have nothing against a harmless flirt once in a while. They enjoy this sort of attention. If she feels she is already spoken for, however, she will never let it get out of hand.

Although she may not be as handy as you'd like in the kitchen, you'll never go hungry for a filling and tasty meal. She's as much in a hurry as you are, and won't feel like she's cheating by breaking out the instant mashed potatoes or the frozen peas. She may not be much of a good cook but she is clever. With a dash of this and a suggestion of that, she can make an uninteresting TV dinner taste like a gourmet meal. Then, again, maybe you've struck it rich and have a Gemini who finds complicated recipes a challenge to her intellect. If so, you'll find every meal a tantalizing and mouth-watering surprise.

When you're beating your brains out over the Sunday crossword puzzle and find yourself stuck, just ask your Gemini mate. She'll give you all the right answers without batting an eyelash.

Like you, she loves all kinds of people. You may even find that you're a bit more particular than she. Often all that a Gemini requires is that her friends be interesting—and stay interesting. One thing she's not able to abide is a dullard.

Leave the party organizing to your Gemini sweetheart or mate, and you'll never have a chance to know what a dull moment is. She'll bring the swinger out in you if you give her half a chance.

A Gemini mother enjoys her children, which can be the truest form of love. Like them, she's often restless, adventurous, and easily bored. She will never complain about their fleeting interests because she understands the changes they will go through as they mature.

LIBRA MAN
CANCER WOMAN

If you fall in love with a Cancer woman, be prepared for anything. They are sometimes difficult to understand when it comes to love. In one hour, she can unravel a whole gamut of emotions. Her moods will leave you in a tizzy. She'll always keep you guessing, that's for sure.

You may find her a little too uncertain and sensitive for your liking. You'll most likely spend a good deal of time encouraging her, helping her to erase her foolish fears. Tell her she's a living doll a dozen times a day, and you'll be well loved in return.

Be careful of the jokes you make when in her company. Don't let any of them revolve around her, her personal interests, or her family. If you do, you'll most likely reduce her to tears. She can't stand being made fun of. It will take bushels of roses and tons of chocolates—not to mention the apologies—to get her to come back out of her shell.

In matters of money managing, she may not easily come around to your way of thinking. Money will never burn a hole in her pocket. You may get the notion that your Cancer sweetheart or mate is a direct descendant of Scrooge. If she has her way, she'll hang onto the first dollar you earned. She's not only that way with money, but with everything right on up from bakery string to jelly jars. She's a saver. She never throws anything away, no matter how trivial.

Once she returns your love, you'll have an affectionate, self-sacrificing, and devoted woman for keeps. Her love for you will never alter unless you want it to. She'll put you up on a high pedestal and will do everything—even if it's against your will—to keep you there.

Cancer women love home life. For them, marriage is an easy step to make. They're domestic with a capital D. She'll do her best to make your home comfortable and cozy. The Cancer woman is more herself at home than in strange surroundings. She makes an excellent hostess. The best in her comes out when she's in her own environment.

Cancer women are reputed to be the best mothers of all the signs of the Zodiac. She'll make every complaint of her child a major catastrophe. With her, children come first. If you're lucky, you'll run a close second. You'll perhaps see her as too devoted to the children. You may have a hard time convincing her that her apron strings are too long.

LIBRA MAN
LEO WOMAN

If you can manage a partner who likes to kick up her heels every now and again, then the Leo woman was made for you. You'll have to learn to put away jealous fears when you take up with a woman born under this sign, as she's often the kind that makes heads turn and tongues wag. You don't necessarily have to believe any of what you hear. It's most likely just jealous gossip or wishful thinking.

The Leo woman has more than a fair share of grace and glamour. She knows it, generally, and knows how to put it to good use. Needless to say, other women in her vicinity turn green with envy and will try anything to put her out of the running.

If she's captured your heart and fancy, woo her full force if your intention is to eventually win her. Shower her with expensive gifts and promise her the moon if you're in a position to go that far. Then you'll find her resistance beginning to weaken.

It's not that she's such a difficult cookie—she'll probably boast about you once she's decided you're the man for her—but she does enjoy a lot of attention. What's more, she feels she's entitled to it. Her mild arrogance, though, is becoming. The Leo woman knows how to transform the crime of excessive pride into a very charming misdemeanor. It sweeps most men right off their feet. Those who do not succumb to her leonine charm are few and far between.

If you've got an important business deal to clinch and you have doubts as to whether you can bring it off as you should, take your Leo wife along to the business luncheon. It will be a cinch that you'll have that contract—lock, stock, and barrel—in your pocket before the meeting is over. She won't have to say or do anything, just be there at your side. The grouchiest oil magnate can be transformed into a gushing, obedient schoolboy if there's a Leo woman in the room.

If you're rich and want to see to it that you stay that way, don't give your Leo spouse a free hand with the charge accounts and credit cards. When it comes to spending, Leos tend to overdo. If you're poor, you have no worries because the luxury-loving Leo will most likely never recognize your existence let alone consent to marry you.

A Leo mother can be so proud of her children that she is sometimes blind to their faults. Yet when she wants them to learn and take their rightful place in the social scheme of things, the Leo mother can be strict. She is a patient teacher, lovingly explaining the rules the youngsters are expected to follow. Easygoing and friendly, she loves to pal around with the kids and show them off on every occasion.

LIBRA MAN
VIRGO WOMAN

The Virgo woman may be too difficult for you to understand at first. Her waters run deep. Even when you think you know her, don't take any bets on it. She's capable of keeping things hidden in the deep recesses of her womanly soul—things she'll only release when she's sure you're the man she's been looking for.

It may take her some time to come around to this decision. Virgos are finicky about almost everything. Everything has to be letter-perfect before they're satisfied. Many of them have the idea that the only people who can do things correctly are Virgos.

Nothing offends a Virgo woman more than slovenly dress, sloppy character, or a careless display of affection. Make sure your tie is not crooked and your shoes sport a bright shine before you go calling on this lady. Keep your off-color jokes for the locker room; she'll have none of that. Take her arm when crossing the street.

Don't rush the romance. Trying to corner a Virgo woman in the back of a cab may be one way of striking out. Never criticize the way she looks. In fact, the best policy would be to agree with her as much as possible. Still, there's just so much a man can take. All those dos and don'ts you'll have to observe if you want to get to first base with a Virgo may be just a little too much to ask of you.

After a few dates, you may come to the conclusion that she just isn't worth all that trouble. However, the Virgo woman is mysterious enough to keep her men running back for more. Chances are you'll be intrigued by her airs and graces.

If lovemaking means a lot to you, you'll be disappointed at first in the cool ways of your Virgo partner. However, under her glacial facade there lies a hot cauldron of seething excitement. If you're patient and artful in your romantic approach, you'll find that all that caution was well worth the trouble. When Virgos love, they don't stint. It's all or nothing as far as they're concerned. Once they're convinced that they love you, they go all the way, tossing all cares to the wind.

One thing a Virgo woman can't stand in love is hypocrisy. They don't give a hoot about what the neighbors say when their hearts tell them to go ahead. They're very concerned with human truths. So if their hearts stumble upon another fancy, they will be true to that new heartthrob and leave you standing in the rain.

Virgo is honest to her heart and will be as true to you as you are with her. Do her wrong once, though, and it's curtains.

The Virgo mother has high expectations for her children, and she will strive to bring out the very best in them. She is more tender than strict, though, and will nag rather than discipline. But youngsters sense her unconditional love for them, and usually turn out just as she hoped they would.

LIBRA MAN
LIBRA WOMAN

You'll probably find that the woman born under the sign of Libra is worth more than her weight in gold. She's a woman after your own heart, your other half in the astrological scheme of things.

With her, you'll always come first—make no mistake about that. She'll always be behind you 100 percent, no matter what you do. When you ask her advice about almost anything, you'll most likely get a very balanced and realistic opinion. She is good at thinking things out and never lets her emotions run away with her when clear logic is called for.

As a homemaker she is hard to beat. She is very concerned with harmony and balance. You can be sure she'll make your house a joy to live in. She'll see to it that the house is tastefully furnished and decorated. A Libra cannot stand filth or disarray. Anything that does not radiate harmony runs against her orderly grain.

She is chock-full of charm and womanly ways. She can sweep just about any man off his feet with one winning smile. When it comes to using her brains, she can outthink almost anyone and, sometimes, with half the effort. She is diplomatic enough, though, never to let this become glaringly apparent. She may even turn the conversation around so that you think you were the one who did all the brainwork. She couldn't care less, really, just as long as you wind up doing what is right.

The Libra woman will put you on a high pedestal. You are her man and her idol. She will share the decision making—large or small—with you, although you both have trouble in this area. She's not interested in running things, but she will offer her assistance if she feels you need it.

Some find her approach to reason masculine. However, in the areas of love and affection the Libra woman is all woman. She'll literally shower you with love and kisses during your romance with her. She doesn't believe in holding out. You shouldn't either, if you want to hang on to her.

She is the kind of lover who likes to snuggle up to you in front of the fire on chilly autumn nights. She will bring you breakfast in bed Sunday. She'll be very thoughtful about anything that concerns you. If anyone dares suggest you're not the grandest guy in the world, she'll give that person what-for. She'll defend you till her dying breath. The Libra woman will be everything you want her to be.

The Libra mother is well-balanced and moderate, like you, so together you will create a harmonious household in which young family members can grow up in an environment sensitive to their needs. The Libra mother understands that children need both guidance and encouragement. Her youngsters will never lack for anything that could make their lives easier and richer.

LIBRA MAN
SCORPIO WOMAN

The Scorpio woman can be a whirlwind of passion—perhaps too much passion to suit the moderate Libra man. When her temper flies, you'd better lock up the family heirlooms and take cover. When she chooses to be sweet, then she is on your wavelength. But then her mood mysteriously changes, and you don't have a clue.

The Scorpio woman can be as hot as a tamale or as cool as a cucumber, but whatever mood she's in, she's in it for real. She does not believe in posing or putting on airs.

The Scorpio woman is often sultry and seductive. Her femme fatale charm can pierce through the hardest of hearts like a laser ray. She may not look like Mata Hari (quite often Scorpios resemble the tomboy next door), but once she's fixed you with her tantalizing eyes, you're a goner.

Life with the Scorpio woman will not be all smiles and smooth sailing. When prompted, she can unleash a gale of venom. Generally, she'll have the good grace to keep family battles within the walls of your home. When company visits, she's apt to give the impression that married life with you is one great big joyride. It's just one of her ways of expressing her loyalty to you, at least in front of others. She may fight you tooth and nail in the confines of your living room. But during an evening out, she'll hang onto your arm and have stars in her eyes.

Scorpio women are good at keeping secrets. She may even keep a few buried from you if she feels like it.

Never cross her up on on even the smallest thing. When it comes to revenge, she's an eye-for-an-eye woman. She's not too keen on forgiveness, especially if she feels she's been wronged unfairly. You'd be well-advised not to give her any cause to be jealous, either. When the Scorpio woman sees green, your life will be made far from rosy. Once she's put you in the doghouse, you can be sure that you're going to stay there awhile.

You may find life with a Scorpio woman too draining. Although she may be full of the old paprika, it's quite likely that she's not the partner you'd like to spend the rest of your natural life with. You'd prefer someone gentler and not so hot-tempered, someone who can take the highs with the lows and not bellyache, someone who is flexible and understanding. A woman born under Scorpio can be heavenly, but she can also be the very devil when she chooses.

The Scorpio mother is protective yet encouraging. The opposites within her nature mirror the very contradictions of life itself. Under her skillful guidance, the children learn how to cope with extremes and grow up to become many-faceted individuals.

LIBRA MAN
SAGITTARIUS WOMAN

You'll most likely never come across a more good-natured woman than the one born under the sign of Sagittarius. Generally, they're full of bounce and good cheer. Their sunny disposition seems almost permanent and can be relied upon even on the rainiest of days.

Women born under the sign of the Archer are almost never malicious. If ever they seem to be it is only a regrettable mistake. Archers are often a little short on tact and say literally anything that comes into their heads—no matter what the occasion is. Sometimes the words that tumble out of their mouths seem downright cutting and cruel. Still, no matter what she says, she means well. The Sagittarius woman is quite capable of losing some of her friends, and perhaps even some of yours, through a careless slip of the lip.

On the other hand, you will appreciate her honesty and good intentions. To you, qualities of this sort play an important part in life. With a little patience and practice, you can probably help cure your Sagittarius of her loose tongue. In most cases, she'll give in to your better judgment and try to follow your advice to the letter.

Chances are she'll be the outdoors type of date and partner. Long hikes, fishing trips, and white-water canoeing will most likely appeal to her. She's a busy person. No one could ever call her a slouch. She sets great store in mobility. Her feet are itchy, and she won't sit still for a minute if she doesn't have to.

She is great company most of the time and, generally, lots of fun. Even if your buddies drop by for poker and beer, she won't have any trouble fitting in.

The Sagittarius woman is very kind and sympathetic. If she feels she's made a mistake, she'll be the first to call your attention to it. She's not afraid to own up to her faults and shortcomings.

You might lose your patience with her once or twice. After she's seen how upset her shortsightedness or tendency to blab has made you, she'll do her best to straighten up.

The Sagittarius woman is not the kind who will pry into your business affairs. But she'll always be there, ready to offer advice if you need it. If you come home with red stains on your collar and you say it's paint and not lipstick, she'll believe you.

She'll seldom be suspicious. Your word will almost always be good enough for her.

The Sagittarius mother is a wonderful and loving friend to her children. She is not afraid if a youngster learns some street smarts along the way. She will broaden her children's knowledge and see that they get a well-rounded education.

LIBRA MAN
CAPRICORN WOMAN

If you are not a successful businessman or at least on your way to success, it's quite possible that a Capricorn woman will have no interest in entering your life. Generally, the Goat is a very security-minded female. She'll see to it that she invests her time only in sure things.

Men who whittle away their time with one unsuccessful scheme or another seldom attract a Capricorn. But men who are interested in getting somewhere in life and keep their noses close to the grindstone quite often have a Capricorn woman behind them, helping them to get ahead.

Although she can be a social climber, she is not what you could call cruel or hardhearted. Beneath that cool, seemingly calculating exterior there's a warm and desirable woman. She happens to think that it is just as easy to fall in love with a rich or ambitious man as it is with a poor or lazy one. She's practical.

The Capricorn woman may be keenly interested in rising to the top, but she'll never be aggressive about it. She'll seldom step on someone's feet or nudge competitors away with her elbows. She's quiet about her desires. She sits, waits, and watches. When an opening or opportunity does appear, she'll latch onto it. For an on-the-move man, an ambitious Capricorn wife or lover can be quite an asset. She can probably give you some very good advice about business matters. When you invite the boss and his wife for dinner, she'll charm them both.

The Capricorn woman is thorough in whatever she does: cooking, cleaning, making a success out of life. Capricorns are excellent hostesses as well as guests. Generally, they are beautifully mannered and gracious, no matter what their backgrounds are. They seem to have a built-in sense of what is proper. Crude behavior or a careless faux pas can offend them no end.

If you should marry a woman born under Capricorn you need never worry about her going on a wild shopping spree. Capricorns are careful with every cent that comes into their hands. They understand the value of money better than most women and have no room in their lives for careless spending.

Capricorn women are usually very devoted to family—their own, that is. With them, family ties run very deep. Don't make jokes about her relatives; she won't stand for it. You'd better check her family out before you get down on bended knee. After your marriage you'll undoubtedly be seeing lots of her relatives.

The Capricorn mother is very ambitious for her children. She wants them to have every advantage and to benefit from things she perhaps lacked as a child. She will train her youngsters to be polite and kind and to honor traditional codes of conduct.

LIBRA MAN
AQUARIUS WOMAN

If you find that you've fallen head over heels for a woman born under the sign of the Water Bearer, you'd better fasten your safety belt. It may take you quite a while to actually discover what this woman is like. Even then, you may have nothing to go on but a string of vague hunches.

Aquarius is like a rainbow, full of bright and shining hues. She is like no other woman you've ever known. There is something elusive about her, something delightfully mysterious. You'll most likely never be able to put your finger on it. It's nothing calculated, either. Aquarius women don't believe in phony charm.

There will never be a dull moment in your life with this Water Bearer woman. She seems to radiate adventure and magic. She'll most likely be the most open-minded and tolerant woman you've ever met. She has a strong dislike for injustice and prejudice. Narrow-mindedness runs against her grain.

She is very independent by nature and quite capable of shifting for herself if necessary. She may receive many proposals for marriage from all sorts of people without ever really taking them seriously. Marriage is a very big step for her. She wants to be sure she knows what she's getting into. If she thinks that it will seriously curb her independence and love of freedom, she'll turn you down and return your engagement ring—if indeed she's let the romance get that far.

The line between friendship and romance is a pretty fuzzy one for an Aquarius. It's not difficult for her to remain buddy-buddy with an ex-lover. She's tolerant, remember? So, if you should see her on the arm of an old love, don't jump to any hasty conclusions.

She's not a jealous person herself and doesn't expect you to be, either. You'll find her pretty much of a free spirit most of the time. Just when you think you know her inside out, you'll discover that you don't really know her at all.

She's a very sympathetic and warm person. She can be helpful to people in need of assistance and advice.

She'll seldom be suspicious even if she has every right to be. If she loves a man, she'll forgive him just about anything. If he allows himself a little fling, chances are she'll just turn her head the other way. Her tolerance does have its limits, however, and her man should never press his luck at hanky-panky.

The Aquarius mother is bighearted and seldom refuses her children anything. Her open-minded attitude is easily transmitted to her youngsters. They have every chance of growing up as respectful and tolerant individuals who feel at ease anywhere.

LIBRA MAN
PISCES WOMAN

Many a man dreams of an alluring Pisces woman. You're perhaps no exception. She's soft and cuddly and very domestic. She'll let you be the brains of the family; she's contented to play a behind-the-scenes role in order to help you achieve your goals. The illusion that you are the master of the household is the kind of magic that the Pisces woman is adept at creating.

She can be very ladylike and proper. Your business associates and friends will be dazzled by her warmth and femininity. Although she's a charmer, there is a lot more to her than just a pretty exterior. There is a brain ticking away behind that soft, womanly facade. You may never become aware of it—that is, until you're married to her. It's no cause for alarm, however; she'll most likely never use it against you, only to help you and possibly set you on a more successful path.

If she feels you're botching up your married life through careless behavior or if she feels you could be earning more money than you do, she'll tell you about it. But any wife would, really. She will never try to usurp your position as head and breadwinner of the family.

No one had better dare say one uncomplimentary word about you in her presence. It's likely to cause her to break into tears. Pisces women are usually very sensitive beings. Their reaction to adversity, frustration, or anger is just a plain, good, old-fashioned cry. They can weep buckets when inclined.

She can do wonders with a house. She is very fond of dramatic and beautiful things. There will always be plenty of fresh-cut flowers around the house. She will choose charming artwork and antiques, if they are affordable. She'll see to it that the house is decorated in a dazzling yet welcoming style.

She'll have an extra special dinner prepared for you when you come home from an important business meeting. Don't dwell on the boring details of the meeting, though. But if you need that grand vision, the big idea, to seal a contract or make a conquest, your Pisces woman is sure to confide a secret that will guarantee your success. She is canny and shrewd with money, and once you are on her wavelength you can manage the intricacies on your own.

Treat her with tenderness and generosity, and your relationship will be an enjoyable one. She's most likely fond of chocolates. A bunch of beautiful flowers will never fail to make her eyes light up. See to it that you never forget her birthday or your anniversary. These things are very important to her. If you let them slip your mind, you'll send her into a crying fit that could last a considerable length of time.

If you are patient and kind, you can keep a Pisces woman happy for a lifetime. She, however, is not without her faults. Her sensitivity may get on your nerves after a while. You may find her lacking in practicality and good old-fashioned stoicism. You may even feel that she uses her tears as a method of getting her own way.

The Pisces mother has great faith in her children. She makes a strong, self-sacrificing mother. She will teach her children the value of service to the community while not letting them lose their individuality.

LIBRA
LUCKY NUMBERS 2009

Lucky numbers and astrology can be linked through the movements of the Moon. Each phase of the thirteen Moon cycles vibrates with a sequence of numbers for your Sign of the Zodiac over the course of the year. Using your lucky numbers is a fun system that connects you with tradition.

New Moon	First Quarter	Full Moon	Last Quarter
Dec. 27 ('08)	Jan. 4	Jan. 10	Jan. 17
2 4 0 8	8 1 6 4	4 3 9 5	2 4 9 7
Jan. 26	Feb. 2	Feb. 9	Feb. 16
1 6 3 4	8 5 1 0	4 6 6 2	3 9 4 9
Feb. 24	March 4	March 10	March 18
3 2 8 8	8 4 9 6	7 1 3 5	5 7 9 7
March 26	April 2	April 9	April 17
5 4 1 0	6 2 8 9	0 3 5 9	9 2 7 5
April 24	May 1	May 9	May 17
0 7 3 8	5 6 9 9	2 6 8 2	2 4 2 1
May 24	May 30	June 7	June 15
0 2 7 4	4 5 8 1	1 0 5 7	3 7 1 9
June 22	June 29	July 7	July 15
4 1 0 2	5 7 2 0	0 4 9 7	6 3 8 4
July 21	July 28	August 5	August 13
1 1 0 4	4 6 1 3	3 8 6 5	2 7 3 9
August 20	August 27	Sept. 4	Sept. 11
9 1 0 4	1 0 5 7	3 1 9 6	2 7 4 4
Sept. 18	Sept. 26	Oct. 4	Oct. 11
5 8 1 2	2 0 8 4	2 1 7 3	8 5 6 6
Oct. 18	Oct. 25	Nov. 2	Nov. 9
6 9 2 6	8 2 7 5	4 1 6 2	8 9 3 3
Nov. 16	Nov. 24	Dec. 2	Dec. 8
5 9 2 7	7 1 8 7	4 9 5 2	3 6 8 8
Dec. 15	Dec. 24	Dec. 31	Jan. 7 ('10)
8 3 5 4	3 9 5 5	1 0 7 9	9 2 4 8

LIBRA
YEARLY FORECAST 2009

Forecast for 2009 Concerning Business
and Financial Affairs, Job Prospects,
Travel, Health, Romance and Marriage
for Persons Born with the Sun
in the Zodiacal Sign of Libra.
September 23–October 22

For those born under the zodiacal sign of Libra, ruled by Venus, planet of romance, money, and the good things of life, the year ahead offers compelling and dynamic changes that could lead to your receiving a wealth of recognition. The year 2009 can be very successful as long as everything is kept in perspective and an overly optimistic approach is avoided. The universe is also encouraging you to get out and about, have fun, and enjoy yourself.

Erratic conditions continue in your daily routine and employment sector. A new job, promotion, resignation, or retirement could find you doing something entirely different at the end of the year from at the beginning. If your job doesn't provide the autonomy or flexibility you want, look to self-employment or working from home to earn a living. Keep your resume up to date so that you are ready to take advantage of opportunities that crop up unexpectedly. Work that doesn't offer sufficient challenge or the chance to be innovative is unlikely to appeal. Libra employers looking for people who have technical and scientific skills should be happy with the workers you hire this year. Restlessness might be harder to control. If feelings of being restricted or constrained occur, it might be easy for you to lapse into laziness and disorganization. Working abroad to advance your knowledge as well as volunteering services to a community or humanitarian program would be a wonderful experience. Travel this year may be more for vacation than for work, although a mixture of travel for business and pleasure would be ideal.

Stern Saturn, the zodiac taskmaster, puts a number of responsibilities on your agenda but also offers amazing opportunities. Saturn transits Virgo, your twelfth house of hidden affairs, until October 29. Then Saturn moves into your own sign of Libra. With Saturn in Virgo endeavor to complete outstanding projects so that you are ready to begin new ones later in the year. People will come and go in your life, and a mentor could provide just the advice or guidance you need to keep you on the right path. The health of someone close could be a worry. Decisions regarding an elderly parent or other relative might need to be made, with ongoing responsibility possibly falling on your shoulders. Saturn in Virgo represents the end of a cycle. The new one begins once Saturn settles into your sign of Libra and your first house of personality. Responsibilities will still be heavy, but accomplishments for the next three years will be significant. Now is the time to analyze who you are and where you want to be next year.

Unconventional Uranus continues to pass through Pisces, throwing a few curveballs in the health and work sector of your solar chart. Energy levels will fluctuate, much as they have done the last few years. You could experience high vitality one day, feeling you could conquer the world, and the next day prefer to curl up and stay in bed. You will have more nervous energy, with restlessness and fidgety behavior more common. Participating in sports, working out at the gym, or maintaining a regular fitness program can help you to counteract agitation and has the added bonus of maintaining your body in top shape. Keep a close watch on your nutritional intake and diet. Digestion problems could be prevalent, as well as intolerance to certain food that never bothered you before. A health problem could flare up, requiring professional services.

An attraction to new methods of staying healthy is likely, with complementary and alternate therapies of interest. You may decide to learn more about natural medicines for your own benefit or to set up a practice helping others. The kidneys are an organ that need special care for Libra folks, so be sure to drink plenty of fluids. Meditation can be a wonderful form of stress relief. Making time for self-nurturing is also essential. Libra folks must balance work, family, and home life with play and creative expression. Otherwise Uranus could give you a wake-up call with an ailment that makes you stop and think. If depression becomes an issue at the end of the year, it may signal that something in your life needs changing. When the Sun moves through the sign of Pisces from February 18 to March 20, you should begin a new diet or exercise program that will be successful and long lasting.

The last week in April and the first week of May are times when you may be more accident-prone. During this period be very aware of your surroundings. Steer clear of dark alleys, don't go out alone, and be careful when handling hot and sharp instruments. Another tricky month for Scales to navigate is September. Then cosmic aspects will be sending contradictory influences to upset your equilibrium. Your ruler Venus is also more active during September. So expect pleasant surprises along with a few shocks.

Early in January Jupiter, planet of abundance, visits Aquarius, signaling that it is Libra party time for the next twelve months. When Jupiter delivers, it is always big. So it is essential this year to avoid overdoing everything. Both Jupiter and Neptune in Aquarius are calling on Libra to have fun but stay within your boundaries. Moderation is definitely the word to add to your vocabulary to lessen the chance of problems. Gambling, speculating, and investing could generate great financial rewards, but losses are possible if a prudent approach is not taken. Women of child-bearing age should take more precautions if pregnancy is not on your agenda this year. Fertility is high, so the chance of conceiving increases in 2009.

This year your creative juices will be flowing freely thanks to Jupiter and Neptune in Aquarius. There should be a greater awareness of your talents and skills. All 2009 can be a period when your expertise and your productivity soar and will be acknowledged by the paying public. As your self-confidence and esteem rise, regularly buying lottery tickets and entering raffles and competitions could bring financial gains.

Neptune's transit through Aquarius further reinforces the importance of luck, creative interests, children, and hobbies in the year 2009. Your sensitive and compassionate nature is to the fore. Relationships with children should be easygoing, and Libra parents will experience a glow of pride at the accomplishment of a child. A new hobby may become a passion with the possibility of generating extra income. A leisure pursuit or hobby is also relaxing, a great way to reduce stress. The influence of Neptune in Aquarius can increase gullibility and warns against putting a lover on a pedestal. Beware becoming a martyr, continually bending to the needs of your mate or children. Parents should be more aware of children's activities, vigilant about the hours youngsters spend on the computer.

With Jupiter and Neptune in Aquarius, the year ahead holds plenty of opportunities for romance and love. Affection is always high up the scale for Libras. You will be in your element as an abundance of admirers arrives on the scene. Those of you unattached have an excellent chance of becoming partnered, and the wait will not be long. This is a year when you will be celebrating major milestones and happy family occasions. Engagements, weddings, and births of children are all possibilities adding to the excitement of 2009. A torrid or secret love affair could be both thrilling and upsetting, and you might have to decide whether to continue on or sever the ties. Social activities, invitations, and trips may be more frequent. An overseas journey holds promise. Libra in a happy, committed union should find that the relationship develops and deepens. But if a partnership is rocky, there are times in 2009 when the possibility of separation is strong. Mid-September is a particularly risky period and not the time to push a partner for any type of commitment.

Passionate Pluto is in Capricorn, your house of home and family, all year. Libra home owners should continue building or remodeling projects begun last year. This is also a starred year to enter into the home or property market. Relocation for work or to move to a larger or smaller home is very possible. There are apt to be many changes in your living arrangements as people come and go. There could also be more conflict as housemates struggle over who rules the roost. Young Libras are likely to experience more battles with parents or a parent figure.

To the uninitiated, a retrograde planet seems to stop before apparently moving backward in the zodiac. All planets except the Sun and Moon appear to go through this optical illusion of retreating, which in astrology is called retrograde motion. Your ruler Venus goes retrograde from March 6 to April 17 in your opposite sign of Aries, impacting your house of partnerships. All one-on-one relationships, both personal and professional, can be the focus of your review, reconsideration, and revision while Venus is retrograde in Aries.

It is planet Mercury that causes the most chaos when retrograde. Misunderstandings, delays, and confusion are possible. Breakdowns in electronic equipment, communication, and transportation are also possible. Making decisions, signing important paperwork, and purchasing expensive items are not recommended. However, you don't need to hibernate during a Mercury retrograde. Instead, review, rethink, and reconsider situations, choices, and current goals to ensure that you are working toward your main aim. Mercury usually goes retrograde three times a year, but in 2009 Mercury is retrograde four times: January 11–February 1, May 7–30, September 7–29, December 26–January 15, 2010.

The phases of the Moon can be a guide to decision making and appropriate action. Beginning a venture during the New Moon phase can increase the chances of obtaining a fruitful conclusion. Completing a venture during the Full Moon phase can bring the desired end results. People, including yourself, are likely to be cranky and agitated during Full Moon phase. This is the time to steer clear of risky behavior.

The unusual and the unpredictable will shape Libra daily routine, employment, and service to others this year. Luck and good fortune will most certainly be your friend as long as you remain alert to the many opportunities coming your way. The most important advice of all sent by the cosmos for Libra is to make sure that your work and your play are equally balanced.

LIBRA
DAILY FORECAST

January–December 2009

JANUARY

1. THURSDAY. Bright. Happy New Year! Living in a world without too many obstacles to hinder your progress might be a preferred option, but unfortunately this is unlikely. Consider making resolutions for the year ahead by formulating goals and deciding what changes are needed to increase your emotional comfort. These could include an updated image, relocating to a new area, or seeking a better-paying job. Continuing with the social and party atmosphere should appeal as communicative Mercury slips into inventive Aquarius, sending encouraging vibes for Libras to indulge in creative and leisure pursuits and to express extra affection toward children, nearest, and dearest.

2. FRIDAY. Happy. Enthusiasm and opportunity meet up today. Life will be even better if you don't have to head off to work, because there are splendid stars for lovers. Libras who are currently apart from their significant other should be able to express affection and longing over the phone, by e-mail, or in letter form. If on the job, keep your nose to the grindstone. With the Sun and energetic Mars linking in industrious Capricorn, you can forge a niche for yourself at work by performing tasks in a particularly efficient and effective manner. Home owners will find that renovating or redecorating is a labor of love. Put your heart and soul into it.

3. SATURDAY. Constructive. If you are still on vacation and are considering making changes around the house, now is a good time to check out the latest trends in the market. Your ruler, luscious Venus, visits placid Pisces, accentuating your employment, health, and daily existence until February 2. Positive, harmonious interactions with coworkers and clients should increase, and love could be found on the job. Weight gain may be an issue for those who are inclined to overindulge. This is a period when the desire for rich and sweet foods increases. Try to be on the same page as your mate or partner to avoid conflict this afternoon, or at least agree to disagree.

4. SUNDAY. Affectionate. Love is in the air, continuing to fire up the flames of passion for all those in love. Your ruler Venus is making a powerful and positive link to Pluto. This can produce wonderful transformations if you know what you would love to do and who you would love to do it with. This is an excellent period to become engaged or to walk down the aisle. A new romance could be just around the corner for the unattached Libra. Networking can be very beneficial. For the self-employed, plans to mix business with pleasure should lead to better than expected profits. A shopping spree with a daughter or a female relative could strengthen ties.

5. MONDAY. Spirited. A bevy of cosmic action will keep you on your toes. A joint financial venture started now could pay off in a spectacular manner in the future providing all facts and figures have been verified and ample effort is put into the project. Be prepared to break out the bubbly tonight in order to celebrate a promotion, salary increase, or unexpected windfall with someone close. Jupiter, planet of abundance, is now visiting Aquarius, your house of romance, creativity, leisure, and speculation. Luck and good fortune will increase, but so will overoptimism and enthusiasm, warning Libras to be diligent when it comes to taking risks.

6. TUESDAY. Mixed. You are likely to encounter a number of obstacles. Frustration and angst could be felt more keenly until mid-afternoon, when the lunar goddess sends a few positive trends to lighten the atmosphere. Before that time take steps to prevent a situation from blowing up into a possible confrontation. Libras who are of childbearing age are in a higher fertility period now, increasing the chance of pregnancy. Helping other people might be a dream, but figuring out exactly how to do this could lead to a few muddled ideas. First sort out what area would benefit most from your energy, then move ahead with idealistic plans.

7. WEDNESDAY. Sensitive. Libras are often discontented with romance and love, having high expectations that can be difficult to meet. Consider your life right now and endeavor to be happy with what you have. Chasing perfection is futile and will only increase your level of dissatisfaction. Financial pressures could leave you feeling trapped by seemingly ever-increasing obligations. Concentrate on overcoming one problem at a time rather than worrying about every situation and issue. Life is to enjoy, not to be overburdened by stress and strain. Casting your eyes on the far horizon might appeal if you are looking for a new destination for a family vacation.

8. THURSDAY. Tricky. A wanderlust attitude could overtake you, making it difficult to focus on today's tasks. Educational, religious, and cultural projects will proceed smoothly if you utilize your talent, expertise, and experience. Be patient with people in close proximity; your level of tolerance may be limited even for the usually serene Libra. A serious problem with in-laws could require attention. Tact and diplomacy, at which you excel, will be essential if certain people think they know what is best for you and your family. However, don't give in just for the sake of peace. If you are not comfortable with a decision, stand up for your rights and express your feelings.

9. FRIDAY. Variable. Socialize, network, and catch up on communications. Although positive trends prevail, you might feel you are in a rut and yearn to break free. Doing daily tasks in a different way or order can help reduce boredom while increasing variety. An issue that seemed to be clear-cut could begin to bother you, and second thoughts about a project could develop. A friend whom you don't see on a regular basis might turn up out of the blue, giving you a chance to catch up with each other's news. Tread warily during the afternoon, when misunderstandings could cause upsets or intense tension with a senior authority figure or an older family member.

10. SATURDAY. Emotional. Plans and projects come to a head as the Moon waxes to the full in the sign of cranky Cancer. Avoid jumping too quickly into any discussions on the job because the chance of arguments increases due to highly charged emotions. Clashes with an authority figure are possible because of demands to put your work before family obligations, which won't sit well with you. An impending new arrival could find you making changes around the house to accommodate a nursery. Pregnant Libra women who are nearing full term should pack a suitcase and stay close to home, aware that babies often make an appearance when a Full Moon occurs.

11. SUNDAY. Tentative. With the Sun and logical Saturn in a friendly link, practical projects can be completed. Home renovations and maintenance should proceed without too many problems, and you should be pleased with the results of your efforts. Social arrangements will be more enjoyable during the morning than this afternoon. Put off signing anything on the dotted line, making major decisions, or purchasing large items. Tricky Mercury begins moving into retrograde motion for the first time in 2009 and will continue to retreat until February 1. Expect crossed wires and muddled communications along with equipment breakdowns, computer failures, and cancelation of travel plans.

12. MONDAY. Efficient. Your competent, businesslike mood continues, although the urge to display ambitious tendencies might not be pronounced today. If someone isn't pulling their own weight, you may decide to say something or to take other action. Environmental concerns might be the encouragement you need to join a group of like-minded people working together to make a difference in the community, country, or abroad. If you would prefer a quiet night relaxing at home, getting together with a few favorite companions can be comfortable and pleasant, even just sitting around drinking coffee, sharing jokes, and exchanging news.

13. TUESDAY. Eventful. Avoid volunteering your services if this means you will have to exert extra energy over the next few days. A new proposition or opportunity could be just what you need to advance your long-term goals. Just make sure that everything is aboveboard and no one is trying to lure you into something that isn't as it appears. Focus on what is going on in your own body rather than on external situations from midafternoon onward. That is a time when the Moon drops in to visit Virgo, your zone of solitude. Checking out the January sales could reveal a few bargains that you cannot pass up.

14. WEDNESDAY. Wary. Dissatisfaction with the external world could find you withdrawing from the social circuit for a couple of days. Channeling your energy into spiritual or mystical directions may help to increase peace and harmony, with meditation or yoga a good choice to begin the process. Let bygones be bygones, especially if past resentments are holding you back in any way. Cleaning up the mistakes and messes made by other people could be frustrating, but at least by performing the job yourself you can be sure it will be done correctly. Steer clear of intrigue in the workplace; it would be wiser not to become involved.

15. THURSDAY. Low-key. A reserved mood prevails. You may wish for the day to amble on without any major dramas or disruptions. You will be inclined to make only a halfhearted attempt at strenuous tasks and, if you cannot make headway, you are apt to give up entirely. This would probably be the best option because your energy remains low and motivation even lower. If you need to make some progress, formulate a clear plan of what is required, devise a strategy, and stick with it. Communicating with folks who were important in your past could be enlightening as both you and they realize how far you have come.

16. FRIDAY. Stimulating. Although the lunar goddess is sending unhelpful trends, the next two days are a special time of the month as the Moon glides through your own sign of Libra. A resurgence of fresh new energy floods your body, motivation increases, and Lady Luck is on your side. If you need a makeover, now is the time to get started. Being well groomed is important, so arrange for a massage, beauty treatment, or a new hairstyle. In addition, dress to impress. A new or improved exercise program could help shift the few extra pounds that you accumulated over the festive period. Do something special for a loved one without expecting anything in return.

17. SATURDAY. Charming. This is another day when personal objectives move into the realm of strong possibilities rather than maybes. Performing several tasks at once shouldn't be a problem. However, remain at a steady pace rather than rushing and more can be accomplished by the end of the day. Dealing with officials or superiors should be a breeze because your charm and tact are pronounced. New connections can be made, ranging from a new addition to your social circle to the possibility of a new love interest for singles. Turning heads at a social function is probably not something new for you, but this evening you can carry it off with more aplomb than usual.

18. SUNDAY. Auspicious. Luck arrives at your doorstep, aided by the merging of informative Mercury and Jupiter, planet of abundance. Although keeping spare cash in your wallet is advisable over the next few days, purchasing a lottery ticket, entering a competition, or placing a small wager could produce some benefits as well as increasing the excitement of the day. Sporting Libras with a special talent could receive a sponsorship offer. If this involves a binding contract, wait if possible until the beginning of February before signing paperwork. Otherwise seek legal advice to ensure that everything is in order and your best interests are being taken into account.

19. MONDAY. Significant. Overspending is not the way to increase happiness, even if an urge for luxury items is compelling right now. With prudence there should be enough cash to keep your checking account in the black. Don't allow anyone to goad you into saying or doing something that you are not comfortable with. Your love life should remain constant, although bells are unlikely to be ringing loudly today. The Sun joins Mercury, Jupiter, Chiron, and Neptune in Aquarius, further highlighting your creative, leisure, and romance sector. The next four weeks favor inviting friends to enjoy your hospitality and spending more quality time with children or other young relatives.

20. TUESDAY. Productive. Present trends increase your administrative abilities. Put your nose to the grindstone and you can handle tasks effectively and efficiently. Taking charge and persuading other people to do your bidding should be easier. Singles who have been interested in someone from afar could now make tentative overtures to determine if the feeling is returned or if it is time to look further for a new romantic potential. A social mood encourages getting out to meet and greet those in your immediate environment. Plan to get together with friends or a partner for lunch, introducing variety and excitement into your day.

21. WEDNESDAY. Diligent. Unless you pay close attention to details and timing, you risk having to repeat important duties tomorrow. Opt for an employment task that offers mobility rather than being stuck inside at a desk all day. An ally or supporter could come forward and help put one of your good ideas into practical form. An urge to further open up your mind and spirit could lead to learning another language or enrolling in a hobby group or course to increase your expertise and provide stimulation. You are the perfect person to intervene in a dispute between friends because negotiation and the ability to mediate tricky situations are innate Libra skills.

22. THURSDAY. Unexpected. Venus, your ruler and the feminine goddess, and Mars, the masculine god, are linking to erratic Uranus today, so you can expect anything to happen. Making changes around the house or working environment can be a positive way to utilize current cosmic influences, especially if you are tired of the same old decor or routines. Novel new ideas could come from seemingly nowhere, offering the potential of making life a lot easier. A casual encounter during the next few days could put the unattached in close contact with a romantic possibility, but move slowly. Although romance will be available, this doesn't necessarily mean that love will last forever.

23. FRIDAY. Stable. Staying close to home or being surrounded by familiar faces is most suitable for today's mood. Because of increased efficiency, home and family matters can be dealt with easily and in a practical, sensible manner. Discussions about upcoming home improvements can be exciting, but make sure everyone has some input into the changes that are going to occur. This is the perfect evening for a gathering with loved ones and extended family members. Special food, playing games with children, and watching an interesting movie would be an ideal beginning to the weekend.

24. SATURDAY. Lucky. As several celestial influences descend today, you might not know if you are coming or going. Abundant self-confidence and energy could find you taking on tasks normally left to others. Just be sure to take care. Pace activities to ensure you have enough vim and vitality to complete everything you start. Luck abounds in most areas of your life. A small financial risk taken now has the potential to produce a significant gain. If a relationship has lost some of its zest, take advantage of current trends for physical passion. Companionship is strong even if romance and affection are missing. For singles, a potential partner could be met at a nightclub this evening.

25. SUNDAY. Easygoing. Although you will be eager to socialize later in the day, your energy may be low. If possible, consider staying in bed a little longer than usual this morning to catch up on your sleep. Libras with young children could ask their partner to take a turn at babysitting early in the day. Check the fridge and freezer; visitors could arrive unannounced, staying long enough that a meal might need to be shared. If venturing out on an unplanned trip, choose entertainment that offers relaxation and provides amusement. Talented Libras might prefer to focus on an artistic project.

26. MONDAY. Renewing. A great day arrives. You will probably prefer to stay home and do your own thing rather than head off to work or school, but do what you must. Whatever is on the agenda should work out well. Being acknowledged for how creative or brilliant you are can be a huge ego booster. This morning a New Moon falls in Aquarius, your solar sector that relates to children, romance, and creative pursuits. Libras who are in a new love affair can expect sparks to fly. Those in a long-established union can be more adventurous, seeking exciting ways to spice up love. Beginning a creative project within the next two weeks increases the chance of success.

27. TUESDAY. Creative. Take advantage of the prevailing congenial atmosphere. If life has been a little tough lately, finding someone to talk to shouldn't present a problem. Your life ruler Venus continues to connect harmoniously with chatty Mercury. Libras who are lucky enough not to have any pressing responsibilities can use the day to seek activities that stimulate thinking processes. Hobbies or activities that you once enjoyed could be revisited now. Your imagination is enhanced and artistic juices should be flowing freely. A mood for love continues. The solo Libra may be thrilled by the way a romance is blossoming. A child could benefit from increased attention.

28. WEDNESDAY. Helpful. Good headway can be made as cosmic influences provide support. New incentives on the job offer the chance to take up a challenge that you never considered before. Amicable relations with coworkers or employees ensure that a consensus can be found quickly and easily with most problems that arise throughout the working day. Your ideas to improve employment techniques and processes should receive a positive hearing from higher-ups. Focus on good eating habits, especially if remaining slim and sexy is your aim. Your willpower probably isn't as strong as usual.

29. THURSDAY. Useful. The lunar goddess sends helpful vibes this morning, allowing Libras to move ahead with work and daily chores without obstacles to slow progress. A change in company policy might not appear to be in your favor right now but could prove advantageous at a future date. Later in the day an issue with an older person could be difficult to discuss. However, if you wish to deal effectively with the problem, getting it out into the open might be the only way to resolve frustrations and clear the air. Allowing the matter to drag on will just increase upset and stress. Carefully handle personal treasures or expensive items belonging to other people to reduce the risk of accidental breakage.

30. FRIDAY. Promising. Morning hours are the best time to seek help, favors, or cooperation from colleagues and customers. That is also the best time to shop for office equipment, clothes, a pet, or artistic supplies. Try to be on time if you have a meeting to attend or somewhere important to be, and factor in possible delays and interruptions to your schedule. A partner could veto plans for home improvements or a new purchase, so be sure to consult your significant other before moving ahead with plans. Taking an interest in alternative health methods such as mind or body therapies, yoga, or reflexology could be a great benefit.

31. SATURDAY. Favorable. Expect a good day ahead. Any legal proceeding entered into now should have a good outcome, especially if connected to an adult child or a lover. Libras are often viewed as generous and willing to do whatever it takes to be popular or to keep the peace. Cater to the needs of your partner or loved ones if that makes you happy, but take care not to bend too far to their demands and wants, especially if this is detrimental to your own personal aims. Social functions should be fun and enjoyable, so look forward to a great night out. The currently single should keep alert for that special someone to come along.

FEBRUARY

1. SUNDAY. Happy. A relatively easy day is being sent by the universe. Speak up if you have something important to impart. Tension could develop in a relationship if you lean toward keeping emotions and feelings to yourself instead of sharing them with your mate or partner. Reconsidering your overall financial position and balancing income received with current expenditures can be beneficial, particularly because Libras tend to spend a lot on the good things in life. Small cost-saving measures made now could put more money into your savings, providing a sense of relief knowing that bills can be covered each month without having to enter into a juggling act.

2. MONDAY. Appealing. Mixed fortunes prevail. Unanswered questions relating to the finances of your mate or partner could intensify current family problems. However, these worries and fears could prove unfounded, so it would be wiser to wait to see how matters work out before getting too wound up. Although the weather may be cool the same won't be said for your love life right now. Later tonight your ruler Venus enters your opposite sign of Aries, lighting up the relationship sector of your solar chart. Take advantage of your ruler's presence here. For the currently unattached, love could arrive out of the blue. In addition, this is an excellent period to ignite an affectionate spark in a longtime relationship.

3. TUESDAY. Positive. Planet Mercury began moving forward again on Sunday, so by now you should be experiencing positive trends. Family matters will flow more easily. Libra homeowners waiting for building or landscaping plans to be approved by local authorities should receive good news soon. If you have been clinging to a large number of trinkets and knickknacks, consider decluttering your house and working area. Consigning items to a charity thrift shop or to a yard sale can clear some space and make way for new things to come into your life. If you have been burying your head in the sand over monetary concerns or a deep secret, don't be surprised if information coming to the surface forces you to address the issue.

4. WEDNESDAY. Heartening. The universe is sending extra oomph to further brighten up Libra love life. Mars is now galloping through Aquarius, your solar zone of romance, so you can expect matters relating to past or current love to come to the fore. You have extra energy to make your mate happier than ever before. From now until March 14 while Mars is in Aquarius, speaking plainly and simply can help avoid outright confrontations with loved ones. This is an excellent period to clear away ongoing arguments as long as you are careful with both how you broach the subject and the words you choose. If it has been some time since your last vacation, obtain travel brochures and start planning a trip with family members or your current love.

5. THURSDAY. Restrained. Your energy could be depleted and confidence at a low ebb as a major pattern forms in the sky between somber Saturn and erratic Uranus. Find ways to reduce stresses and strains, and place your health and general well-being first and foremost. Weariness could overcome you unless you endeavor to keep life as simple as possible. Handling tricky issues might be more than you can cope with right now. Be careful of displaying aggression toward anyone because they might not see what you are trying to accomplish. Steer clear of controversial subjects that have the potential to cause discord or a dispute. Tread warily when it comes to love and romance. If partnered, avoid flirting.

6. FRIDAY. Bumpy. Astrologically speaking, this is not a great day. Don't expect much support or cooperation on the job. Higher-ups are apt to be cranky and colleagues unhelpful. Refrain from asking for a pay raise, time off, or any special favor from those in charge; your request is unlikely to be viewed favorably. The form of a relationship may have changed, but for you it may never end, at least in your mind. Such an attitude is not always healthy, so if the love has gone from a union perhaps you should consider moving on as well. Different obligations are likely to clash, causing concern over the coming days. Put aside daily pressures and relax tonight.

7. SATURDAY. Variable. Although achievements and progress can come from your own effort, today will be a mixed bag. This morning you should freely share your happy mood with other people. If off to work you should enjoy assigned tasks early in the day. By midafternoon, however, challenges that arise will test your patience and resolve. At that time it might be necessary to eliminate insignificant chores so you can make some progress. Be prepared for opposition to your plans from a colleague who isn't as enthusiastic about a project as you are. Social plans will provide the enjoyment and entertainment that you are seeking this evening.

8. SUNDAY. Restful. This is a perfect day for Libra folks to stay in bed longer or loll around at home, enjoying the chance to relax. Keep recreational pursuits simple. Refrain from participating in strenuous or tedious chores. Sports-loving Libras will enjoy watching a child or a favored team play basketball or some other athletic pursuit. Getting together with kindred spirits for a casual meal or before dinner cocktails may be enough social activity for now. If you would prefer a really quiet day, consider putting your feet up and unwinding with a favorite book or movie, refusing to even answer the phone.

9. MONDAY. Sensitive. This is one of those days when emotions are close to the surface and dilemmas and dramas continually cross your path. You can expect troubles to occur with the Leo Full Moon affecting your relationships with friends, a lover, or children. Youngsters are apt to be more temperamental than usual, and no amount of pleading or threats from you are likely to produce peace and harmony at home. There may be very little romance in a committed union. It would be wise to just accept that many people exhibit crankiness when the Moon is full, not only Libras. Be wary during the afternoon hours in case someone tries to pull the wool over your eyes.

10. TUESDAY. Interesting. Although you need to remain alert to the sensitive feelings of other people, progress can be achieved if you are flexible. Concentration is enhanced as the Moon slides through Virgo. This is an excellent period to work alone, moving at your own natural pace rather than rushing through tasks. However, be prepared for plans to be punctuated by delays or other unanticipated obstacles. Take extra care if involved in some type of financial deal. Someone could try to take advantage of you or undermine your authority or confidence. Make up your own mind about a situation this evening, and don't allow anyone to instill doubts in your mind.

11. WEDNESDAY. Subdued. You are apt to experience lackluster feelings throughout the day. Start slowly and move at a comfortable pace. Trying to hurry through tasks or actions could cause mistakes, mishaps, or breakages to occur. This is definitely not the day to leap into strenuous projects or chores because your enthusiasm is likely to run out before those projects are completed. Working for the underprivileged could appeal. Volunteering your services to a local charitable organization could be the way to fulfill this urge and receive emotional gratification. Your romantic relationship requires a little extra give-and-take but should be well worth the effort.

12. THURSDAY. Opportune. Cosmic trends are mixed. There may be much that you want to achieve and you won't take too kindly to interruptions or attempts to disrupt your flow. Hang a sign on the door if you need peace and quiet in order to act on tasks. With the Sun merging with inspirational Neptune, any venture that requires a creative touch should turn out better than expected. Be alert. Keep in mind that if something appears too good to be true it probably is. Bold and beautiful are apt descriptions for Libra, one of the most well-groomed signs of the zodiac. Think about adding a few mix-and-match additions to your wardrobe, items that won't break the bank but look as if they had.

13. FRIDAY. Productive. As a Libra you are not generally prone to superstitions, but in any case you don't need to worry about today's day and date. Expect to be in the spotlight. Your personal touch should work like magic on a chore that other people could find too difficult. Pride in a job well done could spill over into some type of reward for the diligent Libra. If you are looking forward to celebrating Valentine's Day in style tomorrow, ensure that all preparations have been made so you are not disappointed. Libras who hold a responsible position need to anticipate obstacles later in the afternoon that have the potential to delay your departure from work.

14. SATURDAY. Tender. Positive influences and mainly easy vibes illuminate most areas of your solar chart on this day made for lovers. If you are expecting a candlelit dinner, wine, roses, and chocolates, you might have to put in extra effort this evening because your partner could be frugal or even distracted. It might be better if you make the arrangements so you get what you want. Mercury has reentered Aquarius, your house of love, enabling you to display emotional warmth through body language and to verbally express desires and affection to that special person. A favorite hobby that you can share will help to reduce stress.

15. SUNDAY. Unsettled. The universe is requiring a little more of you right now. Making an effort to go the extra mile to make other people happy will also increase personal contentment. If without kids or commitments, indulging yourself this morning will be particularly soothing. Extra rest, a long soak in the tub, reading, or watching a romantic comedy could relieve a furrowed brow. Shopping might not be a good form of entertainment if your bank balance is looking strained. However, if a positive effort has been made to address this issue, search out a few bargains. Be prepared for an argument to erupt this evening if the household budget is currently stretched to the limit.

16. MONDAY. Promising. A much happier day appears on the horizon today, although money matters could continue to cause some stress. A prudent approach is necessary if finances are shaky. You can expect a number of lucky opportunities and events to come your way as your lifetime ruler Venus harmonizes with Jupiter, lord of fortune. Taking a moderate approach will help to reduce the possibility of future problems. Pursuing your own professional goals and enlisting support from others can produce worthwhile financial results. Meeting with a child's teacher should be a positive experience for Libra parents.

17. TUESDAY. Lucky. You are likely to experience the Midas touch. You are also likely to be charm, sweetness, and light personified. Take advantage of this to push forward with personal plans, particularly those that involve expansion. Positive gains are foreseen. A short journey should be pleasant, and relations with those at a distance will be amicable. Teaching children, either your own or in a volunteer position, can be emotionally fulfilling, especially if you are utilizing creative talents. This is a good period to take up a new hobby or recreational pursuit if you are growing bored with current interests.

18. WEDNESDAY. Social. With your ruler Venus happily entwined with energetic Mars, social life should sparkle as many invitations arrive. Libras who are setting off on vacation can expect to enjoy a happy getaway. Love is also in the air. This is an ideal time to turn up the temperature on romance, demonstrating to your lover just how much you care. Everyday relationships with neighbors or family members could be a little tricky. Issues that arise won't be as straightforward as you would prefer. It might be wise to avoid contact as much as possible, at least for a day or two. For the next four weeks the Sun will be resting in the peaceful sign of Pisces, bringing health and employment conditions to the fore.

19. THURSDAY. Successful. A determined approach can find you diligently working toward achieving goals and completing tasks. If you need to reorganize household accounts, assign chores, or re-arrange furniture, energy to complete these activities should be in plentiful supply. With the Pisces Sun now impacting your health sector, this is an excellent period to consider beginning a new diet or exercise regime. Mustering the willpower to stick to a strict pro-gram shouldn't be difficult. With effort, a new you could emerge in time for the many social gatherings that will be on your summer-time agenda. Plan to be alone together with your significant other, arranging a date or scheduling a weekend away for two.

20. FRIDAY. Guarded. Be extra careful. If planning to shop during the morning hours, guard against confusion over the price of pur-chases or the amount of change you receive. Keep a smile on your face and don't argue with coworkers. A higher-up may be watching from the sidelines and evaluating your potential. Work or other daily patterns might need some thought and consideration. The urge to spend more time with your family could be at odds with the need to earn money to supplement the family budget. Seeking ways to reduce hours spent on the job or taking work home might help ease concerns. Don't borrow money unless absolutely necessary.

21. SATURDAY. Empowering. Quiet satisfaction should come from events that take place today. It is a time when you can afford to take a chance, providing you don't take on more than you can comfortably handle. Lucky breaks will only turn into opportunities if you are prepared to act at the right time, so be alert and success should be yours. With the Sun in a strong link to Pluto, planet of power, your charisma is higher and leadership qualities enhanced. Be ready to guide and counsel other people, even if this only entails organizing tonight's social arrangements. If you have been applying for a job you may hear news to your advantage. This is also an auspicious time to go on employment interviews or send off your updated resume.

22. SUNDAY. Pleasurable. Good influences will surround you for most of the day, and evening hours bring lucky vibes. Take it easy through the morning, puttering around and completing weekend chores. By lunchtime you should be ready to actively socialize. Taking children to an educational show or historical site should be fulfilling for you and them. Inspiration to revive creative talent is in plentiful supply, and you could utilize this talent by making improvements around the house. Feelings will run high for those in love, making it easy to enjoy the idealistic ambience. Singles have a good chance of meeting and impressing an older romantic potential.

23. MONDAY. Satisfactory. This isn't a good day to leave anything to chance. Unexpected situations could arise, leaving you wondering what went wrong. Unless you focus on work that offers some variety or stimulation, boredom could make this a long day. Talented Scales might have an opportunity to invent something that can make life easier or to use original ideas to launch some type of venture. Give gambling and other games of chance a miss this evening, and be careful of possible deceitful action by other people. Your creative inspiration is enhanced, so if you have free time consider pursuing a favored hobby.

24. TUESDAY. Excellent. Behold the Pisces New Moon and the merging of chatty Mercury with generous Jupiter. These celestial influences promise an excellent day ahead. With your positive attitude and the conviction that matters will turn out as they should, beginning new projects or applying for a better paying job could meet with instant success. Going on interviews or auditions, implementing new employment processes, or following up on a new development with a health condition over the next two weeks should lead to the positive results that you are seeking. If there are a number of new employees at your place of business, consider arranging a social outing so you can all mix, mingle, and get to know each other better.

25. WEDNESDAY. Superb. This is another starred day for working at activities that give you pleasure and contentment. Informative Mercury happily engages your lifetime ruler Venus, boosting your imagination and creative aptitude. If you wish to learn new skills, consider enrolling in a course or finding a mentor. Solo Libras actively seeking new love could find an attraction that is your intellectual equal, providing the necessary mental stimulation as well as the romance that you desire. Open, honest communication between couples can be entered into with the assurance that discussions will be conducted with love and warmth.

26. THURSDAY. Good. As a Libra you are usually very particular with personal grooming and appearance. If your health or exercise regime has gotten off track recently, now is a terrific period to take corrective action. If exercising alone isn't providing the inspiration required to work out regularly, consider hiring a personal trainer or joining the local gym or health club. Employees should ensure that working conditions are fair. It is vital not to be taken for granted by the boss. Enforced overtime without receiving mandated pay or time off could lead to resentment as well as having a detrimental effect on your family relationship. Beware of conflicts this evening.

27. FRIDAY. Manageable. Morning trends are unhelpful, but you will fare better later in the day. Associates, business partners, and clients may be contrary, making it difficult to retain a peaceful and harmonious environment. No matter what is happening on a personal level or in the domestic quarters, be the consummate professional in the working arena. You should have little difficulty coping with whatever situations arise. If you or your significant other has been experiencing problems with jealousy or freedom issues, mattes may come to a head. If you desire more personal space, ask for cooperation and understanding. If it is your mate or partner who requires more independence, be ready to give it without complaint.

28. SATURDAY. Slow. You may sense that what you are aiming for is not completely fulfilling in the way originally anticipated. However, this is not the day to make any major decisions. Lack of vitality and staying power reduces your enthusiasm and motivation. Use a liberal amount of laughter and humor to diminish the chance of tension and frustration spoiling your day off. If worries or problems persist, seek assistance or guidance from parents or someone who fills the parental role. A problem shared is usually a problem halved. Socializing might not provide expected rewards. You might have more fun staying home and inviting friends over to share your hospitality and company.

MARCH

1. SUNDAY. Rewarding. On this day of contrasts, having fun is as important as showing other people your serious and responsible side. Your sharp mind and wit combine with an enhanced ability to think before speaking, conveying a sense of being both practical and trustworthy. Avoid gossip and don't ask questions if you are not prepared to hear the unvarnished truth. If presenting hobby workshops or a creative seminar, you can inform and entertain your audience most successfully by injecting elements of humor. The appreciation you receive should boost your self-confidence. Worries relating to tax issues might need to be addressed, at least when it comes to better record keeping.

2. MONDAY. Industrious. Keep an eye on your personal and business finances. If there is a need to apply for a loan or search for better interest rates or a credit card deal, this morning is a favorable period to begin. Increasing the amount of your life insurance, especially if you have young children, or adding more home and contents coverage would be prudent. If seeking amusement, do something productive and utilize artistic skills. A dance class, learning to sculpt, or creating your own unique jewelry can be an innovative way to let off steam in a constructive manner. Steer a loved one away from any form of gambling if money is an issue; a loss is more likely than a win this evening.

3. TUESDAY. Helpful. Today's favorable trends urge broadening your horizons in areas of special interest. As a Libra, learning is important to you. Libra folk are eternal students, constantly seeking fresh experiences, understanding, and insight. Colleagues and customers should be in a good mood, making it easier to sell a product, project, or even your own virtues. This is a favorable day to make an appointment with a specialized physician or health practitioner. When you are on the job, don't ignore ideas that pop into mind. With a little more thought and effort, implementing inspired thoughts could produce financial gains. You may go on an actual trip or take a journey through reading.

4. WEDNESDAY. Interesting. Today you can expect to experience as many ups as downs. A change of scenery might do you a world of good if you begin to feel stuck in a rut. With the Moon in Gemini, research the possibility of enrolling in a course that ignites your interest. Or browse the Internet for interesting travel packages. These pursuits give you something for you to look forward to in the future. Playing basketball with a friend or getting together with a few colleagues for a team sporting event after work can be both relaxing and an investment in your health. Unwind tonight by immersing yourself in love, romance, and social activities.

5. THURSDAY. Confusing. Staying grounded and realistic will be difficult as imagination and inspiration come to the fore. Confusion abounds. If you have a number of options or possibilities, making a choice may be almost impossible. Postpone projects that require concentration and focus. Artistic Libras can expect to be very productive as creative juices flow freely. Relax in your spare time by indulging in fantasy, daydreaming, or listening to music that motivates and inspires you. With messenger Mercury merging with dreamy Neptune, this is not the time to reach any major decisions, confront complex situations, or enter into spirited debates.

6. FRIDAY. Balancing. Celestial trends send a few obstacles that must be overcome first thing this morning. The pressure of organizing children or driving your mate to work could cause extra strain or clash with your own agenda. Try not to hurry or become stressed, which will only slow progress even further. Venus, your lifetime ruler, will be retrograde from now until April 17 in Aries, your house of personal and professional partnerships. Take this opportunity to review past decisions regarding important relationships, and be prepared to implement changes if you feel that they will increase contentment. Social plans could disappoint you this evening.

7. SATURDAY. Tricky. Over the next few days there is increased potential for self-delusion or deception. Creativity and intuition are heightened, and this is a great time to display what you have made to the public. Before setting a price for your goods, ask a knowledgeable friend or associate for advice. Right now there is a tendency to allow domineering people to manipulate or intimidate you. Continue to put off important decision making. Your energy is apt to be depleted, so opt for a lazy weekend. Put off physical chores that require extra exertion, which could drain your vitality even further. If socializing, dress warmly if the weather is chilly or wet to avoid an infection, virus, or the flu.

8. SUNDAY. Conflicting. A wide array of planetary trends forms in today's skies, sending contradictory influences. Libras could float around aimlessly rather than jumping into action. Physical energy will probably remain at a low ebb. Staying in bed an extra hour can add to your vitality if you have been suffering from tiredness or exhaustion. Libras employed in a retail outlet should be alert not to accidentally overcharge a customer, give the wrong change, or order the wrong product. Talkative Mercury visits Pisces, your zone of general well-being and daily grind, encouraging you to take a deeper look into new diets, exercise programs, or a health issue.

9. MONDAY. Disconcerting. Unsettled feelings are likely, so try to remove yourself from any situation that could escalate into outright conflict. Around midmorning the Moon slips into Virgo and things seem difficult, or at least it might appear that way to you. If a feeling of being overwhelmed begins to develop due to a heavy workload, delegate tasks so work can be completed on time. Rules and regulations could cause frustration. However, they are there for a reason, so you just need to chill out and go with the flow. Otherwise your stress level is likely to soar. This evening a touch of romance will add some excitement and help you put aside your worries and relax.

10. TUESDAY. Sensitive. There seems to be more negative trends prevailing than positive ones, but this just means that you need to work a little harder to make progress. An ability to impress other people with your verbal skills will be a great help for those presenting a training seminar or delivering a lecture. Productivity is likely to flourish for Libras focused on writing a report or speech. Withdrawing inwardly and thinking about the spiritual or mystical aspects of life could be comforting tonight. The Full Moon in Virgo stirs up sensitivities and emotions, warning Libras to be gentle with the feelings of loved ones. Hidden thoughts or secrets could finally come out into the open, bringing an issue to a close.

11. WEDNESDAY. Excellent. This should be a pleasant day complete with a large dollop of love and luck. Your lifetime ruler Venus is smiling happily at the abundance that flows from jolly Jupiter. Libras who have been experiencing problems with willpower will need to call on all possible self-discipline to reduce the risk of going overboard with credit cards, fine food, or an inability to say no to loved ones. Dress to impress in the most sophisticated outfit in your wardrobe if attending a gala social affair tonight or in the near future; you will be noticed. A child's sports or academic achievement can give parents immense pleasure. Singles are in for a busy time as a potential suitor appears on the scene.

12. THURSDAY. Variable. Alter your daily schedule to avoid settling into a rut. Ignore routine methods and tackle work from a different angle. If working part-time or from home appeals, talk to the boss to see if something can be arranged so you can take advantage of a more flexible employment arrangement. There is strong potential for a disagreement because feelings are running close to the surface. You might discover that a business or professional partner is eager to face an issue head-on while you prefer to take a more conciliatory wait-and-see stance. Some exercise and a healthy meal will help you retain balanced emotions.

13. FRIDAY. Good. This day should improve as the hours pass. Worry about important customers and irritable coworkers this morning, not black cats and potential bad luck. Later in the morning participating in a creative project could give you pleasure. Inspirational ideas are likely to flow without much effort on your part. A physical task or pursuit gains momentum after work. Athletic Scales should be happy with success on the playing field; there is a good chance of being on the winning side. Committed couples can share happy rapport, and singles who mingle can expect an exciting evening.

14. SATURDAY. Challenging. If you had a late evening last night, a grumpy mood is bound to set off an argument with your mate or kids. If you can stay cool and calm, domestic accord should remain relatively harmonious. Don't allow financial worries to get you down. If you have taken appropriate action to resolve problems, continually obsessing will not solve the overall situation and may just increase stress. The warrior planet Mars visits Pisces, your house of health and working conditions, from now until April 22. Mars in Pisces conveys extra vitality and motivation for Libras who work long hours on the job.

15. SUNDAY. Smooth. Most of the day should fall effortlessly into place. Just avoid shopping this evening, when you could be shortchanged or purchase something that looks great in the store but is less than perfect once installed in your home. Take it relatively easy, visiting friends, going for a walk, or puttering around home base. You need to maintain a reserve of energy for the working week, when you could be inundated with extra duties and a pace that is likely to be quicker than usual. This evening is an ideal time to sort out financial paperwork, write checks, or pay monthly accounts via the Internet or snail mail.

16. MONDAY. Manageable. Look forward to a gradual improvement of lunar trends as the day progresses. Morning vibes warn Libras to be careful when talking with or about coworkers or clients. Conflict could quickly erupt over a seemingly minor point, or you might blurt out words that annoy your listeners. The ability to concentrate and pick up on the smallest of details will assist those involved in selling, writing, or communicating in any form with the public. This is an excellent time for an intimate discussion with your mate or steady date. Bring concerns out into the open. Forming mutual goals should proceed smoothly, with both parties prepared to cooperate and to compromise if required.

17. TUESDAY. Mixed. Communication is to the fore. If you become annoyed over a minor issue, there is a possibility of speaking first and thinking later instead of the other way around. Straight talking is fine as long as you walk the talk. This morning you need to put your money where your mouth is. Although plans are unlikely to fall easily into place, blaming other people will be futile. There is always a reason why things don't proceed smoothly. You may need to review details and find a better way to take action. An invitation could bring a wide smile, making you feel that life is indeed wonderful. However, a conservative atmosphere could put a damper on tonight's activities.

18. WEDNESDAY. Difficult. Today's definitely gloomy atmosphere stems from a large number of lunar influences. With trickster Mercury rubbing restrictive Saturn the wrong way, remaining positive may be difficult even for the optimistic Libra. A self-critical attitude could be on display, with nothing you do seeming to be good enough. Purchase a raffle chance or a lottery ticket and you may find that your luck is changing for the better. This isn't the day to initiate any important discussions, especially with an older person or someone in a position of authority. Notice warning signals from your body, and seek medical attention if a problem becomes severe or is ongoing.

19. THURSDAY. Energetic. You should be brimming with energy, motivation, and self-confidence. Ferreting out information should be easy in your detective mood. Carrying out research or conducting an investigation can be a breeze while energetic Mars happily combines with Pluto, planet of the underground. Love and romance might not fare too well, and it would be prudent to refuse to be drawn into any arguments. If you can just agree to disagree, you might escape discord or tension. Decluttering your home will give your spirits a definite lift. Removing books, magazines, or items that have outlived their usefulness can be freeing.

20. FRIDAY. Renewing. Home, family, and property matters are under review. Libras who have a house for sale could hear positive news, and those seeking a new tenant or roommate should have success with the interview process. The golden light of the Sun is now shining on assertive Aries, your opposite sign signifying the people in your life. The spring equinox is a period of celebration, the time to begin fresh activities and projects. Both intimate and professional partnerships will strongly benefit because relating to other people and building rapport should be easier. Although you may be happy in the company of that certain person, don't surrender your identity completely during the next four weeks while the Sun transits Aries.

21. SATURDAY. Bright. Creative juices are flowing, and the stars promise a delightful day ahead. Lady Luck is smiling your way, but don't wager your whole paycheck because good fortune is fleeting. An issue close to your heart may finally be resolved, or a problem with a child sorted out to everyone's satisfaction. Athletic prowess continues to improve for the dedicated sportsperson. You as well as others may be amazed at what you are able to achieve in a competition. Your social life continues to expand. The chance of meeting unusual, interesting people increases. Let your hair down tonight and relax. If a social function is not as exciting as expected, find a way to make your own fun.

22. SUNDAY. Restless. Today's planetary patterns encourage getting out as restless trends continue throughout the day. Unless you refuse to stick with the same old routine, irritability and frustration could result. Don't place extra demands on yourself; just go with the flow and do what feels natural and right. This is a favorable day to attend a class or present a lecture that can boost your career or your income potential. Aim to begin and finish one chore at a time, because concentration may be limited and energies scattered. Choose entertainment that provides movement and diversity to keep boredom at bay.

23. MONDAY. Demanding. Imagination and inspiration will surge forth as long as you relax and let the stars be your guide. With the Sun and intense Pluto forming a challenging influence, your equilibrium could be threatened when emotions come to the surface. Conflict, which peace-loving Libra folk try to avoid at any cost, might accost you at home. You may be surprised and also dismayed at the depth of your anger toward a partner or parent. Be prepared for household equipment to break down. If you are hosting a special function, have a backup plan ready. Complaints from an associate or an important client should be taken seriously, immediately implementing action to restore their good humor.

24. TUESDAY. Reassuring. Take your time on the job, particularly during the early morning. Steer clear of hazards. Walk instead of run in order to avoid any mishaps. Energy and confidence are up, assisting Libras to aim high and to successfully complete difficult or strenuous duties. If an ongoing health problem is not responding to standard medical treatment, this is an excellent period to look into various alternative therapies to bring needed relief. Shopping for groceries should be easy and quick, and you could pick up a few more bargains than usual in the food department. If in a committed relationship, special attention shown to your significant other can lead to loving rewards in return.

25. WEDNESDAY. Revealing. Unforeseen situations are likely to occur, especially on the job. Sticking to an agenda or schedule could be more effort than it's worth. Abandon your plans and allow the day to run itself. If you have been cooped up for too long at home or in the office, get out and enjoy fresh air and open spaces. From now until April 9 communicative Mercury zips through Aries, your solar sector of all one-to-one relationships, including both your business and marital partnerships. So be prepared for many discussions with partners and associates. Skip routine chores and enjoy a favorite recreation tonight.

26. THURSDAY. Eventful. Don't expect a peaceful morning unless sleeping late is part of your usual daily routine. Make sure to put your best foot forward on the job. A superior is apt to be watching your every move, ready to jump on any little or big transgression. As a Libra, striving for harmony in all relationships is important. However, sometimes an outburst erupts that requires fixing. During the next two weeks you can begin new projects and obtain a clearer picture of a current partnership. An Aries New Moon can help you start fresh and restore balance if a personal or professional relationship has become a little rocky.

27. FRIDAY. Varied. Romance and leisure pursuits are under positive trends, but the same cannot be said for a number of other areas in your life. You could be at odds when it comes to the bigger picture, becoming enmeshed in unimportant details. Competitive urges may be more obvious than usual. It is not like you to rock the boat, but this could change today. Holding your tongue may be more difficult than usual, especially with a family member or a close associate. Try to avoid cutting or sarcastic remarks; you might say something that you later regret. Loving vibes abound, and singles could attract someone that stirs mutual interest.

28. SATURDAY. Agreeable. Life offers a playful touch. Love is in the air, although it might be more about passion and lust than romance. A desired opportunity or option could come to fruition. Taking action with joint money or resources is the way to make things happen. If you are secretly considering some type of new investment, this is an excellent time to investigate it further. Mixing business with pleasure can be fortuitous. Socializing with a potential business partner, agent, or major client can help further career or commercial plans. An enchanting date could have singles shouting from the rooftops. Effort applied to organize a social occasion should pay dividends.

29. SUNDAY. Diverse. Mixed fortunes are in force. Happiness and fun will not come quickly or easily and will need to be actively pursued. You might be your own worst enemy in this regard, feeling that for every step forward you are taking two steps backward. Sorting out complicated family business should be done midmorning. This is also the best time of the day to organize financial paperwork and pay bills. Wheeling and dealing could return a small profit, which may be enough to generate feelings that the effort was worthwhile. Prearranged social plans could be canceled or postponed, leaving you with free time for personal pursuits.

30. MONDAY. Deceptive. Beware today's general air of deception and dishonesty. Charlatans and con artists are on the prowl, looking for easygoing Libras to swindle, so take extra care. Don't become involved in a deal that is suspect, and keep an eye on personal possessions and cash. There may be no stopping you if you have made up your mind about entering into a new business partnership or franchise deal. Just make sure that all the legalities have been covered and that you have thoroughly investigated all angles. Issues concerning your love life are happily few and far between. Couples should share bliss and contentment, while singles could meet a romantic match.

31. TUESDAY. Distracting. This high-pressured morning brings changes and delays, causing frustration and stress. However, by the time the working day ends, happier lunar influences will provide support for whatever activities you have planned for tonight. If you have done the studying, you shouldn't experience any difficulties taking an exam or writing a research paper. Exciting plans for a long-distance trip could find you pleasantly occupied arranging the final details of your accommodations and itinerary. Discussions with that special person in your life can bring better understanding of where your relationship is currently heading and where you want it to go.

APRIL

1. WEDNESDAY. Uneasy. Throughout this week you need to look after your physical and emotional well-being. If your energy slumps you may succumb to a virus, cough, or cold, even though the weather is warming up. Decisions might not go your way, and a female may be intent on making life difficult for you. Your mate or partner could be very sensitive over the next few days, inclined to start an argument at the slightest provocation. Either turn on your Libra charm or turn the other cheek to help deflect disharmony. Most people like to flirt, and especially Libras. However, right now you need to take care as there is a possibility of becoming involved in a clandestine or obsessive love affair.

2. THURSDAY. Fair. Life could be a little dull and slow. Libras in a committed relationship are unlikely to have a rosy time when it comes to love and affection. On the job, the unstable emotions of a coworker may shatter your nerves and leave you on edge, not knowing what to expect next. Throughout the next few days keep your feet firmly planted on the ground when it comes to romance. Otherwise you could be drawn into an intense but ultimately unhappy relationship as your ruler Venus disputes with passionate

Pluto. A secret admirer may be revealed, which can boost the confidence of both single and attached Libras.

3. FRIDAY. Passionate. Steer clear of situations that threaten your personal emotional stability. Avoid a romantic entanglement that is not straightforward, unless living on the edge incites a sense of adventure. Secret financial deals or issues that have elements of intrigue should be deferred right now. Your patience could be stretched to the limit, and you might be exhausted from trying to carry a heavy workload over the past week. A spur-of-the-moment fling or one-night stand is possible as physical desire and passion reach a crescendo. Spending time with friends at home might appeal if you prefer a quiet night.

4. SATURDAY. Mixed. Intensity continues to permeate your romantic life. Spending leisure time with friends over the weekend should give you desired companionship as well as stimulation. Energy and motivation to complete routine chores or physical tasks might be in limited supply over the next few days. Active Mars is currently being constrained by serious Saturn, reducing enthusiasm and drive except for the good things of life. A luxury outing or purchase that is well deserved and overdue could be a wonderful extravagance, making you feel good. For single Libras, the idea of turning a friendship into a love affair could be irresistible.

5. SUNDAY. Wearisome. Prepare for a trying day in which you are likely to come up against obstacles and blocked progress. Carry on with a gentle approach and engage in some self-nurturing. As a Libra you will need a large dose of soothing relaxation and tranquillity over the next few days. Staying in bed a little longer than usual this morning could provide an energy boost. You might need to seek out a friend or professional adviser to obtain support or crisis management if a situation threatens to become overwhelming. Psych yourself up throughout the day so you are prepared to deal with a difficult task that you have been avoiding.

6. MONDAY. Interesting. Let go of unhelpful anxieties this morning. Turn to distractions, variety, and diverse activities throughout the day to help reduce restless tendencies. Issues or people from the past could come out of the woodwork, but don't worry. Finding the right words and actions to handle tricky situations should be easy. Whether a personal or a business partnership issue is causing concern, meeting the other person halfway and making concessions can produce a positive solution without anyone feeling that they lost the argument. An early night is definitely called for if you can swing it.

7. TUESDAY. Sensitive. Drifting into a world of your own might be your preference. Sensitive influences are in force as tricky Mercury meets up with idealistic Neptune. Remaining practical and grounded in order to keep the boss or teacher happy is essential. Not keeping your mind on the job at hand could cause problems later on. Imagination and creative vibes should be strong. However, robust labor or a complex discussion will seem like too much work for you. Contradictory messages could activate feelings of anger. You might wonder at the ungrateful attitude of a friend.

8. WEDNESDAY. Problematic. Difficulties are likely to land at your doorstep. Even though the Moon is in your sign of Libra, this isn't the day to begin anything new or to implement plans. Better results are likely if you wait to act until tomorrow. Taking your time will help everything fall more easily into place. Remaining cool and going about your normal business can keep problems to a minimum. A bargain that is irresistible could require a little juggling of finances before calling it yours. Socially, be versatile and make your own fun this evening or you are likely to be disappointed.

9. THURSDAY. Emotional. A bevy of cosmic action lights up the sky. Don't hesitate to demonstrate loving feelings as the Full Moon in your own sign shines brightly. Practical common sense will help you in discussions about the future and when making plans or formulating a list of current aspirations. Talkative Mercury visits Taurus and your solar house of shared resources and partnership assets. From now until April 30 projects requiring dedicated research skills are favored and your powers of persuasion will be enhanced. This is an excellent period to consult a professional financial adviser, banker, or tax attorney.

10. FRIDAY. Fortunate. Not only is there a celestial emphasis on luck and finances, but Libras should exude charisma and charm. However, big ideas could find you getting out of your depth with excessive spending and grandiose plans unless caution is the watchword. Keep some money in the bank in case unexpected expenses shoot holes in the household budget. Purchase a lottery ticket or a raffle chance; a win could boost your bank balance. Relaxing amusement might be the preferred option this evening. If interested in meditation, practicing this medium will become easier now. Affection from someone you love could speak volumes, and you will be inclined to return the action.

11. SATURDAY. Volatile. If you are going out early this morning, dress to impress. You could be feeling a little down as you prepare to greet the day, and looking your best can help raise your confidence and boost self-esteem. There may be no limits when it comes to using your mind. An employment plan you are currently involved in could require rethinking and extra research to come up with a more promising option, but may open up a whole new area to develop and explore. Curb an inclination to cling to a point of view or opinion. Don't be insistent in discussions with other people. Leave credit cards at home if heading out to shop or socialize; the impulse to buy now and worry later is strong.

12. SUNDAY. Expressive. Mental stimulation remains strong, although concentration and focus might be difficult through the morning hours. As a peace-loving Libra, bossiness is not one of your innate characteristics. Today, however, could be an odd period, with many Scales being overly opinionated. This could result in seeking out only those who will listen and agree rather than using your powerful verbal ability in a more positive manner. Being able to impart worthwhile advice through words or writing will help if you are addressing the public, sending a letter to the editor, or leading a seminar or workshop. A leisurely trip to a nearby scenic destination could be a relaxing excursion.

13. MONDAY. Tricky. Over the next few days go with the flow. Entering into battle will just increase stress. During this period planet Mercury is likely to cause a few issues when it comes to communication, so wait it out. The universe will send calmer influences later in the week. The best way to avoid upsets is to think before voicing concerns or complaints. Also guard against stinging comments or sarcastic remarks. It might be wise to steer clear of family members with whom you don't always see eye-to-eye. This should lessen the chance of irritations and annoyances getting the better of you. If tonight is not usually scheduled for social activities, do something different by taking your mate or steady date out for dinner.

14. TUESDAY. Disconcerting. Avoid obsessing over minor issues because more important situations will arise that need attention. Unexpected financial problems could develop on the job or in the domestic arena. Put on your thinking cap if your boss decides that costs have to be reduced. You could come up with novel methods to achieve this aim, which could earn you a bonus. Travel or traffic could be subject to delays, and you need to steer clear of any potential altercation on the road. Misunderstandings with associates or a partner can be cleared up midafternoon, and customer complaints can also be successfully resolved then.

15. WEDNESDAY. Balanced. Steady as she goes is the best advice to heed so that the day proceeds without too many hassles. A domestic issue is likely to test your patience and resolve. However, if irritation is quelled, you can deal with it successfully. Shoppers should double-check prices charged for purchases and carefully examine merchandise to avoid future disagreements if you discover a problem once you leave the store. Someone in your immediate environment may be fired up and argumentative. Be the mediator on the job, not the one who causes disputes. Comments made in the heat of the moment toward coworkers or employees can lead to loss of productivity and greater tension.

16. THURSDAY. Calm. Emotions should begin to cool down a little, with tension disappearing and amicable vibes returning. The most probable cause of arguments today relates to business or personal finances. Although there may be opportunities to forge ahead with a career plan, this isn't the best time to talk to a superior about a pay increase or ask for any favors that involve company cash. Put your foot down gently with a demanding partner, child, or sibling. Explain that you cannot always be at their beck and call. If it is a request for money, make it clear that you are not a personal banker.

17. FRIDAY. Eventful. The day begins with a busy time in the celestial heavens. With mainly positive trends prevailing, moving forward and completing your regular work should proceed relatively smoothly. The highlight of the day is your lifetime ruler Venus getting ready to move forward. This can be especially profitable if you do business with the general public or are waiting for the outcome of a legal matter. Give yourself a treat and enjoy favored indulgences, without infringing too much on a healthy diet or lifestyle. An attempt to collect a personal or professional debt should succeed expectations.

18. SATURDAY. Moderate. There isn't a lot of activity in the cosmos, but mainly minor irritations and pesky obstacles will hinder progress. Children's activities could be a feature for Libra parents, and running youngsters to ballet, baseball, or to visit friends could occupy a lot of time. The reaction of a child may be unexpected this morning. You might need extra patience before learning the reason for unusually bad behavior. If you have time on your hands, you should have ample energy to engage in favored leisure or creative pursuits. Don't expect an exhilarating evening if attending a social occasion from a sense of duty rather than for pleasure.

19. SUNDAY. Constructive. Diverse planetary influences exist, but this doesn't necessarily mean that the day will be dull, boring, or problematic. Celebrating a child's special achievement or important milestone can bring joy for Libra parents. It may be difficult to think a certain situation through to a logical conclusion, causing confusion in serious communication. Be discerning with your manner of speech involving family property, shared assets, and financial resources. The next four weeks, while the Sun visits Taurus, your zone of marital income and expenditure, will be an excellent period to turn over a new leaf with fiscal management.

20. MONDAY. Varied. Mixed conditions exist. Activities that need an extra boost of passion should be worthwhile. Implement better time management procedures, streamlining efficiency in order to successfully cull the amount of work piling up in your in-basket. Pace all activities. Your energy and self-discipline will more than likely be limited. Refuse to allow irritable employees or working conditions to negatively affect your emotions. Otherwise this can affect both job performance and health. Focus on facts and avoid wishful thinking. Stating your case clearly and succinctly can help you obtain more positive results regarding a family issue or decision.

21. TUESDAY. Intense. Over the next few days passion and desire rule. You might not be inclined to deal with the reality of life or with any unpleasant situations. Your ruler, feminine Venus, merges with masculine Mars, bringing excitement, zeal, and fervor to the mix. If you are drawn to someone on the job, someone who makes your heart beat faster, progress can now be made in this area. Entertaining or cultivating clients, as well as mixing business with pleasure, can expand your networking circle and increase your profit margin or take-home pay. This is an excellent day to search for the ideal pet that suits your current lifestyle.

22. WEDNESDAY. Active. A plethora of lunar influences should keep you on your toes. A social gathering or a function where attendance practically commanded through duty or professional reasons may not be thrilling but should at least be interesting. Increased focus centers on business and intimate relationships, and steady progress can be made. The Libra entrepreneur should be more alert because there will be chances to sign a major client or take on a new partner, which could provide promising future financial gains. Warrior Mars marches into the sign of pioneering Aries, energizing your relationships with other people. Mars in Aries impacts your house of marriage and partnerships until May 31.

23. THURSDAY. Compelling. A surge of personal power and confidence makes this a great day for Libras. You can jump right in and do whatever needs to be done. Your ability to lead and guide other people is enhanced. Prepare to be asked a number of tricky questions that no one else has been able to answer satisfactorily. Perception is heightened, making it very hard for anyone to trip you up or pull the wool over your eyes. Rededicate yourself to cherished goals and personal ambitions. Throughout the next week schedule time to play a sport, use your gym membership every day, and engage in other enjoyable physical pursuits.

24. FRIDAY. Insightful. Intuition and intellectual abilities are heightened as Mercury meets up with Uranus. The negative aspect is that you might not be very grounded or focused. Unconventional tasks or unusual activities hold the most appeal as your curiosity about the world around you increases. Your ruler Venus reenters Aries, your relationship house, conveying a romantic overtone when it comes to relating to your intimate partner. And tonight's New Moon culminates in the sign of determined Taurus, representing your house of finances and assets shared with other people. The next two weeks is an excellent period to apply for a mortgage, focus on fiscal security, or pay off a long-standing loan.

25. SATURDAY. Confusing. A dreamy, deceptive, very impractical atmosphere prevails. In order to be successful, stick to imaginative and creative pursuits. Clarity of thoughts may be missing, replaced by muddled ideas and confusing concepts. Confirm all facts and figures. Also guard against a tendency toward misunderstandings. Reading between the lines could mean you don't really understand the message that someone hopes to impart. This is a day when you could be taken for a ride unless you remain attentive. Someone close may be a little sneaky or prone to telling falsehoods. It might be tempting to overspend, so exercise self-restraint when it comes to your cash flow.

26. SUNDAY. Vigilant. With a major planetary aspect forming in today's sky, take extra care now and over the ensuing days. Aggressive Mars is in dispute with powerful Pluto, leading to an overflow of energy. It is essential to use this in a productive manner, which will lessen the chance of an accident or mishap. Moving from place to place is great as long as you are aware of where you are going and are careful of your personal well-being. Steer clear of danger areas. Remove dangerous hazards around the house. Conflict with a partner or associate could develop, particularly if praise and appreciation are not being conveyed for your work and extra effort.

27. MONDAY. Focused. Today's lack of lunar influences allows time to concentrate on study, research, or reading in order to gain more knowledge and understanding. Focus on philosophical beliefs, religious topics, or profound mental topics that will expand your wisdom and insight. If you have had trouble recently with a business partner, expect another round of heated arguments with no punches pulled. Be vigilant when it comes to locking up your home; check that doors and windows are tightly secured. Postpone business matters with legal implications. This is an unfavorable period for involvement with law enforcement or the courts.

28. TUESDAY. Intriguing. Gaining knowledge is important as a positive way to further develop your identity. Researching various philosophies or new hobbies could appeal, and you may discover what later becomes a passion. Rather than rushing out and purchasing a bundle of expensive books or CDs on a topic that sparks your interest, borrow from your local library in case interest wanes. Avoid chores in which you are required to perform a number of different tasks at the same time; concentration lapses are likely. Locate a new restaurant that serves exotic cuisine, then go out to enjoy something different from your usual fare.

29. WEDNESDAY. Bright. The Moon is now moving through Cancer, your professional and career zone. Over the next two days show other people how capable and resourceful you can be. Reach high and challenge yourself to go the extra mile. If you take this approach with all that you are doing, a positive outcome is assured. You are likely to be in the right place at the right time, so take advantage of the good timing. Conversely, there is the potential to become tangled up in red tape if you don't abide by the rules. A congenial atmosphere should prevail at home this evening, so relax and take comfort in your own snug surroundings.

30. THURSDAY. Challenging. Dissatisfaction with employment conditions or your current pay could be the encouragement you need to begin hunting for a job that is more fulfilling. Begin the process of applying for employment, but don't take any definite action. Also refrain from confiding your plans to other people. Once the search begins, you may realize that your current position is not too bad after all. Information gatherer Mercury slips into Gemini, one of the signs this planet rules. This can be the boost that Libra students, writers, and teachers need to complete an important report, thesis, or manuscript. This is also the time to edit work, contact a publisher, or look for a literary agent.

MAY

1. FRIDAY. Disconcerting. You could use some type of adventure today to add a dash of excitement into what otherwise may be a dull day. Be wary of charging ahead with challenging tasks that require strict focusing on details, particularly on the job. Delays in promised cash flow could trigger frustration if you are relying on receiving those funds. Joining a hobby group whose members share a common bond with you can inject new interest into your world. Visiting interesting Internet sites could raise your current level of awareness. This is a good time for younger Libras to take an exam or to apply for a driver's license. Lack of confidence is all that might hold you back.

2. SATURDAY. Fervent. Embrace your own talents and identity, rather than staying in the shadows of your mate or partner. Your lifetime ruler, sensuous Venus, disagrees with passionate Pluto over the next few days, so take extra care when it comes to matters of the heart. Manipulation, jealousy, and possessiveness are possible negative manifestations of this influence for those in a committed union. Singles might become involved in risqué behavior, a one-night stand, or an intense love triangle. Don't allow an annoying financial situation to get you all worked up; remain cool and calm, and resolving the problem should be easier. A challenging social situation could tax you emotionally, but valuable alliances may be forged.

3. SUNDAY. Lethargic. Emotions could overwhelm you as tiredness or lack of motivation takes hold. Let go of control and allow good things to manifest themselves in their own time. Current conditions favor resting and recharging spent batteries. Romantic vibes are still intense, but they can be used to your advantage if you go all out to make love, not war. Although getting out and about could be costly, this could be the perfect opportunity to do what you have always promised yourself or to purchase a long-desired item. Rendezvousing with an acquaintance might not seem important right now but could turn out to be beneficial in the future, so be sure to exchange contact details.

4. MONDAY. Demanding. The tempo may be a little quicker than you prefer. Your idea of heaven might be to curl up on the couch and do as little as possible. Unfortunately this may not be possible if you need to face the day and work for a living. Pace your activities, and try to limit labor-intensive tasks or you could quickly run out of steam. A little friction is occurring between aggressive Mars and over-the-top Jupiter, so stay within set boundaries and don't go overboard or become overly opinionated. This is an excellent period to confirm facts and figures, then stand back and survey the situation before taking action. An early or lazy evening would be the wisest choice.

5. TUESDAY. Starred. Fortunately you should have ample energy to face this busy day. Just be careful not to push yourself too hard. Doing so could result in irritation if other people cannot keep up. Or you could suffer a strained muscle if you are a sporty type or a minor mishap around the house. Libra charisma and magnetism are boosted. This is a starred time to decide on a course of action and immediately put it into action. Associates and family members should be more than willing to help you achieve desired aims. If you are unsure about a relationship issue, a decision made this morning has a better chance of being successful than delaying until later in the day. Morning is also the best time to finalize travel or educational arrangements.

6. WEDNESDAY. Productive. If you have anything important to sign, do so today before Mercury moves into retrograde motion tomorrow. Back up computer data and check to be certain virus software is up to date. Choose your words and timing carefully if attempting to diffuse a tricky situation. Follow up on an offer that should solidify your financial position. This is not the day to worry and stress. Instead, let life flow, and the universe will take care of the rest. A mini makeover might be in order if creating an entirely new look is on your wish list. A luxurious body massage or a long soak in the hot tub could also soothe, calm, and wash away the worries of the daily grind.

7. THURSDAY. Enticing. Although willpower is usually in ample supply when the Moon is in your own sign of Libra, this characteristic might be missing today. Unless you take a more assertive approach, you are apt to go along with the wishes of other people even if not in your own best interests. Informative Mercury begins retreating through Gemini, your solar zone of adventure and education. This poses more chances of travel delays, stalled legal action, and issues surrounding academic studies. While Mercury is retrograde for the next three weeks, don't sign anything important unless verified by a legal adviser. But this is an excellent period to reexamine and reassess a project already started.

8. FRIDAY. Chancy. A challenging influence between the Sun and Pluto might require an ego adjustment. If you can resist the temptation to insist on having everything your own way, there shouldn't be much to worry about. However, if this is ignored, be prepared for conflict to arise, especially around the domestic quarters. Avoid using credit cards even though the inclination to wave the plastic around this afternoon will be strong. If you stop and consider when the payments will come due, you might realize that this is the time to be cautious with your money rather than carefree. Be prepared for an arguments about money if socializing later this evening; better to escape to bed early and miss possible negative issues.

9. SATURDAY. Fine. The bank balance or cash flow of Libra folks could be on the lean side, but everything else in your life should be good. Replacing household items that have seen better days could put more pressure on the budget. However, if certain items are dangerous, if will be better to discard and replace them rather than risk personal safety. A gift for a special person could set you back considerably unless you spend extra time searching out an item a little different from the usual run-of-the-mill. Socially, an important occasion should provide enjoyment and an emotional lift as well, allowing you to network with those who could prove helpful in the future.

10. SUNDAY. Good. The lunar goddess is not very busy in the sky, so you can expect a day when problems should be few and pleasure plentiful. Tackling challenging chores won't faze the industrious Libra. A home project that requires a creative touch should be as enjoyable as it is constructive. Locating the perfect mode of transportation, whether this is a car, motorcycle, skateboard, or bicycle, can be easy. You know what you want and how much you are prepared to pay. Being with friends can appeal. A desire to speak your mind is enhanced. Conversing or debating can be a pleasant way to spend the day. Other people are apt to see you as wise and well-informed.

11. MONDAY. Distracting. You are apt to have quite a few things on your mind. As a Libra you are not known to make quick decisions; sitting on the fence is more your style. Today you probably won't know what to do, so taking your time is the correct action. If on the job do not underestimate a commitment because minor details could make it more time-consuming than you first thought. In order to do your best, take one step at a time. On the domestic front be careful that tempers don't become frayed. Depleted energy will lower your tolerance and patience significantly below your normal level. Think twice before asking someone for advice because they could offer discouraging guidance rather than positive help.

12. TUESDAY. Positive. A quick mind can be a hindrance or a help, depending on how you use it. Exploit your own quick wit positively and refrain from sarcasm. Laying the foundation for a plan or venture that has the potential to pay dividends in the future should proceed smoothly. If you have been feeling pressured, this could continue today. The ideal is to obtain balance, but sometimes the status quo needs to be upset in order to build a more stable and steady future. Family infighting is never the preference of peace-seeking Libras; however it might need to be confronted. The line between work and play may be skewed, requiring that you inject more fun and enjoyment into daily work.

13. WEDNESDAY. Constructive. Discard worry today. Think about where you're going and the best way to get there. You can do the planning and strategizing without rushing ahead too fast. A practical mood can be utilized to get much of your to-do list checked off and finalized. Get routine chores out of the way early. If you have ideas on how to brighten your home environment, put these into place now. The urge to spend more time with your loved ones could drive you to reconsider a current position. But if this involves your personal partner, it would be wise to avoid a discussion this evening because you are unlikely to agree.

14. THURSDAY. Diverse. Today's forecast involves family members and those with whom you are in partnership. You might be inclined to take it easy, but you will still have to deal with daily pressures, chores, and the reality of life. Making loved ones feel special will act as a gentle reminder of current priorities. Being in love can be a great experience, especially for the naturally romantic Libra. Right now, however, you may have some doubts regarding the affections of your lover. Put these aside and just enjoy what you have. Avoid making a mountain out of a molehill. Take a moderate approach if socializing tonight, avoiding too much contact with anyone or anything.

15. FRIDAY. Easygoing. The Moon sailing through Aquarius can be a time when restlessness takes ahold of Libras. If you are feeling trapped by responsibilities and pressure, consider taking some time out to play. Concentrate on enjoying yourself, even if that is just window-shopping, strolling through the park, or going for a leisurely drive. Do something different to add variety to your routine. Also release the reins a little and allow life to unfold in its own good time. Beware putting anyone on a pedestal. You may be naive or gullible, refusing to believe that someone could be two-faced or deceitful. For peace of mind, clarify gossip or hearsay so you know where you stand.

16. SATURDAY. Surprising. This is a day of mixed influences. As long as common sense is to the fore, the Aquarius Moon favors letting your hair down and being both creative and experimental. The Sun is challenging Jupiter, increasing the chance of egos becoming overblown. The Sun is also friendly toward Uranus, conveying the possibility of pleasant surprises and opportunities. Your charming nature can help deflect any trouble spots you encounter providing you avoid an overly opinionated approach. Lean toward an outlandish or unique approach rather than old and stale ways and everything should progress better. Luck is smiling on you. Social activities should be surprisingly enjoyable.

17. SUNDAY. Varied. Today's misleading stars warn Libras to double-check everything at least twice. Recent confusion or changes could find you still trying to adapt, but if things are not working out don't force the issue. Bide your time and improvements should occur. You may initiate your own mini rebellion but this shouldn't affect anyone else. Serious Saturn has now turned to forward motion in Virgo, which can help you get on with many of the jobs you have put on hold. Delays with a health issue could disappear. If you have been waiting for a vacancy to open up for yourself or for a relative, news should be received soon.

18. MONDAY. Supportive. Act on important tasks this morning, when celestial vibes are most supportive. Beginning a new financial project or entering into a business partnership can be a positive move for the savvy Libra eager to get ahead. Proceed steadily without being too expansive. If your focus is maintained, your labors will bear fruit in the future. Good news for your mate or partner could come in the form of an inheritance, large bonus, or a significant salary increase. By midafternoon the day could begin to go downhill. Stomach or nervous problems may hinder your progress. Coworkers might be irritable or emotional, and communications with them are problematic. A soothing massage could work wonders tonight.

19. TUESDAY. Variable. Minor luck prevails as long as you are positive and alert for opportunities. As the day goes on, a gloomy atmosphere could develop. You will need to remain upbeat to fight off negative feelings. If a romantic relationship has lost its zing, you can do one of two things. You can take action to add some magic back and revitalize your feelings, or you can let things be. However, don't expect your relationship to improve without effort on your part. Any action taken regarding employment or working conditions should produce a good outcome. This is an excellent time to try doing something new on the job. Libras seeking employment or a better-paying job can take steps to make this happen.

20. WEDNESDAY. Important. On this day of shifting energies you need to be careful and not let your guard down. A sense of guilt if you have fun pervades the air. You may be inclined to hide or suppress feelings for your loved ones. Refrain from displaying a cold emotional front. This is not your usual style, and the current planetary influences encouraging this type of behavior will soon pass. The golden Sun now beams in the sign of Gemini, accentuating your house of foreign vistas and educational pursuits until June 21. The urge to explore, whether through travel or gaining more knowledge, becomes stronger. Seeking adventure can help calm restless feelings.

21. THURSDAY. Misleading. Be wary of the impulse to speak your mind. Even though you want everything to be out in the open, deceptive influences surround you and things might not be as they seem. A vigilant approach is required with money matters. This is not a favorable period to act on a hunch when it comes to any type of investment. Keep your money in the bank is the best advice to follow now. Loads of interesting ideas and plans could form in your mind, and the challenge will be to remain logical. Your ability to see the larger picture is enhanced, but you are likely to overlook minor but important details. Libra couples can share happy rapport. Socializing should be fun.

22. FRIDAY. Agitating. Issues involving a lover, child, or money can increase your angst throughout the day. Reconfirm travel arrangements and costs; there may be a discrepancy between your expectations and what you have paid for. Verify a child's whereabouts if they are old enough to go off alone but not old enough to keep specific details of their activities secret. Property owners could receive good news concerning the sale of a house. Libras seeking to become a home owner might find just the right place at an affordable price. This is also a good time to advertise for a new tenant or to interview a potential roommate to help you cover current costs.

23. SATURDAY. Challenging. If you have ongoing disagreements with a father figure, in-law, or someone in authority, this isn't the day to try to ease tensions or to reconcile. In fact, it would be wise to put off a visit if problems still exist because there is strong potential for conflict. Important apparatus or everyday household products may break down, so have an alternative available if you are relying on certain equipment for a social event. With computers also at risk, all data and photos should be backed up in case of a crash. A revision of tactics might be required before you are able to achieve a desired breakthrough.

24. SUNDAY. Helpful. Because it is Sunday, float along rather than push yourself or other people for results. Choose companions that don't jar your sensibilities but are exciting and stimulating to be with. This is a good time to get together with travel-minded friends and plan your next vacation. With a New Moon lighting up your Gemini zone of long-distance travel, organizing a major journey, enrolling in a school or university, or sending a manuscript off to a publisher should produce desired results. Legal matters implemented within the next two weeks should culminate in the results you envision. You could be lucky at the racetrack or saddled up at a horse show.

25. MONDAY. Excellent. You should feel uplifted and on top of your game. There is bountiful energy for a new project or venture that has the potential to produce financial gains. This opportunity is likely to give you a large adrenaline rush and added self-confidence. Libras on vacation or enjoying time off can expect to share a happy and lively day with that special person, putting a big smile on your face. Singles looking for love could find it while traveling, at school, attending a church event, or in connection with the law. Someone from another country or culture could also tug on your heart-strings.

26. TUESDAY. Spirited. Put your versatility on display as assertive Mars happily hooks up with Jupiter, Uranus, and Neptune. Confidence surges forward. Career-minded Libras can take full advantage by positively harnessing current planetary influences. If you keep your feet firmly planted on terra firma, dreams could come true. An unexpected romantic proposal could bring a thrill of exhilaration. Moving into a committed union can be the first step toward a lifetime of happiness and shared experiences with your significant other. Even with today's positive flow, it is essential to guard against overoptimism and the inclination to take on too many commitments.

27. WEDNESDAY. Insightful. Conditions urge you to look within so you can learn more about yourself. Luck continues to smile on Scales, and doors that you didn't even know existed could magically open up. Career and professional matters will benefit strongly. Libras with creative expertise can realize the true potential of these talents. As your intuitive side emerges, activities such as reading poetry, drawing, researching spiritual writings, or listening to a motivational speaker can be the inspiration to seek even higher aims. If you are looking for a new love, current elevated self-confidence can help target the right person who is waiting for you.

28. THURSDAY. Active. An urge to clear up, declutter, and beautify your current surroundings could be overwhelming. Utilize this energy to your best advantage by launching some spring cleaning. Hidden talents could be uncovered if you go outside your comfort zone and get involved in experimental activities. Idealistic Neptune is retreating through Aquarius, your romance zone, until November 4. During this period you need to keep in mind the saying about love being blind; there might be an element of truth in that statement. Make sure you are aware of what is happening right in your own backyard, and this includes actions of children as well as your mate, partner, or steady date.

29. FRIDAY. Renewing. This is a good day to redo a project or complete one that was started some time ago. A long-awaited phone call or get-together can revitalize a relationship. However, if you expect everything to be as it once was you may be disappointed with the outcome. As a Libra making decisions can be excruciatingly difficult, often leading to lengthy procrastination rather than justing making a choice. Evaluate and consider options during the early part of the day; you should be happy with the decisions you make and the results you achieve. A friendship may be under scrutiny, but wait a few days before reaching a conclusion about whether to continue or to sever ties.

30. SATURDAY. Flexible. A go-with-the-flow attitude is the positive way to make the best of current influences. Rest and relaxation are vital. If you have a hectic social evening planned, put off strenuous tasks for another day. An afternoon nap, preferably with your mate or partner, could provide the extra oomph needed to paint the town red later on. If you are a happily attached Libra, you and your significant other can create magical moments and make lasting memories from today's vibes. Chatterbox Mercury turns around and begins moving in a forward march, releasing any delay with a property settlement, payment of an insurance claim, or matters involving a legacy.

31. SUNDAY. Steady. Conditions still favor slowing down and taking life as it comes, especially for those who socialized long and hard last night. If you don't have to do anything special today, it could be worthwhile doing nothing at all, or at least performing only insignificant tasks. Confidence may be down a little as the day begins, so make an effort not to get drawn into self-doubting which can be a depressing energy. As mighty Mars zooms into Taurus, your solar zone of health, the pressure and the pace of life are likely to slow down considerably. From now until July 11 your energy level should be stable and can be dedicated to transforming matters dealing with joint finances and resources.

JUNE

1. MONDAY. Happy. The new month starts for Libra folk with a positive, happy atmosphere prevailing. Over the next week love and romance may occupy your free time, moving your thoughts to a higher plane. Yearning for the ideal partner might have singles in a spin. Libras in a permanent union could experience a new lease on life in the relationship. This is an excellent period to tie the knot, move in together, or celebrate a long-term commitment. Listen to your instincts, but go easy when it comes to spending since going over the top is a distinct possibility. Lady Luck is smiling, and a financial windfall could come your way.

2. TUESDAY. Promising. Dreamy romance continues to pervade the air as your lifetime ruler Venus pleasantly links to unique Uranus, idealistic Neptune, and excessive Jupiter. As a Libra you are one of the best-looking signs. This combined with your abundant charm gives you the ability to make an impressive impact on other people. Dress in your best and set about enticing someone who takes your fancy or can help you get ahead. Good news should arrive soon. New romance is promised for the unattached single. You could experience some good fortune at the racetrack, on the stock exchange, or with a game of chance. Just be sensible, however, and keep your wagers small.

3. WEDNESDAY. Favorable. Good news continues for Libras as active Mars entwines with Pluto, increasing your energy, drive, and motivation over the ensuing week. The hectic pace of the day is unlikely to let up until early evening, so focus on your to-do lists and get cracking; accomplishments should be plentiful. An initiative taken regarding family property or an investment could pay off, with the possibility of also significantly increasing your bank account. With the Sun still in the travel sector, the desire for physical or mental adventure continues, encouraging research of distant vacation destinations or of exciting exploits closer to home.

4. THURSDAY. Pressured. Up-and-down emotional influences are in force. Take your time making decisions, especially when it comes to matters regarding your financial status. This is not the best day to finalize or pay for vacation travel or accommodations; you could find out later that guarantees have changed or adjustments have been made to the originally quoted price. Self-employed Scales may find it hard trying to collect an outstanding debt, so it might be wise to postpone this task until Saturday at the earliest. A surplus of energy assists most projects or tasks on your schedule. A work challenge could be something you relish even if you have never performed a similar job before.

5. FRIDAY. Frustrating. You are apt to feel restrained and limited. Your energy could be depleted and enthusiasm in short supply. Being ready and willing is your key to success. Patience and preparation will also be essential in order for progress to be made. You might be inclined to jump from one thing to another without making any headway. With the Sun challenging taskmaster Saturn, frustration increases and problems with authority figures are very likely. Serious discussions with a trusted friend or older adviser could be worthwhile, with valuable information being imparted. Your cash flow might be a little tight, but have faith that the pressure will ease soon.

6. SATURDAY. Versatile. Clear, concise, and to the point will be the way to get a message across to other people. Ideas that come to mind should be recorded; these might be valuable at a later time. Face up to a fear now rather than trying to hide from self-doubts. It is time to look to the future and not remain in the past. Get together with friends or neighbors for a lively exchange of ideas and information. From now until July 5 your ruler Venus visits Taurus, your house of sex, and transformation, and other people's money. You might lose your heart to a romantic potential or to an activity that captures your imagination.

7. SUNDAY. Crotchety. You are likely to begin the day a little under the weather or slightly agitated. There may be a lot of talk or activity around home base as the Full Moon culminates in freedom-loving Sagittarius. Be sure to steer clear of controversial topics of conversation. Endeavoring to change opinions or attitudes is fraught with difficulties, and making any appreciable headway in this regard is highly unlikely. Hassles with a personal activity may be frustrating, but a conscientious approach could produce a positive result. Over the next few days would be a good period to arrange a romantic getaway. Partnership activities should be exciting and inspiring.

8. MONDAY. Ardent. Intense, passionate trends are in play. You can expect an intimate relationship to be hot and steamy. Libras desiring the power of decision and the benefit of choice can take advantage of opportunities being presented now. Singles might meet a future partner. Those in a relationship that is currently strained should exert extra effort to help restore harmonious vibes. Over the next few days self-deception or not facing up to issues that are staring you in the face might create problems. Be realistic if information passed on by a child or a lover doesn't seem to have the ring of truth. Someone might not be averse to telling a few lies if doing so suits their purpose.

9. TUESDAY. Unsettled. Don't expect an ordinary day. Communicative Mercury is in dispute with dreamy Neptune and over-the-top Jupiter while happily linked to erratic Uranus. A multitude of events are possible, with many beyond your control. If there was a day to expect the unexpected, this is it. Delays could occur, happy surprises might appear, and long-arranged plans may be disrupted by unforeseen problems. You might feel no one understands what you are saying, so be patient if asked to repeat instructions or questions more than once. Be careful that other people don't take credit for your efforts, and remain alert for someone trying to pull the wool over your eyes.

10. WEDNESDAY. Cautious. A little moderation is a good thing today. A roving eye could lead to difficulties for those already in a committed relationship. Even if life is not working out as expected in the love department, seek closure before moving on. Strong feelings and ideas might be conveyed by other people and will need to be addressed. Listening to their point of view can be helpful to understanding the message they are trying to convey. An expected benefit from an investment could be a disappointment, making you realize that profit projections may have been too high. Nurturing vibes can be found at home in the company of loved ones.

11. THURSDAY. Strained. Life is high-pressure now, with tricky cosmic trends making it hard to progress. Turning your back on a problem won't make it disappear. If it has been easier to ignore rather than confront and resolve a certain situation, time might be running out. Ask for help if difficulties with a wayward child are becoming overwhelming. Other people can often see what a parent doesn't see or won't acknowledge, or they may have already experienced similar problems. Keep travel arrangements simple; a delay or cancelation might upset the best of plans. A romance that has been casual and flirty could move in another direction.

12. FRIDAY. Demanding. Today's bumpy road is likely to prove annoying. Your usual placid and gentle demeanor might be missing. You are likely to balk if too many demands are being made, especially by loved ones. Although romantic trends remain strong, joy and contentment with your love life depend on thought processes and approach. Favorite leisure activities or hobbies could provide the perfect entertainment if you prefer a quiet evening at home. Libras who are eager to chase excitement and nightlife should take it easy and be careful when it comes to personal safety. Don't go out unaccompanied, and steer clear of dangerous places.

13. SATURDAY. Contented. Creative and artistic juices should run free this morning. Take advantage of this before other people arrive on your doorstep and take up valuable leisure time. Partnered Libras could find changes in romance increase contentment and are very pleasing, although these feelings might not last all day. As the hours pass, conflict could develop, particularly if shared finances are a topic of discussion. Singles in a blossoming new love affair should avoid overexpressing words or actions, which may be misunderstood or given too much weight. Steer clear of speculating with your cash, and give the casino a miss.

14. SUNDAY. Calm. Peace and tranquility reign throughout the day. Quick decisions might be called for, and you will be able to make choices without agonizing over which is right. A friend or family member could add great pleasure to your day. Spending time outside can be a very pleasant diversion. Libras with a green thumb might want to work in the garden. Swimming in a pool can be therapeutic, or take a trip to the beach and float in the ocean to your heart's content. If children are included in an outing, don't forget essential items to keep them protected from ultraviolet rays.

15. MONDAY. Chancy. Debates, deliberations, and discussions are likely to be numerous, but not all communication will be pleasant and helpful. Intense conversation requires insightful handling and understanding if you are to break through barriers, especially if an employee or coworker is involved. You might respectfully listen to the arguments of other people, then ignore their advice if your mind is set on a predetermined course of action. Don't be impulsive. However, if you feel you are right, then refuse to allow anyone to persuade you otherwise. Resistance to what you want to do may be strong, and you may decide that it would be wiser to make changes yourself rather than rely on relatives to adapt.

16. TUESDAY. Disruptive. Don't rush into anything. Your ability to compromise and work as a team member is important to career progress but could be undermined if you become irritated or agitated. The brush between warrior Mars and explosive Uranus can bring aggression to light, particularly when dealing with coworkers, employees, or customers. Try to keep the atmosphere lighthearted to reduce the risk of a situation degenerating into an all-out argument. Defer negotiations with a business partner if money is to be the focus of discussions. Later in the day being with those you love takes on added importance, with an older relative anxious to be included.

17. WEDNESDAY. Opportune. The Sun is busy making aspects to nebulous Neptune, disruptive Uranus, and jolly Jupiter. Expect to be on the go and to be creative, with a number of lucky breaks to help you along. However, it could be difficult to remain logical and practical because restlessness and impulsive action could reduce your productivity and efficiency. With your naturally sympathetic and compassionate nature, your awareness of the feelings of other people is enhanced. Nevertheless, guard against becoming too emotionally involved in anyone else's affairs. Try to maintain a discreet distance if a coworker starts venting about colleagues, clients, or the boss.

18. THURSDAY. Inspired. Libra imagination will be vivid, elevating your enthusiasm for creative work. Success with a spiritual or artistic project is foreseen. The occult or other New Age topics could appeal as a form of relaxation. From now to October 12 giant Jupiter retreats through Aquarius, your solar house of romance, children, and leisure pursuits. Jupiter retrograde gives you an opportunity to reexamine recent decisions you made in these areas. A favored hobby that you put aside some time ago could appeal once more. Pull out the craft equipment or paraphernalia and determine if the old spark is still there. You should experience an increase of funds if contact is made this afternoon with someone who owes money to you or your company.

19. FRIDAY. Strategic. This is a favorable day to reconsider your financial position. Don't hesitate to put in place new strategies that are designed to positively affect fiscal stability and security. Self-employed Libras contemplating taking on a new business partner, associate, or major client should not have any difficulty making a decision in this regard. Although balance and keeping the peace are usually your style, a competitive spirit may find you operating with a code of silence and confidentiality so that other people won't learn of your plans. Your business instinct is especially good this afternoon. If you need mental savvy to negotiate a special deal, you should have plenty in reserve.

20. SATURDAY. Uplifting. Libra shoppers might be inclined to use credit cards too freely this morning unless a more frugal approach is taken. If you are burdened with unexpected assignments or urgent work projects being added to your never-ending to-do list, slow down, take it in stride, and just do the best you can given current circumstances. Head out to a restaurant or marketplace featuring cuisine from other countries this evening. The flavors and smells of foreign food could bring back sweet memories of trips you have enjoyed. Libras who have yet to embark on world travels might be fascinated by the tang of unfamiliar aromas.

21. SUNDAY. Lively. Look forward to a very eventful day. The summer solstice marks the entrance of the Sun into the nurturing sign of Cancer, bringing Libra vocation, business affairs, and reputation into the spotlight for the next four weeks. This can be a terrific period for the career-minded Libra to push ahead with ambitious goals. Accomplishments are more than likely. Getting up close and personal with your mate or partner may be a priority. Action in your love life might have more to do with lust and passion than with love and romantic exploits, as saucy Venus smiles engagingly at dynamo Mars. Singles should mix and mingle; encountering a potential partner is definitely possible.

22. MONDAY. Busy. There is an abundance of planetary action in today's skies. Although you may covet a quieter life and peace of mind, these might not be readily available. A new source of happiness could emerge. This is an important period for single Libras. Your ruler, luscious Venus, happily meets up with sober Saturn and dynamic Mars but encounters friction with intense Pluto. An older or more mature lover, or even your soul mate, could enter into your life now. Perseverance is the key to achievements. Following the advice of a person wiser than you could bring the financial or emotional rewards that you are currently seeking.

23. TUESDAY. Stressed. Expect a tense day when taking care of personal safety is essential. The Sun is opposing powerful Pluto while rubbing Mars the wrong way, increasing the potential for tension and conflict. There may be changes to your duties and responsibilities that cause some additional anxiety. A diplomatic but assertive approach is the best way to stand up to someone who is in a vociferous and opinionated mood. Keep the amount of your monthly salary to yourself, especially if there is a chance that you earn more than coworkers, which could cause hard feelings. Business affairs look good, although you might find that your obligations increase.

24. WEDNESDAY. Satisfying. This should be a mainly positive day as long as you don't allow too many distractions to take you away from essential tasks and duties. You might get bogged down in minor details, which can impede progress. Opportunities exist in unlikely places, so be adventurous, broaden your scope, and don't concentrate only on the obvious. If you display special talents and skills on the job you may soon reap well-deserved rewards. Don't try to persuade other people to follow your lead because this could make them even more eager to prove you wrong or to go their own way. It is a good time to form or strengthen new friendships, especially with an important official or with a colleague.

25. THURSDAY. Useful. Extra work is required over the next few days to ward off a pessimistic mood. If this serious atmosphere is utilized productively, a lot of good work can be completed. Balancing personality differences on the job or at home could be difficult, but if anyone can arouse cooperation and harmony it is a Libra. Key issues could come out into the open, and this may be positive rather than negative. Clearing the air can often be cathartic. As a Libra you are the eternal romantic. However, expecting romantic bliss could be a bit of a letdown this evening. Don't despair; good times are not far away.

26. FRIDAY. Staid. This is another day when gloom and doom may seem to wrap around you. Daily duties are unlikely to provide desired stimulation, which could encourage behaving in a rash, impulsive manner. Don't dive into the depths of despair, but on the other hand don't try to push yourself into being jovial and socially outgoing. Just accept that it is a slow and somber atmosphere, and be aware that these influences will pass in a day or two. Problems with electrical equipment are foreseen, so put safety first and seek advice from an expert rather than trying to make repairs on your own. Be sure the refrigerator and kitchen are well stocked in case unexpected visitors appear on your doorstep, ready to be fed and entertained.

27. SATURDAY. Slow. With the Moon in your hidden twelfth house of Virgo, pace your activities to conserve energy. Putting your feet up and daydreaming could be what you prefer to do. The right amount of physical energy combined with sufficient rest and relaxation can help to maintain a healthy body and fitness level. Also be sure to eat light and right. Normally Scales are not known to be fastidious and pedantic, but today you could go against the trend and display a picky attitude toward other people. An important person from your past may reappear, which may be the catalyst to finally making a decision that you have been trying to avoid.

28. SUNDAY. Restful. If it is too hot to enjoy extra sleep this morning, at least take things slow. With the Moon still in your Virgo house of solitude until later in the afternoon, a gentle approach is needed to recharge rundown batteries. Ease up a little and find pleasure in the simple things of life. You have a lot to say, and plenty of folk are prepared to listen. Your concentration should be excellent, and your ability to communicate is better than usual. A sympathetic and spiritual approach could find you visiting the aged or ill to brighten up their lives a little. Fun and enjoyment can come from getting involved in a pleasant hobby or going out with your honey.

29. MONDAY. Bright. With the Moon in your own sign of Libra, you can shine until the end of the month. Self-improvement on all levels is not something you shy away from, in fact just the opposite. Opportunities for you to advance are likely to be offered. An awareness of your personal attributes can help you exploit these to your best advantage. Updating your image can be easier now. You know what is needed to convey the impression you want to make to other people. If it has been some time since you changed your hairstyle, its color, or its length, make an appointment and get ready to surprise people with a more modern you. You may also benefit from an appointment with a cosmetic dentist.

30. TUESDAY. Good. Concentrate on personal projects and aims. Advancement seems promised by today's stars. This is a good day for spontaneous action, which is unlikely to end negatively. Minor luck beams down on the Scales, and you can expect a welcome surprise to brighten your day. If money matters haven't been too bright, the possibility of a shift in this area is strong. This might come in the form of a pay raise or a promotion. Your persuasive ability is enhanced, and you could probably achieve record sales. This is a good day to go on a job interview or to hire new employees. Libras who are looking for work should take time to update their resume and seek out prospective employers.

JULY

1. WEDNESDAY. Erratic. An abundance of cosmic activity creates an atmosphere of chaos, confusion, and creativity as you begin the new month. There is a restless quality and the erratic desire to be a wanderer, if only for the next few days. Venus, your life ruler, is stressed. Unfavorable developments are likely regarding shared finances and assets. You might need to renegotiate a mortgage payment. Or an inheritance could fall short of promised funds, possibly because of increased legal fees. Uranus the planet of excitement and disruption, goes into retreat in Pisces, your solar zone of work and service. Uranus retrograde gives you an opportunity to reconsider your current employment situation.

2. THURSDAY. Diverse. Variety is definitely the spice of life for the adventurous Libra, and life continues to arouse the unexpected. Problematic predicaments are likely, but remaining realistic and setting boundaries can help you get through the day fairly smoothly. With egos on display, someone could try to make life a little difficult if you allow this person to get the upper hand. A joyous bond between Venus and excitable Uranus infuses a dash of spontaneity into the love life of Libras who are in a committed union. Singles can look forward to meeting an exhilarating new romantic interest. Enjoy the moment without expectations of a long and enduring relationship.

3. FRIDAY. Fair. The celestial heavens will continue to shake you out of your comfort zone. A number of difficulties may arise throughout the day, but putting on a happy face can lessen the likelihood of a major fallout. Financial issues involving an academic pursuit could be worrisome this morning. Put off taking action on this matter until later in the day when good ideas to resolve the issue could pop into mind. Mercury, the divine messenger, is now visiting sensitive Cancer until July 17. Fame, reputation, and professional matters come to the fore for Libras and can lead you to new opportunities and advancement.

4. SATURDAY. Tricky. The planets are not supportive even though it is a special holiday. With trickster Mercury opposing intense Pluto, you need to choose your companions carefully. Otherwise the day could be spoiled by tension pervading the air. Other people may be somewhat argumentative, and someone might try to verbally battle with you. A large dose of diplomacy and a willingness to turn the other cheek might be required to avoid a major confrontation from developing. Increased duties may be expected of those on the job. This is a favorable period to work toward a promotion or pay raise. Attend a daytime social gathering with friends or family members if you have the day off.

5. SUNDAY. Social. The feeling of being on vacation continues, and today should be a much more social day than yesterday. Mixing and mingling with other people can be stimulating. Meeting friends at a local coffee shop or special restaurant can provide a good dose of gossip. Libras who want to purchase a new home or property, or who are hoping for a promotion at work, should enter into negotiations. Talks should proceed as envisioned aided by your quick thinking. Your ruler Venus enters Gemini, your solar sector of adventure, travel, and academic pursuits. Venus here raises the chance of an impeding legal matter finally being settled in your favor.

6. MONDAY. Bumpy. Emotions are likely to be unstable. Your lifetime ruler Venus is in a cosmic dispute with intense Pluto, indicating that the day could begin and end on a low note. A lovers' quarrel or domestic disruption could create an atmosphere of heated exchanges. You will need to remain cool and calm in order to make any sort of progress. Just when you think that life is beginning to run smoothly, past indecisiveness could come back to haunt you. Even if you are drowning in a sea of paperwork, don't rush through tasks or you are likely to make mistakes. More haste equals less speed. Watch personal possessions carefully.

7. TUESDAY. Tumultuous. Aggressive Mars may be causing Libra folks a few problems. Necessary energy to move forward should be in plentiful supply, but remain alert when it comes to personal safety. This isn't the day to become involved in any risky business or to participate in any dangerous leisure pursuit if you have limited experience. Intense feelings are leveled at the domestic quarters as a Full Moon culminates in Capricorn, your zone of family and home. Stay cool under pressure, especially if you are struggling with meeting the demands and expectations of your boss and also of family members. If it is all becoming too much, now is the time to look for ways to make life easier.

8. WEDNESDAY. Edgy. Talkative Mercury is causing strife and unrest. Confusion and misunderstandings are a certainty and will require care. Be explicit when in discussions with other people or when giving instructions. A tendency to exaggerate, embellish, or waffle could confound your listeners. Record important meetings or messages. Check your calendar to avoid overlooking an important task. Forgetfulness could be a major problem. Colleagues or a lover may be evasive, vague, or extremely unreliable so it would be wise to handle urgent tasks yourself rather than waiting for their help. Productivity with creative pursuits should be high, but don't allow your imagination to run too wild.

9. THURSDAY. Constructive. This promises to be a better day than yesterday, although the lunar goddess is unsupportive when it comes to leisure and pleasure. Fortunately the Sun and serious Saturn will make up for this lack, so you should have a productive day. The career-minded Libra can make good progress with activities that require secretiveness, and also with behind-the-scenes projects. Someone older or wiser could offer good advice, so be prepared to listen and learn. This is not the time to abandon the tried-and-true way of fulfilling career or business obligations. Attending an important public meeting can be informative. Recognition in some form could be bestowed on you or your organization for past efforts or performance.

10. FRIDAY. Productive. Your creative talents could increase your popularity and garner added respect. You can make huge inroads with a special talent. Take full advantage of the opportunities that materialize to showcase your special skills and expertise. Social life should continue to expand. If you are organizing a party or other gathering, add a touch of fantasy and inspiration to invitations, catering, or decorations. Relationships might not be as agreeable on the job. A colleague may be more angry than usual, ready to dispute the slightest critical comment or negative situation that arises. Opt for a relaxing evening listening to music, attending a concert, or going to the movies. Steer clear of dangerous substances.

11. SATURDAY. Mixed. Libras who hold a position of authority should find that life is definitely getting better and better. On the other hand, Libra employees may find work responsibilities taxing; taking one step at a time can help overcome hurdles. Formulating long-term plans should not be difficult. However, ambitions could lead to overwork, so do only what you can cope with in order to avoid possible burnout. Dynamic Mars moves into Gemini, your zone of higher learning, teaching, and travel. Mars here directs your energy into favored topics of interest that both inspire and motivate you. From now until August 25 is a good period for writing, publishing, and fighting a legal battle.

12. SUNDAY. Good. Collecting facts, forming opinions, and disseminating knowledge are currently enhanced. This is an excellent day to conduct research or work on the Internet. Scales eager to pursue academic areas could get help with this aim. Libra students who apply effort should be well rewarded. Stretching brain cells a little bit more can help retain required facts, figures, and focus. An emphasis on domestic matters might be the encouragement you need to clean and declutter. Warm sunshine and loving feelings toward your nearest and dearest can be a great excuse to invite some friends to come over for dinner and to share your hospitality. Just avoid late-night entertaining.

13. MONDAY. Rewarding. Put off implementing legal action if this involves travel or real estate. A challenge to increase productivity can be positive providing you avoid pushing yourself or other people too hard. Partnership stress is likely, although it could be averted by better communication, compromise, and cooperation. This is a good day to make a career move designed to enhance your reputation and status. Libras with a high profile, especially if connected to the media, film, or television, can expect positive feedback from an important appearance, lecture, or involvement in a publicity campaign. Look for new ways to get your message across to the public at large.

14. TUESDAY. Tense. Watch your fuse. Mars could trigger disputes and conflict throughout the day. It would be better to go out for some fresh air or take a deep breath and count to ten every time a crisis occurs or there is a threat of an argument. Remain above pettiness. Look at the bigger picture, particularly if associates or a business partner are creating tension. You could feel you are at the beck and call of loved ones, but this too should pass fairly quickly if you handle demands in a mature, calm manner. Reviewing a current situation to see how you want to proceed can be constructive if you are not sure of your next move.

15. WEDNESDAY. Demanding. By tonight you may feel that this wasn't your finest hour or day. Difficult matters and erroneous situations are apt to arise, but try to take them in stride, particularly if making progress seems impossible. Be clear and concise. Words could be misconstrued making it tricky for those who are trying to follow your instructions. Paying strict attention to all details, no matter how trivial they seem, can keep important items from being overlooked. Talk over your plans beforehand. Volunteering services or donating cash to the less fortunate could cause issues with your mate or partner, who might feel that this increases pressure on family resources.

16. THURSDAY. Volatile. Restlessness, impulsiveness, and rash behavior may mark this day. Flexibility and going with the flow will be required as unexpected situations make this an exciting but exhausting period. Have confidence and the courage of your own convictions if beginning a new journey or venture. With thinking Mercury linking to chaotic Uranus, thought processes are accelerated. People close to you could have trouble keeping up with what you are saying, doing, and expecting. A different approach, or the assistance or intervention of another person, could help smooth over any upsets on the job. Don't be shy when it comes to asking for assistance if required.

17. FRIDAY. Eventful. Anticipate another roller-coaster day. If you have done your homework, you can look forward to good luck with a business venture or with achieving a worldly desire. Career-minded Libras shouldn't shy away from taking on extra obligations or duties. The ensuing challenges should make employment conditions more to your liking. Mercury, messenger of the gods, slips into Leo, your sector of groups and friends. Leo here enlivens social activities and further enhances your popularity. Serious discussions and casual chats are likely to increase. Make sure that other people get a chance to express their views and opinions, toning down your own inclination to hog conversations.

18. SATURDAY. Exciting. The need to add more excitement and adventure to your life could encourage taking off to explore new sights and unseen places. With the Sun shining brightly toward erratic Uranus but frowning at nebulous Neptune, boredom with daily routine will quickly set in unless you include a large dash of variety in your usual activities. The energy for meeting an interesting new romantic potential in a social setting is positive for singles. A special gathering tonight could be the beginning of an increasingly hectic social schedule. Teenagers should listen to their parents when it comes to the subject of suitable friendships and companions.

19. SUNDAY. Slow. Libras could have some difficulty becoming motivated this morning. This might have more to do with a late night, although enthusiasm may also be down and the inclination to think pessimistically up. An innate curiosity to know about worldly events could lead serious-minded Libras to study, conduct research, or enroll in a course that can advance educational qualifications. If academic study is out of the question or doesn't appeal, there are other choices such as looking into astrology and philosophical subjects. If the thought of a vacation getaway appeals, check local travel agents and the Internet to find a package to suit your budget.

20. MONDAY. Expressive. Your need to express thoughts and emotions may be strong. Speaking openly and frankly to friends and loved ones can make you feel happier and less burdened. Your wit should be sharp, but so could your tongue. Beware speaking or acting before considering the consequences of both your words and actions. A matter very close to your heart could be settled, or long-term issues resolved with good humor and grace. You have an abundance of ability to work hard to reach your desires. Be quick to take advantage of new opportunities that arrive. The possibility of a wonderful chance for a relative could have you waiting eagerly for their good news.

21. TUESDAY. Contrasting. Diverse trends make for a day of mixed emotions. The New Moon in Cancer, your house of status and prominence, illuminates Libra vocational and career matters. Over the next week your business sense and salesmanship skills should be heightened and acute, providing new chances to move forward. Unusual or original ideas should flow, increasing the number of potential opportunities that unfold. However, matters pertaining to your cash flow and love life might not be so lucky, with a bleak atmosphere affecting your romantic relationship and finances. Look at the way money is currently being handled and try to find a more prudent approach to spending and saving.

22. WEDNESDAY. Important. Long-term goals, cherished aims, and members of your friendship circle take center stage with the Sun lighting up Leo from now until August 22. Libra energy to socialize with friends, business acquaintances, and family members increases. Take advantage and accept appealing invitations as soon as they arrive. Attracting important support to further your aims should be easier. You could be pushed into a leadership role of a club or organization. If you are uncertain about the smartest approach to take with a certain problem, put on your thinking cap and search for a clever shortcut.

23. THURSDAY. Irritating. Exasperation marks this day. You are unlikely to be at your sparkling best, as red tape, rules, and regulations test both your determination and resolve. Discussions and debates could become loud. People with overblown egos may oppose your long-term plans and opinions. A power struggle could erupt within your network of friends, requiring mediation. You may be the one asked to try to restore amicable vibes in the group. Arrange to meet up for coffee or lunch with a special friend so you can mull over your life, loves, and future aspirations. Libras with humanitarian inclinations could determine that more facts are needed before giving time or money to a certain charity.

24. FRIDAY. Sentimental. Most productive activities will occur behind closed doors. An urge to spend more quality time on your own, which isn't usual for you, could have other people pondering why you are withdrawing. The reason is that as the Moon glides through your solar twelfth house, solitude is more eagerly sought. Direct your energy to creative pursuits, wrapping up loose ends, or working on a venture that is scheduled to be launched at a future date. Nostalgia for the ways things were in the past could become almost overwhelming, but this is the time to review what was learned from the experience. Look to the future for happiness and success.

25. SATURDAY. Supportive. Seek satisfaction from privacy and catching up with outstanding obligations and chores. Over the next few days lovely Venus bonds with Jupiter, planet of good luck, putting you in your element. Energy may still be somewhat limited, so taking it easy shouldn't be a problem for even the most energetic, let alone the lazy Libra. The sweet smell of love permeates the air. This is a day when you could pop the question, or a romantic proposal could come your way. For Libras who are walking down the aisle this weekend, the stars are extremely supportive.

26. SUNDAY. Pleasant. Romance and expansion are strong motivating forces again today. Vim and vitality could still be below par, even though the Moon is now slipping through your own sign. An urge to splurge on beautiful things, including sweets, chocolates, or take-out food could test the resolve of even the most health-conscious Libra. Fresh challenges could attract you. However, this is a time to be very wary of taking on more than you can comfortably handle. Financial trends are favorable, although it may be prudent to put the reins on spending. Issues involving moderation and knowing your limits can be of concern.

27. MONDAY. Vigorous. You should have ample vim and vitality as you greet the new day. All systems are ready to go, and you will be both physically and mentally alert. Find time to handle personal tasks as well as your usual responsibilities. Events occurring in the romance department should be viewed as positive even if that judgment isn't obvious. Realize that it is not the number of friends that is important but the quality of special friendships that is significant. Someone you haven't seen for a while could call and share interesting news. Rent a romantic film and relax with that special person tonight.

28. TUESDAY. Lucky. Good fortune and warm feelings surround Libras. Your ruler is happily engaging with imaginative Neptune but disputing with disruptive Uranus. If you are half of a partnership you are likely to see only the best in your partner, which can strengthen loving bonds. Try to arrange time together, but beware putting your mate on a pedestal, which can be a recipe for future disaster. Singles could enter into a relationship with a partner very different from the usual type. Although this may be an exciting love affair, it is apt to last a short while. Be super savvy with your money. An unrealistic or idealistic approach to spending could blow the budget.

29. WEDNESDAY. Complex. The cosmic sky sends a number of blockages and obstacles to hinder advancement. The receipt of a special invitation could be a big thrill but could also add extra pressure to the household budget. Seek ways to reduce costs so you can look forward to the event without worry and reservations. Home could be the source of conflict during the afternoon hours, but tension should pass quickly if tempers remain under control. Confidential information obtained this evening can lead to modest gains if you follow the advice you are given. A night on the couch or a stroll around the neighborhood might appeal if you prefer a relaxed evening.

30. THURSDAY. Cautious. Be careful. An inclination to go to extremes is strong. Tricky Mercury challenges happy-go-lucky Jupiter, but this day could be anything but pleasant and easygoing. Avoid matters involving the law. Nor should you sign important legal documents because overlooking what might appear to be a minor detail could result in future losses. Seek professional advice if important paperwork has to be handled. Even if this help is costly, it might save you a lot of money in the long run. Although your fertile imagination can produce lots of inspirational ideas, you might lack the practical approach needed to utilize them in a productive manner right now.

31. FRIDAY. Variable. Expect another day of ups and downs. There is an element of deception, warning you to take extra care. This is not the day to believe everything you hear. Disregard gossip at least until facts have been confirmed. Restlessness could hinder progress unless you exert extra effort to remain focused. Tonight your lifetime ruler Venus enters Cancer, the sign ruling your midheaven and accentuating your professional matters and status. Until August 26 socializing with superiors, other important people, or associates has the potential to increase your profile. Self-employed Libras can make financial gains by mixing business with pleasure during this period.

AUGUST

1. SATURDAY. Starred. A good mood prevails and should rub off on those in close proximity to you. If someone you know well is down in the dumps, do your best to cheer them up for their sake and also to keep their negativity from transferring onto you. A number of short journeys could lead to driving around a lot, running errands, chauffeuring children, and going to various other venues and activities. Intense energy in the romance department is being sent by the universe as your ruler Venus clashes with powerful Pluto over the next few days. Be wary of a one-sided infatuation. A close encounter of the romantic kind could take you to a peak of passion never experienced before.

2. SUNDAY. Profound. Deep feelings continue to highlight your romantic life. Libra couples who have experienced a lack of zest in the love department can take action to invigorate this important emotional need. If socializing with work colleagues, make sure your behavior is appropriate. If you are already in a romantic union, jealousy and possessiveness could cause problems. Mercury, the planet of thought and communication, begins touring Virgo, your twelfth zone of hidden issues and solitude. From now until August 25 your need to be alone with your thoughts increases, and you could become more withdrawn and less social. This is not the best time to begin any new projects.

3. MONDAY. Varied. Mixed fortunes prevail. You can now take decisive action on an issue left unresolved for some time, which should give you a strong measure of relief. Words that you utter are apt to be powerful and motivating, as talkative Mercury teams up with powerful Pluto. If speaking to a large group of people, prepare for the unexpected to arise. However, getting your message across should not be difficult because audience appreciation is more than likely. Scales negotiating a confidential contract or business deal should be well rewarded with results as anticipated.

4. TUESDAY. Heartening. A fortuitous turn of events could convey an offer or proposition that puts a smile on your face. Plans to improve living arrangements should move forward without a hitch, and pleasure with the end result is more than likely. Aim to work out a manageable budget that fits your lifestyle and allows you to save for a special purchase. Although this could require some effort, it will be all worthwhile when the dollars begin accumulating in your savings account. Puttering around at home performing minor chores should be pleasurable. Hang out with loved ones or extended family members this evening.

5. WEDNESDAY. Uneasy. A troublesome day arrives with the culmination of the Aquarius Full Moon lighting up your house of creative expression, romance, and children. An artistic project could come to an end, which might make you a little sad but should provide opportunities to become involved in a fresh new challenge. Emotions will be running hot, with a strong likelihood of disagreements. A youngster might need a firmer hand than usual, or one of their tricky issues could require delicate handling. Libras with a talent for interior design should consider developing this skill further. Extend your expertise to add your own special touches around the house.

6. THURSDAY. Mixed. Morning trends are unlikely to provide many laughs or pleasantries. Sensitivities remain highly charged. By midafternoon conditions begin to improve, and a small measure of luck could be your reward. It might be the right time to ask the boss for a raise, apply for a promotion, or seek some other employment perk that you currently covet. A relationship that is still developing may be your primary focus. Action you take this evening can propel the liaison successfully forward. There is a social quality to the evening, and Libras inclined to mix business with pleasure should receive financial benefits for their efforts. Consider taking your significant other out this evening to someplace new and different.

7. FRIDAY. Bright. With your ruler Venus making a number of planetary connections, romance is in the air. Matters of the heart will occupy much of your time. Retail therapy should be relaxing, with the added bonus that you could acquire a number of quality bargains to add beauty to your surroundings. Concentrate on eating nutritional food, including the snacks you choose. Even if you are fit and in good shape, don't take good health for granted. Compliments you receive will probably be very sincere, making you feel great; accept them gracefully. Partnership bonds should be strong, and expressing loving feelings can set the scene for intimacy to grow.

8. SATURDAY. Tricky. Clashes and power trips mark this day. Libras who are on the job could witness unstable emotions of a coworker, customer, or someone else in the workplace. Stay neutral or under the radar, and don't let yourself be dragged into an emotional blowup with a superior or a workmate. To guard your health, it might be time to cut back on rich or fatty foods and reduce consumption of caffeine or alcohol. Someone close may need help with a health problem, or you might have an ongoing ailment to sort out. When socializing make sure you don't step on the toes of other people, either literally or figuratively, or this could develop into a painful issue.

9. SUNDAY. Compliant. Be as adaptable as you can without expecting to make much progress or receive much praise. The morning hours are best suited to performing daily tasks around the house and organizing your week ahead. This would also be the time to put in extra working hours if you are self-employed or working from home and need to catch up. A family concern could become more complicated and be awkward to resolve, requiring your renowned gentle and diplomatic approach to prevent heated exchanges. Deceit and disappointment are ever-present today. Someone you care for might not be completely honest. Make it your business to know exactly where teenage children are hanging out today.

10. MONDAY. Restrained. On this low-energy day feelings of constraint and limitations could impede advancement. Don't try to second-guess what is going on around you. Take a step backward, gain new perspective, and then try to attract the right people and situations into your life. Change can be difficult, but once implemented you may wonder why you didn't act sooner. Discussions might be needed. However, someone close to you may rub you the wrong way, and your patience for how they act or what they say may be in short supply. Unless you can find a way to cooperate or work with current situations on the job, your in-basket could remain full for the whole day. Don't undervalue your time and effort.

11. TUESDAY. Productive. Whatever seemed wrong yesterday could suddenly feel right as the pressure of the last few days fades. The lunar trends promise an easier day. With the Moon in Aries, your partnership house, you can look forward to bigger business profits and improved relations with clients and the general public. A compromising approach can help you earn support from other people. Libras who are part of a team should feel that extra effort is being appreciated by other members. This is a favorable day to negotiate an important contract or business deal. Your routine could be hindered by an unexpected visitor or chore unless you put a do-not-disturb sign on your door.

12. WEDNESDAY. Uncertain. A financial proposition, loan, or transaction that you have been confident about could now hang in the balance, and it may be a few days before you learn its fate. You could find that a major must-have item is a big threat to the budget, stretching your credit card to the limit or emptying your bank account of hard-earned savings. Time spent with someone close can be a starred way to revive lost, sweet memories. If this is an older person, consider recording these recollections for posterity, or at least for younger members of the family to enjoy at a future time. In a social situation you will be the consummate diplomat.

13. THURSDAY. Constructive. Energy to organize finances, find methods to reduce debt, and begin a saving plan is enhanced under the Taurus Moon. Take advantage of the opportunity to wade through bank and credit card statements, check current interest rates, and pay outstanding accounts. Mighty Mars and generous Jupiter are working to your advantage, so try to relax. Even though a few obstacles are crossing your path, most activities that you undertake should work out advantageously. Don't be afraid to combine work with studies. Motivation to learn should make it a breeze to conquer the toughest subject.

14. FRIDAY. Stimulating. Travel pervades your thoughts, so unless you are heading off on a real trip take time to indulge in some fantasy and escapism. International business or diplomatic endeavors should be fruitful. However, a legal entanglement could lead to mixed fortunes. Partnered Libras should ensure a balance between intimacy and independence. There is a chance that you could be drawn into a philosophical discussion, which might get you thinking about volunteering your services or joining a political or humanitarian organization. It would be wise to ponder this idea for a while before jumping into the fray.

15. SATURDAY. Eventful. Act on tasks during morning hours or early this evening to gain the most support from the lunar goddess. These periods are excellent to begin writing a new novel, read a best-seller, or take off to parts yet unseen by you. A loved one who lives abroad may be very glad to hear from you via a phone call or Internet chat. Keep your bags packed. The chance of a lifetime to go on a trip could catch you by surprise, albeit a very pleasant one. Expect confusion with communications for the rest of the day, along with delays involving long-distance travel arrangements, plus issues with a sibling. A cheerful evening is promised for Libras eager to mix and mingle.

16. SUNDAY. Demanding. Inflated egos and power plays might be on display, with disruptive conditions at home upsetting you for much of the day. You will probably need to chill out and back down if retaining peace and harmony is your ultimate goal. Trying to convince other people that your way is right may be a waste of effort. A home project that requires a creative touch and flair should be as enjoyable as it is productive. You might be able to persuade a family member to help you complete a chore that is annoying to you and others. An opportunity to combine socializing with networking should work out well if you are aiming to market your talents.

17. MONDAY. Good. An abundance of diverse planetary action takes place in today's skies. A successful meshing of ideas and methods behind closed doors could enhance your business or professional status. There is a possibility that you may be offered a leadership role. Libras need to watch what is said. Otherwise you could inadvertently let slip information that someone specifically requested be kept confidential. Being neither a borrower nor a lender is a good motto to follow, especially where friends and money are concerned.

However, generosity can be shown to those less fortunate, so dig deep and donate what you can afford to a worthy charity.

18. TUESDAY. Volatile. Prepare for a day when anything could happen, which may be both pleasant but also unfavorable. You might opt to transfer from your current employment. Or you might prefer to take a part-time job that provides increased challenges and has the potential to turn into a full-time position. Either way, these choices should be more emotionally rewarding than your present job. It would be wise to avoid sensitive discussions because an excitable mood could be adversely reflected in your manner of speech and body language. Libra drivers should take extra care on the roads. In particular, guard against rash and impulsive behavior.

19. WEDNESDAY. Comforting. Although there are a few challenges to confront, you should feel secure and comfortable. A display of affection and romance is always a priority for Libra people, and the sense that your love life has entered a more stable phase can be a big relief. You don't need to be too frugal if purchasing a special treat for yourself; you deserve it. Balance your checking account and spend an affordable amount on what you need rather than on trivial items. Joining a new group should work out well. Members are apt to eagerly welcome new blood, and a casual friendship could develop into a much stronger bond.

20. THURSDAY. Refreshing. A bright New Moon in your Leo house of friends and groups can be the catalyst for a large number of social invitations to come your way. Activities involving an organization or a team of people are favored. The next two weeks is a brilliant time to act on dreams and long-term goals. Confusion and unsettled feelings currently surround you, so this is not a good day to speculate, invest, or gamble. Allow more time for a challenging task; it is bound to take longer than you envision. Bide your time if there is a decision to be made. Uncertainty about which direction to take could bewilder even the most assertive Libra. Spend some quiet time alone if you get the chance.

21. FRIDAY. Pressured. Be willing to delegate tasks. Otherwise your restless attitude could hinder progress with employment duties or daily activities. Keep life in perspective. Pressure that is currently being applied may increase strain and nervous anxiety, in turn affecting health and overall well-being. If you are considering giving someone a second chance, keep your eyes open and remember not to expect too much too soon. You cannot force anyone to change unless that is what they want to do. Deciding whether to take it easy and rest or have a night out on the town could have you in a quandary. Make the decision later in the day.

22. SATURDAY. Diverse. A number of exciting possibilities are foreseen for you to enjoy. However, your love life could be subject to disappointment or self-delusion, or it could offer thrilling anticipation, depending on your reactions to situations as they occur. Prepare for unexpected ups and downs, and handle each one as it comes along. The Sun enters perfectionist Virgo and your reclusive twelfth house of private and confidential matters. This is the time of year when signals from your body suggest slowing down and becoming more choosy about social invitations and leisure pursuits. The likelihood that someone will try to bamboozle you over the next four weeks is higher than usual.

23. SUNDAY. Insightful. Welcome a sudden surge of energy as the Moon glides through your own sign of Libra. Someone from the past could act as a guiding light for you. If you are seeking answers to questions, don't be afraid to ask someone who wields more power and influence than you. Although the time to spring clean is long gone, today is a good time to dispose of items no longer used, required or important to your lifestyle. Attending a psychic or New Age fair, or visiting your local palm reader or astrological consultant, could provide increased understanding and insightful information to help point you in the right direction.

24. MONDAY. Satisfactory. Work that has been performed in the past, probably alone, could begin to show signs of paying dividends, so you can flaunt it in a modest way. Matters regarding your personal life need to be seriously considered. Financially an important objective may be achieved. Throughout the week warrior Mars is doing battle with destructive Pluto, which increases the potential for conflict at home and in the working arena. Be careful not to do anything that may be detrimental to your reputation. Be aware of a tendency to damage yourself in some way.

25. TUESDAY. Helpful. A monetary theme runs through your solar horoscope today. If the lack of cash is getting you down, talk to a family member or friend about new methods of handling household income and expenditures. If a number of people provide feedback, you might actually be able to cut expenditures and increase savings.

Libra qualities are shining through brightly, with chatty Mercury entering your sign and giving you the chance to air your ideas and views articulately. You can make other people sit up and take notice. Active Mars has also moved on and is now visiting canny Cancer in your sector of vocation and business matters. Ambitions rise, and it might be time to talk to the boss about a pay raise.

26. WEDNESDAY. Promising. Take extra care if traveling. Walk, don't run. Avoid dangerous situations and areas. You are in an accident-prone period. Unless you are vigilant, cuts, bruises, and burns could be sustained. Both wit and speech may be sharper than usual, assisting writers, teachers, and public speakers. Avoid listening to or spreading gossip. Also be careful of becoming involved in intrigue and rumormongering on the job. Your lifetime ruler, saucy Venus, is now gliding through Gemini, accentuating your friendship circle and group participation. Engaging in teamwork and connecting with groups will increase pleasure for the Libra social butterfly. Falling in love with a friend is a possibility.

27. THURSDAY. Energetic. Your words could flow faster than your thoughts, leading to speaking first and thinking later. Slow down and focus so you are not guilty of saying something better left unsaid. A crucial point may be overlooked, particularly if you sense that someone is keeping important news or information from you. Don't assume anything, or allow arrogance to prevent you from seeing the forest from the trees. However, do trust your instincts. Expressing an unpopular theory or opinion is unlikely to win you any friends, but doing so might be essential to dampen the overblown egos or unwarranted enthusiasm of a higher-up.

28. FRIDAY. Active. On this lively and restless day productivity is only assured if you keep moving and remain on the go. Don't fret over the small stuff. A short trip could take you into uncharted territory, and may bring opportunities to network with some interesting new contacts. Although socializing is something that you could be avoiding, you will enjoy meeting and greeting a diverse mix of interesting people. If you wish to arrange an interview, meeting, or audition, now is a good time to set plans in motion. Singles ready and waiting for romance could meet a dynamic interest that sets heartstrings fluttering.

29. SATURDAY. Happy. Enthusiasm for household tasks might be absent. You could prefer to be out shopping, playing a sport, or participating in some other physical pursuit. Don't force yourself to take action on unappealing chores. You could be less attentive than usual, and this might create an atmosphere for accidents and injuries to occur. For those on the job, the thought of working alone rather than with other people would seem to be a blessing and much more to your liking. Disagreement regarding family obligations could arise. Be sure to take into consideration the feelings of others, both older and younger. If you want to be noticed, flaunt your attractions.

30. SUNDAY. Guarded. You could find this a rather strange day. The desire to escape from the rat race for a little while might become overwhelming. Spending time in the garden, harvesting herbs or vegetables, or trekking through the woods communing with nature can help bring back a sense of tranquillity and peacefulness. Just don't go wandering off alone without safety gear or a cell phone. Starting anything new is unlikely to appeal. More can be achieved by completing chores left unfinished for some time. Concern for someone who is ill or recovering from a fall could bring home the importance of family values and of spending quality time with loved ones.

31. MONDAY. Pleasant. The cosmos sends more action today to keep you amused and on your toes. Libras who are at home could decide that it is a good day to change the decor by adding a new coat of paint, cushions, or plants to brighten up the domain. Be vigilant when it comes to door-to-door salespeople. Otherwise they could charm you into purchasing items that you don't really need or cannot afford. Real estate matters are under positive stars. If seeking to move out of the nest or purchase a new home, you may be surprised by the number of suitable places that are currently available. Unexpected entertainment should delight the family tonight.

SEPTEMBER

1. TUESDAY. Varied. Mixed indications herald this new month. Throughout September your ruler, vixen Venus, is involved in a number of cosmic challenges and harmonious links. This will increase the focus on two things that Libras love most: money and romance. Today it won't take much to work yourself into a major flap possibly to meet an important deadline or to complete all of your tasks before heading home. Mental work will be especially enjoyable. Complicated, complex puzzles or intricate pursuits should be a major source of relaxation and pleasure. Skip any form of competition, except competing to beat your own best performance.

2. WEDNESDAY. Tough. Feeling constrained could lead to lethargy and weariness. As far as work is concerned, expect a nose-to-the-grindstone atmosphere, although there may be a number of stoppages making the job that much harder to do. This is not the day to quit current employment, even though the thought could be very tempting. If disagreements arise, stay focused on the lessons to be learned from the situation rather than dwelling on the negative aspects. You may feel that the cautious approach favored by an older relative is holding you back. However, it would be prudent to listen and analyze the information that is passed on to you.

3. THURSDAY. Surprising. Another day dawns when you will enjoy giving your brain a good workout. A sharp mind enhances concentration, and right now you have the ability to pay close attention to details and to convey great ideas. Your manner of speech should be quicker than usual, but you need to guard against a cynical or sarcastic attitude. Beware of a new romantic encounter, especially with an employee or coworker; sincerity may be lacking. An unexpected turn of events could provide you with an item you have long desired, or a situation may be cause for a joyous celebration.

4. FRIDAY. Sensitive. A touchy, emotional day is likely unless sensitivity can be kept under control. It might be hard to be optimistic if you don't know whether you're coming or going, and with a Full Moon in Pisces this could definitely be the case. The focus is on health, work, and service, with the potential for an ending in at least one of these areas. Avoid letting petty frustrations be distracting, focusing straight ahead instead. You have the potential for breaking a negative or unhealthy habit. The resignation of a coworker could cause stress and anxiety if you suspect or know that the bulk of their work is likely to fall on you.

5. SATURDAY. Laid-back. A relatively easy day is being sent by the universe, although there may be a tendency toward a moment of gloom this morning. Projects that require precision could be a problem, so it would be advisable to put these aside until another day if possible. Energy may be below par, which could cause problems if you have a hectic schedule or a busy round of social activities. Gentle pursuits will be more appealing. If you want to get out of the house, a slow bike ride, a leisurely walk, or a picnic in the park could be just what you need to relax and chill out for a few hours. By evening your energy rises and you should be in the mood to have some fun.

6. SUNDAY. Uncertain. This usually lazy day of the week might be far from relaxing if you share your home with other people. Find constructive methods of releasing energy to avert potential disputes and disagreements. You might need to allow your mate, partner, or someone close to you to sound off. Providing this isn't criticism being leveled your way, continue to go about your business until things settle down. Pettiness could cause tempers to flair for those who are on the job. Sharp words spoken in retaliation might intensify an already unpleasant atmosphere. From midnight until September 29 be prepared for crossed wires, delays, and frustrating breakdowns as tricky Mercury moves into retreat.

7. MONDAY. Balancing. Be ready in advance, not when it is too late. Take care when signing an important document, remembering to read all of the fine print. This is the time to reexamine past personal decisions with the intention of readjusting what needs to be changed. Ambitions and aims should also be reviewed to ensure that you are on the right track. Discussing plans with a trusted friend or relative will give you more confidence that your current direction is the best one to pursue. Continue to cultivate a potentially large client who could add valued dollars to the bottom line. Singles need to be discerning with their choice of a romantic companion over the next few days.

8. TUESDAY. Focused. Coming to grips with your finances can be a positive way to use the current transit of the Taurus Moon. Sorting out shared assets, paying outstanding debts, or completing bookwork can be very useful. Consult an accountant or tax professional if you need help with more intricate areas of investments and retirement planning. Working out a budget for an upcoming project should proceed smoothly. Your mental alertness, at least until late afternoon, assures that you will dot all the i's and cross the t's. Libra love life can be more delightful if effort is made to spice things up in the boudoir.

9. WEDNESDAY. Problematic. Stressful aspects abound, making this a difficult day. With feisty Mars in friction with dreamy Neptune, your vim and vitality are likely to slump. Dishonest folk could be attracted to you, so take care that a gullible attitude doesn't lead to some type of a loss. Organizing a household budget can be productive if funds are disappearing faster than income is being generated. This could be the catalyst for Libras with high expectations to realize that thoughts of a lavish vacation or a new car should be put on hold until finances are more stable. Shoppers should keep purchases to essential items, steer clear of large department stores, and leave credit cards at home.

10. THURSDAY. Expressive. Expect a better day as your energy begins to return. Legal matters, higher education, or contact with people from overseas can be handled without too many obstacles cropping up to hinder a successful outcome. The publication of an article or book, either in print or on the Internet, could boost your reputation. This is also an excellent time to edit a manuscript, getting it ready to send off to an agent or publisher. Put on paper how much you care for the special people in your life. Libras writing wedding vows should not have any trouble choosing the right words to express emotions and joy.

11. FRIDAY. Moderate. Adverse planetary influences stir up toil and trouble for those who are prone to overindulge in the goodies of life. If moderation is your watchword, all should go well. However, it would be wiser for spendthrift Libras to hibernate at home or in the office. Food and drink can play a major role in the day. An invitation to go out to an expensive restaurant or coffee bar will be hard to refuse. While vacationing, whiz past souvenir stores or risk having to pay for overweight luggage on your return home. An idealistic, generous approach toward the needy is laudable, but keep within the bounds of reality.

12. SATURDAY. Expansive. Motivation to learn another language or increase knowledge of the world is high right now. This can be the encouragement you need to seek a job abroad or to further your education. Seminars and workshops to achieve this aim or to broaden hobby skills can be both informative and stimulating. Working harder might be necessary to ensure that a personal plan doesn't wind up amounting to nothing. Libras applying for a driver's permit should succeed with enough study and behind-the-wheel practice. Pluto, the planet of change, is now moving forward in the house of home and family, easing possible delays with property repairs or a home purchase.

13. SUNDAY. Challenging. Be prepared for a busy day rather than a leisurely, restful one. There is potential for anxiety. However, avoiding an overactive imagination can help curb unnecessary worry about matters that may never come to pass. A major cosmic pattern has formed that can increase your sense of uneasiness and uncertainly regarding what life holds in store for you and your loved ones. Take care of the basics now, and be ready to make adjustments, particularly with matters concerning children or a creative project. Libra singles in a new romance could be floundering and unsure of the strength of mutual affection. Proceed slowly, and don't push for any type of commitment at this time.

14. MONDAY. Variable. This is a mixed day, although confidence with business and professional matters remains intact. When it comes to other areas of your life, particularly romance, you might feel you are in a fog, unsure of the future. Remaining positive and upbeat will be challenging but necessary in order to carry out daily requirements and continue to grow. On the job a challenging project should be successfully completed. Business affairs are likely to move in an upward trend. The unemployed have an excellent chance of finding suitable work, and hardworking Scales are likely to at least receive the promise of a pay increase.

15. TUESDAY. Bumpy. Anticipate a tough day as Saturn, the planet of tradition, challenges the unique expression of Uranus, shining conflicting light into your work, daily grind, and health sectors. Unhealthy patterns of behavior can be broken, but only in a well-planned, structured manner. Changes are unlikely to be instant but should be long enduring. This is a good time to show the courage of your convictions. Face fears that are causing you sleepless nights and headachy days. Unexpected twists with an employment issue or task are likely to prove challenging. However, with a positive approach, developments should work out in your favor. Avoid putting your lover on a pedestal or you risk disillusionment when the inevitable fall occurs.

16. WEDNESDAY. Taxing. Libra love life remains under a cloud. The best way to handle current disruptive energies sent by your ruler Venus is to remain flexible and pliable. Trying to make changes or push anyone's buttons may have the reverse effect from what you desire. A former lover could appear on the scene, but be aware that promises being bandied about could come to nothing. If you are on the job, friendly competition between colleagues can be enjoyable and useful if entered into in the spirit intended, which can reduce stress and anxiety.

17. THURSDAY. Tricky. More upset being sent by the cosmic heavens is stirring the pot for Libras as Mercury retrograde slips back into Virgo, your twelfth house of hidden matters. Logic and innovation are in abundance, but a restless streak and the possibility of speaking out of turn makes this day fraught with problems and difficulties. If you are prepared to listen to the views of other people and can curb your own outspokenness, it is a good time to take part in a debate, discussion, or meeting. You won't be shy in expressing ideas and plans that seem to have merit. At lunchtime go for a walk, head for the mall, or enjoy a relaxing coffee with coworkers or friends to reduce edginess and help clear your mind.

18. FRIDAY. Renewing. Opportunities to make significant headway are usually limited when the Moon is in the sign of Virgo and your house of confinement. Today, however, there is a New Moon culminating in Virgo, which gives you a chance to switch to a healthier diet and lifestyle to replace old habits and behaviors. Alternative remedies, flower essences, and organic foods could appeal and be helpful if you are seeking different forms of natural healing. Social matters should not occupy you as much as usual, but make sure to set aside some time to mix and mingle with family members and friends. Take notice of your dreams and record what you remember; these notes could supply the answers to some nagging questions.

19. SATURDAY. Spirited. As a Libra you are on a roll, with life beginning to look up. Self-analysis can provide important personal discoveries that will help you sort out the important priorities in life. With the Moon in your own sign, you exude personal magnetism. Keeping up appearances assumes more importance for the socially inclined. Pick out the liveliest function to attend this evening; you are bound to be in the center of action. Get ready for the love arena to improve markedly after a period of being in the doldrums. Your sex appeal is on the rise and ardent emotions are heating up.

20. SUNDAY. Tender. As a Libra you should be in seventh heaven. Love is in the air, and it is time to believe in dreams and fantasies. Your ruler Venus, goddess of love and money, moves into your Virgo twelfth zone, remaining there until October 14. Give in to the urge to take time away from your social schedule and concentrate more on private interests and on spending time alone with your lover. Peace and quiet will be coveted and can provide the space you need to organize a special upcoming function or celebration. A former lover could come back on the scene. Also, beware becoming involved in a clandestine romantic affair.

21. MONDAY. Strategic. A cool head is needed when it comes to matters associated with personal finances. Serious consideration of a major purchase should be put on hold. This could increase financial pressure or cause arguments with your mate or partner. Someone who is usually agreeable might not give in to your wants. Struggles could occur in the area of love. Doubts and uncertainties regarding the depth of a partner's commitment may continue to plague those currently lacking self-confidence. Deciding whether to begin an illicit affair or take back a former lover could also be weighing heavily on your mind and heart.

22. TUESDAY. Happy Birthday! With the Sun now glowing in your sign until October 23, Libras whose brightness has been hidden over the past four weeks now have a chance to get noticed, especially by those who count. Even with your ruler Venus hiding out in Virgo, your house of solitude, your spirits should receive a large boost. Unwanted burdens could disappear. Work that is being done behind the scenes should soon be ready to be brought out into the light of day. Taking a steady fiscal approach will reap rewards in the long run if you are prepared to tighten your belt a little now in order to refill your bank account.

23. WEDNESDAY. Disconcerting. A bundle of planetary activity is now occurring in your solar horoscope. Personal issues could become increasingly irritating over the course of the day. Colleagues, friends, or a parent might have a great deal to say, and some of it might not be very complimentary or what you want to hear. Your ability to juggle a number of responsibilities simultaneously could be severely tested as a fidgety mood descends. Ideas and projects need to be properly organized, and data needs to be clear and concise to reduce the likelihood of misunderstandings or unclear messages. It would be advisable to write on paper what you don't want to forget.

24. THURSDAY. Stable. Expect a more settled day. Good news could arrive. The time is right to begin making plans, to be implemented later in the month when Mercury moves forward. No matter how trivial, if you pay attention to details your projects should move ahead favorably. Your natural compassion combined with the ability to listen to the confidences of other people can attract those who are seeking a guide or mentor. Pass on your knowledge and wisdom without becoming too entangled in their problems. A number of distractions could hinder efficiency this evening, and a heavy atmosphere could disrupt domestic harmony. Drive carefully if venturing out to socialize.

25. FRIDAY. Unsettling. Current celestial patterns can affect your personality in a negative way. You need to curb ego tendencies and remain humble, but without putting yourself down. Associates and those in your immediate environment could be uptight and a little hard to handle. Try not to nag or become overly agitated. Displaying this type of behavior is likely to prolong problems and increase stress. Hang back rather than taking the lead in a sports event or challenge, not letting anyone accuse you of being conceited. Entertaining at home would be ideal tonight.

26. SATURDAY. Pleasant. Cosmic activity focuses attention on the home and family sector, urging Libras to act on obligations and household tasks. Consider rearranging furniture to improve ambience or to make room for an office or home theater. If you are seriously considering relocating, begin to make plans now. Check out suitable localities, begin discarding items that won't be making the move with you, and start packing. Wait at least until Tuesday before advertising unwanted goods for sale or hiring a moving company. A new love may be on the horizon for singles who keep expectations to a realistic level. Couples can enjoy a loving evening at home.

27. SUNDAY. Cautious. Take care if launching a do-it-yourself project or home renovations this morning. A gung-ho approach could find you getting into difficulties, possibly requiring a professional to finish the job. If a change of residence remains a priority, scour the Sunday newspaper for leads and ideas. Interviewing a potential roommate should be productive. Libras viewing real estate with the intention to buy could find a number of properties that suit family requirements. A visit to the grandparents can delight youngsters. Social Scales should find plenty of entertainment to keep both body and mind stimulated.

28. MONDAY. Favorable. Creative juices flow freely, and a very active social life should continue to keep you fully occupied. If you don't have enough hours in the day to accept every invitation you receive, opt to please some of the people some of the time rather than trying to get to all social functions. Cranky children could disturb the evening, but don't allow your heart to rule your head. Be firm and don't give in to the whims of youngsters; make sure established guidelines are adhered to. A favored leisure pursuit or hobby could be the best form of relaxation tonight.

29. TUESDAY. Fair. Libra parents need to remain cool and calm again today. Children could be causing tension around the home with their willfulness or by squabbling with siblings. Divorced couples may be caught in the middle, with youngsters playing one parent off against the other. Over the past three weeks you may have experienced issues with repressed expression or the inability to clearly and concisely explain to other people exactly what you mean or what you want. With information gatherer Mercury now moving forward in articulate Virgo, this problem should soon abate. Confusion over a creative project or a spiritual issue will disappear.

30. WEDNESDAY. Interesting. Stay active and adaptable. You should feel more contented and peaceful. The creative Libra should start work early. Imagination, inspiration, and original thoughts will flow freely, increasing productivity and output. Early morning is a good time to smooth out a difference of opinion with a loved one. From midmorning onward, better results are likely if complicated tasks are left for another day. Duties that are pleasant and easy should be performed instead. A secret love affair that you or someone close is involved in could be adding extra stress. It might be time to look at the situation from a more realistic and practical perspective.

OCTOBER

1. THURSDAY. Opportune. The good times continue to roll as the new month begins. With the Sun in your own sign, this is the time of year when the universe opens doors to good fortune and opportunity. With informative Mercury harmonizing happily with energetic Mars, your active mind and strong intellect provide the power to formulate both business and private goals. If matters are not proceeding according to plan, consider revising strategies and targeting new aspirations. Someone on the job might be biased or hold some type of grudge, but you can overcome problems by ignoring barbs and going about your daily affairs in a positive manner.

2. FRIDAY. Harmonious. This day dawns with most things flowing smoothly, promising positive achievement. Relationships with employees and coworkers should be improving, and leftover tension from yesterday can be cleared away thanks to your happy, optimistic approach. Taking steps to increase your fitness level should fare well.

If you wish to trim down in time for the festive celebrations, this is the time to join a gym or start to get serious about using home exercise equipment. It is important not to neglect your diet. If suffering from frequent stress-related headaches, look into new ways to overcome these. Expect a special compliment of surprise this evening.

3. SATURDAY. Tricky. If you are feeling out of sorts, it may be from a combination of a late night and the prevailing downbeat stars. The best advice is to think pleasant thoughts rather than concentrating on the annoying aspects of any situation. Once the day gets started your mind is apt to be more active than normal, and you may go looking for stimulus and action. If seeking fun do some research and choose entertainment that can provide enjoyment at a minimal cost. Over the next few days messenger Mercury is just one of the planets creating havoc. Shopping is one area to watch because you might spend more than you intend or be ripped off by a shopkeeper or even a pickpocket.

4. SUNDAY. Sensitive. A huge day is forming in the skies in terms of planetary patterns, so expect conditions to be anything but ordinary. Emotions are running high, and you will need to exercise care to keep your actions and behavior from going over the top. Keep in mind that the Full Moon lighting up the sign of Aries will intensify the feelings of those around you. Don't allow arguments to develop and spoil your day. Pay extra attention to your significant other. If your relationship is going through a difficult period, a crisis point could be reached at any time within the next two weeks, requiring immediate action. Your words can be misconstrued, warning against issuing ultimatums.

5. MONDAY. Emotional. Strong feelings are close to the surface again today. Business finances should improve substantially. Your ability to overcome opposition to plans and projects is enhanced. Individual accomplishments are foreseen within a working team structure. Be ready to act on short notice. A surprising action by a colleague can work to your advantage, with the potential to increase your prestige and income. Libras who are half of a couple should be in happy agreement about mutual aims. However, recalculate a joint checking account before making a last-minute decision that is likely to put extra pressure on your finances.

6. TUESDAY. Bumpy. This is one of those days when no matter how hard you try, getting started is going to be difficult. Emotions increase the strain this morning. Transportation delays could add a large dash of frustration. Money issues may be a source of irritation between you and your mate or partner. A compromising approach is needed to diffuse friction and disputes. Seeing the humor in a situation and having a laugh can be a great stress buster. A talk with a wayward teenager could be reassuring for Libra parents, confirming that everyone in the family is back on the same wavelength. Add a few extra dollars to your wallet if going out because costs may be higher than anticipated.

7. WEDNESDAY. Busy. Focusing on issues concerning insurance, taxes, and investments should be beneficial. Updating home insurance should be done on a regular basis; be sure to include expensive electronic additions and personal jewelry. Investigating possible business ideas that would suit self-employment or part-time work from home might be of interest if you are anxious to branch out on your own or want to work more flexible hours. Opt for serious discussions rather than superficial conversations. A movie or television program with a mystery theme or deep psychological content could appeal.

8. THURSDAY. Positive. Attentiveness and focus are improved, giving you the ability to concentrate on both major and minor details. This is the time to take control of matters that have been bothering you recently. Discussions with a parent could resolve worrisome issues regarding an illness. Researching care facilities for an elderly relative who seems unable to cope on their own should produce a number of high-quality options. Thorough reading of a lease can reveal any hidden clauses that could be of concern in the world of commerce. A real estate purchase should proceed smoothly. Remain positive and don't allow negativity to invade your thoughts.

9. FRIDAY. Interesting. The desire to gain and expand present knowledge is strong, bringing you to the point of exploring new ideas for further study. Take advantage of your local library or the Internet to research techniques to improve business and professional possibilities. Your ruler Venus is wreaking havoc in your love life now. Excitement, the unexpected, and confusion are possible manifestations of her influences, requiring a temperate approach. Don't give in to rash or impulsive behavior. The unattached should beware hasty judgments or decisions when it comes to a romantic encounter. Your mind may be focused on rebellion and thrill seeking rather than reality and logic.

10. SATURDAY. Fortunate. The universe smiles and good fortune is on your side. With the Sun embracing abundant Jupiter, Libras are blessed with an optimistic frame of mind and strong personal magnetism. Write down personal ambitions. Other people are likely to take notice of you, and your prestige will get a boost. No matter what your current ambition, act on it now. If you have been working on a special project, it should be nearing successful completion. Romance could still be risky but exciting. If you take it as it comes, without expectations of a long-enduring love affair, enjoyment and contentment can be your reward. Socializing should be exceptionally enjoyable.

11. SUNDAY. Upbeat. Positive trends continue to shower Scales with happiness and joy, although weariness may cause a few grumpy moments this morning. Don't rush to get up. Read the newspaper in bed, catching up on world and local events. Problems with a lover or a child could require exerting effort to help. Stay calm and deal with each issue individually until satisfactory solutions are found. Keep a sense of humor to release tension if a depressing atmosphere threatens to become overwhelming. By midday you will be ready to get back into the social scene. A gathering of friends, a reunion of schoolmates, or a party including extended family members should restore happy vibes.

12. MONDAY. Helpful. Today brings a positive merging of brain and brawn along with the ability to think before acting. Logic and understanding are increased, signifying a positive period to forge ahead with occupational matters and commercial activities. Put your best foot forward. A superior will appreciate your commitment and effort, and you could be put in line for a raise or promotion. The good news continues as jolly Jupiter now moves forward in Aquarius, the leisure, pleasure, and treasure sector of your solar chart. Life should begin to take off in a big, pleasant way. A marriage proposal could come along for singles, or a major sponsorship deal might be headline news for athletic Libras.

13. TUESDAY. Bountiful. Scales waiting for a pay increase could find that the delay is finally over. Versatile Venus, your ruler, merges with structured Saturn and smiles at active Mars, bringing financial rewards for past efforts. Emotions are more stable. Libras who are in a committed union will experience more love, warmth, and desirable moments together. Lonely singles should consider joining a group. People who share your interests can provide the comfort of knowing you belong to a community that shares a common bond. Setting a friend straight can be a positive move as long as this is done in a constructive and caring manner.

14. WEDNESDAY. Magnetic. Your ruler now moves in to greet and tantalize the Sun and Mercury in your own sign of Libra. Venus in your sign further enhances your popularity and activates your personal charisma. Your sensual nature is aroused, making this the time for love and romance. Pleasure can be gained by spoiling yourself with a few luxury treats that provide joy but don't break the bank. New clothes, updated cosmetic products, and an occasional massage can make you feel special as well as boost your confidence and self-esteem. Creativity peaks. This is an excellent period to sort though equipment and supplies needed to engage in a favored pastime or leisure pursuit.

15. THURSDAY. Circumspect. The present position of the Moon indicates that energy flow may be lower than usual. This contrasts with the higher sex appeal of Libras. Passion and desire are enhanced due to seductive Venus disputing with intense Pluto. An undesirable romantic liaison could be forged by the currently unattached. Emotional manipulation and issues of control might permeate an established union. An unprovoked incident may be upsetting and could be due to jealousy or the insecurities of your mate or partner. If single and going out looking for a good time, be careful not to make promises that you won't be able to keep. Be discerning when choosing a romantic partner.

16. FRIDAY. Diverse. Guard against complexity and complications. A bevy of cosmic energies is both helping and hindering advancement. Dynamo Mars is now visiting Leo, your house of hopes and wishes, for the remainder of the year. Grasp this chance to take the helm with a group enterprise. You know what needs to be done, and you have the vitality to do it. Mars in Leo can also be constructive for considering future plans and making adjustments to areas that require further action or effort. Libra creative juices are flowing. Enjoy time at home teaching youngsters a craft or pursuing a favored hobby on your own. Social plans should be enjoyable, but limit your consumption of alcohol.

17. SATURDAY. Bright. This ought to be a pleasant day as long as you take extra care when it comes to personal safety. Effort coupled with ambition can lead to stunning success, increasing satisfaction and pleasure. This is the time to shift into high gear, without allowing any obstacle to stand in your way. Libras who are inclined to self-pampering can spend a number of indulgent hours shopping at department stores or having a mini makeover at the beauty salon. An important, deep, and meaningful discussion with romantic overtones could be the beginning of an important change in your life. Before accepting the challenge of a commitment, be sure that you are ready to fully take on more responsibility.

18. SUNDAY. Revitalizing. The cosmos provides a wonderful uplifting energy to begin the day, with a New Moon arriving in your own sign of Libra. This marks the start of a fresh personal cycle when ambitions and aspirations can be fulfilled and future goals put in place. High-quality personal grooming and a pleasing appearance are important, and the next two weeks is the perfect time to plan a shopping expedition to update your wardrobe and also your overall image. Minor or major surgical enhancements of choice can be considered if they will boost self-confidence. If you opt for a more natural look, indulge in frequent massages and a fitness training program.

19. MONDAY. Rewarding. Sun, Venus, and Mercury are gracing your sign and your first house of physical appearance. You will enjoy roaming the stores for what would enhance your style and persona. Unforeseen expenditure could put a small dent in your savings. Having a lot of money doesn't guarantee happiness, and with innovative thinking and buying you can still have a lot of what you currently desire. The good news is that Lady Luck is standing by to give you a hand. Partner with friends to buy lottery tickets or raffle chances, increasing your chances of smiling all the way to the bank. Go out of your way to support a special charity by giving time, money, or both.

20. TUESDAY. Expansive. The day should fall nicely into place and life should be looking up. Data-gathering Mercury and bountiful Jupiter continue to shower luck your way, so make the most of this wonderful chance to move ahead. Enrolling in a class to broaden your outlook and advance your career aims could open up a whole new field of learning that can take you further than you ever envisioned. Opportunities for investment abound. This is also a good time to try your luck with a game of chance or a small speculation. If you have an important topic to discuss with a family member, now is an excellent time to openly communicate.

21. WEDNESDAY. Cautious. Guard against clumsiness and accidental breakages. This isn't the day to make decisions relating to love, cash flow, or issues relating to children. Your judgment is apt to be clouded, increasing the risk of errors. Put off purchasing a designer outfit even if it is on sale. Forget about updating your computer until the bank balance is a little healthier. Your romantic nature comes out in full force. However, expectations of a magical evening that includes a candlelit dinner, expensive champagne, and an attentive lover could be somewhat unrealistic and far-fetched. You probably will have to be content with companionship and cuddling on the couch.

22. THURSDAY. Varied. This is not the day to sit back and rest on your laurels. Abilities that you didn't realize you have could come to the fore. Using enhanced networking skills to your advantage can increase your social status and also assist career and business matters. Pay extra attention to helpful contacts, and make sure to communicate on the same level. Around lunchtime signs of restlessness will have to be managed by introducing new tasks into your routine or keeping on the move more than usual. Unless auto maintenance has been kept up to date, Libra drivers might experience a mechanical failure. Or you could be frustrated by a computer crash that results in lost information.

23. FRIDAY. Comforting. For Libras lucky enough to have time off, lazing around enjoying home comforts could be the activity of choice. For others, time may be devoted to planning ways to improve the overall appearance of your home or clearing space for the arrival of new furniture or electronics. Challenges in the financial arena are more than likely now as the Sun visits Scorpio, your house of material possessions and personal values. The urge to splurge will be strong. Libras with a weakness for shopping could blow the budget a couple of times over. Leave work at the front door and concentrate on those you love over the weekend.

24. SATURDAY. Lively. This is a time to get organized and get moving. Vim and vitality are high, and there will be lots of activity and action around home base. Forget any thoughts of relaxing; your on-the-go mood will have you active from daybreak to dusk. This is a good day to wield a paintbrush, spend some time raking leaves, or conduct a major decluttering in the house and garage. Drawing up plans for a major renovation or home extension should proceed smoothly, with plenty of creative and innovative ideas coming to the fore. A beneficial and interesting connection could be made that will help you take the next major step forward.

25. SUNDAY. Sociable. Be sure to keep track of invitations, appointments, and meetings to ensure that none are overlooked. Mental overload and social fatigue could cause a lapse of memory. A full calendar might be exciting but could cause burnout if activities are not paced. A flirty attitude assists shy singles seeking new love. Confidence is currently boosted, so don't hesitate to mix and mingle more than usual. For those in a partnership, romance receives an extra boost of loving vibes. Socializing should provide ample happy enjoyment. Don't neglect to acknowledge a child's achievement, no matter how small; this will increase their pride.

26. MONDAY. Uncertain. On this uneasy day nothing will go quite the way you'd like or planned. However, with the Moon in quirky Aquarius, a welcome break from routine could appeal even if chaos reigns. Remain alert and you should be able to overcome most of the upsets that slow down progress. Use your time positively by reviewing your strengths as well as areas that could do with some improvement. Focus on your overall well-being, especially the idea of replacing negative habits that are a risk to your health with an improved lifestyle. Current cosmic vibes are strengthening loving ties. The ability for both you and your loved one to compromise increases warmth and contentment.

27. TUESDAY. Carefree. More relaxed trends exist now. A sociable mood increases your spirits. You may prefer to forget chores and just enjoy yourself instead, but this might not be possible. At least plan to go out for a meal or to the movies or a club with a favored companion. If preparing for an upcoming special celebration you can make good progress by contacting caterers, checking out venues, and arranging the many varied minor details that go into making a big day even better. Arranging a future game of tennis or golf with workmates will increase bonds and help you maintain good working relationships.

28. WEDNESDAY. Favorable. Expect an expensive but enjoyable day. Excellent celestial trends are sending good luck and love to provide generous assistance for all your plans. You may be in the mood to spend in an extravagant fashion, which is fine if you can afford it. However, taking a more moderate approach could save upset later on when credit card bills arrive in the mail. Your mind should be focused on generating income now that communicative Mercury is settling into Scorpio, your house of monetary assets and possessions. Plans to make and spend money gain momentum. Increased profits could come through writing, selling, or public speaking.

29. THURSDAY. Major. A significant planetary change takes place now with Saturn, planet of structure and restriction, moving into your own sign of Libra. The urge to stop being a couch potato or to kick a bad habit receives a boost from the cosmic universe. Libras hoping to lose weight before the upcoming festive season can be successful if you begin now. You are being asked to take yourself more seriously, to walk your talk, and to figure out not just who you are but who you want to be. Expect to be busy as you turn away from the past and look to the future. Become more involved with your own life, and take steps to make your goals and dreams become reality.

30. FRIDAY. Promising. Adrenaline is pumping, encouraging you to focus on major plans without holding back. You might be willing to put the needs of other people before your own, but don't give in to the unreasonable demands of loved ones. Difficulties with a business or personal partner are anticipated. A contingency plan may be essential to provide both of you with enough space to stand back from the firing line. There may be conflict over someone's possessive behavior; you won't take kindly to this type of attitude. As the working week comes to a close, try to slow down a little. Avoid an inclination to continue at breakneck speed rather than moving at a more leisurely pace.

31. SATURDAY. Restless. You are bound to feel a little pressured and on edge. Blockages are likely in a number of areas, or you might feel that someone is standing in your way. Appliances and machinery could go on the blink. Libras who are on the job can expect eruptions from workmates or customers. Be discerning if making any purchases or you might end up with faulty merchandise or items that you thought were suitable but don't seem so once you get home. Since it is Halloween, light the pumpkin, dress up in the weirdest costume you can concoct, and slip into a party mood.

NOVEMBER

1. SUNDAY. Taxing. Life could be a little stressful but only if you allow problems to weigh you down. You might think it is best to say exactly what you think, but this isn't the case. It would be wiser to choose your words carefully. If there is a concern about money, it is pointless worrying about how you are going to pay upcoming expenses. Instead, take a proactive approach by recording all income and expenditure to see where cost cutting can be most effective. If planning an outing with friends, make sure everyone knows beforehand about entertainment expenses to avoid objections regarding their fair share.

2. MONDAY. Upsetting. Disruption arrives today, although it isn't all bad news. Your ruler Venus is wearing rose-colored glasses, awakening your emotional side as she showers love and romance in her wake. This is a good time to pop that all-important question. Or you may receive a special ring as a token of love. The Taurus Full Moon can bring you back to earth with a thud as financial problems have to be sorted out. Libras employed in the field of finances, including debt collection, should be prepared to listen to rude and cranky customers sound off. Promises of any kind are not reliable.

3. TUESDAY. Demanding. Money is again the main priority. There may be a pressing need to complete a tax return or other financial paperwork. If this task is outstanding, take action now to lessen the chance of a fine. A relationship could have you highly emotional, but this isn't the time to make any concrete decision or choices. If your energy is drained due to the pressure of too many obligations, duties, or demands of loved ones, consider taking frequent breaks to clear your head. An unexpected gift or compliment should restore your good humor this evening.

4. WEDNESDAY. Expansive. Consider learning a foreign language if this will help you move up the career ladder. Libras who are involved in overseas trading, political interests, or public relations should make excellent progress. A legal decision could be in your favor. However, don't refuse to accept an out-of-court settlement if this would save you or a family member a lot of stress and strain. Meeting a romantic potential from another country could be a highlight for singles, and love on the high seas is possible for the traveling Libra. Exotic fare might appeal to your taste buds this evening, so book a table at an ethnic restaurant and savor tantalizing flavors from another country or culture.

5. THURSDAY. Excellent. Libra folks will be on the financial ball as the Sun meets up with alert Mercury. Your ability for organization and to get everyone working together enhances your profile. Very little will escapes your eagle eye. One problem could be nonstop interruptions from visitors or phone calls, reducing your productivity unless you lock the office and hide away. You have what it takes to excel in an individual sport or a team event, earning better than expected results. Seriously consider an offer to go into business with a relative, which may provide the independence you currently seek.

6. FRIDAY. Satisfactory. Advice, whether solicited or not, from those closest to you might not be what you want to hear but is nevertheless worth listening to. You don't have to rush ahead with a decision. First weigh all your options, which is something Libra folks are very good at doing. At last pressure is easing and creative juices should again flow freely now that Neptune, planet of inspiration, is moving forward again in Aquarius, your house of artistic expression and talents. A sponsorship deal that has been held up, news relating to exhibiting or publishing your work, or a romance that has been stalled could benefit and advance thanks to this cosmic change.

7. SATURDAY. Fine. Be discerning if shopping for electronic products or communication equipment. Check out warranties thoroughly, and compare prices to get the best deal. Libras who are at work should enjoy being singled out for special mention by the boss or another supervisor. There might even be mention of a pay increase or extra benefits coming your way. Luscious Venus joins the Sun to grace your Scorpio sector of material assets and finances. Venus in Scorpio enhances your ability to attract more money as well as the beautiful things of life. Desiring additional comfort, pleasure, and goodies has a downside, however, because spending more than you can afford is likely.

8. SUNDAY. Manageable. Look before you leap, and beware of promising more than you may be able to comfortably deliver. Minor irritations could grow into large annoyances unless you maintain a calm, cool demeanor. Restrictions abound, with energy slightly under par. This suggests a rest rather than running all over would be of benefit. Prudence is in order. Putting money in a savings account could be the best way to begin managing the future instead of heading off to the boutiques or music store. A speech or public address could be enlightening when it comes to trouble in your community or the wider world.

9. MONDAY. Exciting. Love and romance permeate the air as sexy Venus ignites passionate Pluto. The next few days is a perfect period to make romantic plans, arrange a honeymoon, or plan a sensuous candlelight dinner for two. Splurging on fancy luxury items could be difficult to avoid unless you exercise extra willpower. Friends or associates may let you down, so if plans depend on them be prepared to be left to your own devices. Self-employed Libras or contractors who haven't increased fees for their services for some time should consider doing so now. The currently single can expect a dynamic new attraction.

10. TUESDAY. Moderate. Find a quiet place so you can spend some time in solitude. Although as a Libra you are a social sign, you realize the value of peace and tranquillity. Being alone provides the chance to contemplate life in your own good time, without distractions and interruptions. Although your intentions may be exemplary, expectations of what you and others are capable of achieving may be too high right now. A moderate approach needs to be taken. The inclination to eat and drink to excess must be curtailed or it could result in health problems now or in the future. Care with credit is advised. Be sure to include a few early relaxing evenings in your busy schedule over the ensuing weeks.

11. WEDNESDAY. Bumpy. This could be a trying, tiring, but exciting day as Mercury makes a positive connection with erratic Uranus and debates dreamy Neptune. Although major decision making isn't recommended, procrastination by other people could lead to frustration and annoyance. Concentration is limited as restlessness takes hold. The tendency to daydream instead of mentally focusing could cause problems. Spend some time composing a love song or painting an original masterpiece rather than trying to make sense of facts, figures, and an overload of demands and requests. Plan to do something totally different from your usual Wednesday night routine.

12. THURSDAY. Calm. With the Moon still gliding through your Virgo house of solitude, you will still prefer peace and serenity at least until lunchtime. Until then watch and wait rather than beginning any new project or moving into action. Emotions might be close to the surface and could spill over at any time. Virgo is the sign of service par excellence. However, with the Moon here a fussy or pedantic attitude is often seen, which could get people's backs up and create upsets or tension. Later in the day good humor and the urge to socialize return with a vengeance. Take time to pamper yourself without feeling guilty, especially if this is not your normal habit.

13. FRIDAY. Promising. There isn't any need to worry about today's date. Apart from a few minor obstacles, the day should hum along nicely. If you enter a competition, purchase a raffle ticket, or play the lottery you could be surprised by luck turning in your favor. A unique and challenging personal undertaking might be just what you need to display your capabilities to one or more important people. A sudden rise in responsibilities could mean you have to make some minor adjustments. Reschedule where you can to reduce the possibility of stress due to work overload. Social plans this evening should be memorable.

14. SATURDAY. Adaptable. A flexible approach can assist your efforts to overcome hurdles and stay on your chosen path. Before making any financial decisions, consider all of your options and think them through thoroughly. This is an excellent period to research methods of increasing income and reducing expenditure. Your positive spirit and determined effort will be rewarded. Extra exertion to promote your skills and expertise can produce financial advantages. If attempting to demonstrate your talent to the public at large, consider hiring an agent or management team to publicize your work or products.

15. SUNDAY. Exacting. A major planetary pattern has formed in the cosmic sky. Libra folks could be experiencing limitations and transformation of personal desires and ambitions. In addition, unsettling situations are apt to be occurring around home base. To cope with current influences, altering your outlook and perspective is required. Although this is a time of change, don't be persuaded by other people to follow their wishes if this is contrary to your desires. Money that comes in quickly is likely to go out in the same manner unless you can stem the flow and tighten the money drain. Check out the credentials of those with whom you conduct business; taking people at face value is not advisable right now.

16. MONDAY. Renewing. Enjoy today's more optimistic atmosphere. Mercury, planet of information, is now residing in Sagittarius, highlighting your solar sector of short travel and all forms of communication. A business trip to add contacts and customers should lead to desired results, with an increase in sales and goodwill. Be careful of a get-rich proposal around midday. Forget about gambling or playing any games of chance, or prepare to be parted from your hard-earned cash. A New Moon in Scorpio, your personal financial house, increases your focus on monetary matters.

Over the next two weeks take the opportunity to implement new financial ventures and projects.

17. TUESDAY. Disciplined. Ambition and self-control are gifts now promised. Dreams and desires currently being sought could be found where never expected. This is a great day to practice your listening skills. If you are ready to engage in serious discussion with a relative, the stars are supporting your endeavor. Praise for your efforts could come from those higher up the ladder than you, which can be a wonderful boost to your self-confidence. Choose companions who are likely to talk about serious, deep topics rather than merely gossip. You will consider petty issues not worthy of your attention.

18. WEDNESDAY. Active. The atmosphere should be more easygoing today, with Scales optimistic and energetic. A brisk stroll around the neighborhood could get your heart pumping and provide an opportunity to increase your fitness level. If you are not on the job, a gossip session with friends or neighbors could put you in a good frame of mind. Running errands and performing personal tasks might have you on the go. The organized Libra could begin sourcing gifts, cards, and decorations to get ready for the upcoming festive season. A romantic interlude this evening can round off the day nicely, or you might prefer to curl up on the couch with a new novel or DVD.

19. THURSDAY. Passionate. Unless activity involves romance, you probably won't be in the mood for anything too strenuous or demanding. Affectionate Venus is in conflict with assertive Mars, creating tension in your love life. A committed relationship could be tested, challenging the depth of your union. With passion more likely to be on display than affection, couples shouldn't have any trouble adding extra zest in the bedroom. Libras who are in a blossoming new love affair should guard against comparing an old flame with a new one, which will only create tension and dissatisfaction. Being surrounded by those you love most will appeal this evening.

20. FRIDAY. Fair. A number of obstacles are slowing progress, but these are only minor and can be quickly and easily overcome. You may find it difficult to please yourself, let alone others, unless you are in familiar surroundings performing routine tasks. Puttering around at home, cleaning, making minor repairs, and focusing on household chores can be a positive way to utilize current cosmic forces. It might be time to begin cooking and baking and planning for the festive season. Emotional happiness and contentment come from being with family members, so opt for a night at home if possible instead of hectic socializing on the town.

21. SATURDAY. Happy. If your relationship with a family member has been a bit difficult, finding a way to overcome grievances and feel more comfortable should be easier now. A child could be anxious for your attention, which may add extra pressure to your already overloaded schedule. Giving your undivided attention at least for a short period can be helpful. By midnight tonight the Sun will enter the sign of Sagittarius, joining Mercury there until December 21. This provides you with the opportunity to meet and mingle with friends you haven't seen for some time. Socializing moves into top gear as you head into the holiday period.

22. SUNDAY. Enjoyable. A mini sabbatical could appeal this morning. Catching up on your beauty sleep or cuddling in bed can be the perfect beginning to the day. With socializing playing a major role in your life over the next few weeks, this is the time to make plans and become well organized. Bright ideas should be flowing freely, which will help with the many upcoming tasks that need a unique, creative touch. Purchasing gifts, arranging an end-of-year party, or planning a gathering of family members and friends will benefit from your original thoughts. The mood to party carries into activities planned for today, and whatever event you attend should bring pleasure.

23. MONDAY. Cautious. Remain clam and handle one task at a time. There is a lot to fit into your schedule, but rushing around in an uproar will just make matters worse rather than easier. When your ruler Venus is in dispute with excessive Jupiter, the word moderation needs to be clearly etched into your memory. Otherwise you could spend a small fortune without realizing it on food, alcohol, and entertainment. Postpone shopping for gifts; an overly generous attitude could increase the temptation to buy more than you intend. Delays or disappointment regarding a friend could overshadow a planned social event.

24. TUESDAY. Opportune. Life has a lot to offer to those born under the sign of Libra. Patience and self-discipline are abundant. Past efforts and accomplishments may be recognized, raising both your confidence and profile. Methodical planning can be the best way to obtain what is required. Progress comes through practical endeavors. The motivation to set goals and act on tasks that you would normally ignore moves to another level. Take the opportunity to go on a road trip with friends; you never know where this could lead, either now or sometime in the future. Social connections could be particularly useful, and mixing business with pleasure should add more dollars to your bank balance.

25. WEDNESDAY. Pleasant. A sociable, fun-loving frame of mind arrives with the advent of saucy Venus happily linked to excitable Uranus. Expect to receive a pleasant surprise some time within the next few days. For some Libras a marriage proposal could bring a thrill of anticipation. An intimate meeting this evening could excite the currently unattached. However, this is a time to enjoy the moment without holding out hopes of a long-lasting relationship. There is a possibility that a friendship could begin to have romantic overtones. If this is what you desire, it is time to make the first move. Good luck abounds, and finances should be looking up.

26. THURSDAY. Volatile. Conditions do an abrupt turn when it comes to love and money. In romance it is now time to proceed slowly and remove those rose-colored glasses. With a difficult contact between seductive Venus and foggy Neptune, senses and sensibility can be clouded. If in doubt, do nothing at all. Deceitful maneuvers by other people need to be guarded against. Your judgment may not be very sound. Avoid the temptation of shopping in stores that are open. An impractical mood makes you an obvious target. Creative activities will be fueled by the combination of raw talent, inspiration, and enthusiasm, leading to greater output and productivity. Enjoy a get-together, but don't promise anything to anyone.

27. FRIDAY. Tense. Libra folk need all the patience that you can muster now. Other people are unlikely to be cooperative, and a team effort that appeared to be moving along smoothly could come to a grinding halt. Mediation or compromise may be required before relationships can be put back on track. Be firm and sure about what you are seeking in a relationship. Avoid conveying mixed messages to your significant other. If you are not seeing eye-to-eye with a personal or business partner, it might be because one of you wants to handle things differently from the way they were done in the past. Initiate a discussion so you can talk about the best direction to take.

28. SATURDAY. Smooth. If you stay calm and centered, positive results can be achieved. With the lunar goddess sending mainly positive vibes, life should become easier as confusion and uncertainty regarding home and love life begin to disappear. With a

sense of direction regained, and confidence in your own ability returning, this is the time to sort out money issues, research investment opportunities, and prepare to move into a better personal
space. A shopping trip with your significant other or a friend can be
fun, and you should do well when it comes to picking up quality
items at bargain prices. A social occasion certainly shouldn't be dull
or boring.

29. SUNDAY. Interesting. This is another day when there should be
plenty of reasons to smile. An easygoing mood increases your
charm and personality. Spending time with favorite people will enhance your enjoyment of the day. With abundant luck shining your
way, you are likely to be in the right place at the right time. Any involvement with communication, from public speaking to writing out
greeting cards, should proceed well. If you should need to talk your
way out of a tight situation, you shouldn't experience any problems.
It will be essential to keep all dealings aboveboard and avoid any
dangerous areas.

30. MONDAY. Erratic. As the month winds down, you may feel
you have been on a roller-coaster ride, with as many ups as downs.
This trend continues today as talkative Mercury disputes with erratic Uranus. This is exactly how you may feel toward those who
never stop talking or don't know when enough is more than enough.
Restlessness and indecision peak, and negative or insensitive comments could test your patience. Don't take matters personally and, if
possible, look on the funny side. Tomorrow a more peaceful atmosphere should prevail. Avoid haste, drive slowly, and walk instead of
running.

DECEMBER

1. TUESDAY. Restless. Although the beginning of this month
should flow quite smoothly, this is one of those days when you may
feel unsettled and restless without knowing why. Dissatisfaction
with the way your life is heading might be the cause. Adding variety
to your daily routine can break the tedium and increase your enjoyment of looking forward to each day. If your love life has been a
little up and down recently, it should now begin to settle down.
With the transit of Venus in Sagittarius, your third house, from now

until December 25, communication and interaction with friends and children should be more joyous than usual.

2. WEDNESDAY. Sensitive. Scales are likely to be in a hurry today, with one eye on the clock and the other on the overflowing in-basket. If you are trying to meet a deadline, take into account that the Full Moon is culminating in Gemini, increasing not only your sensitive feelings but those of everyone else in close proximity to you. This is an excellent period to complete a special project, sales report, or book manuscript. Keep an open mind and be receptive to other people's points of view. Uranus, the planet of originality, has now moved forward in the Pisces house of work, service, and health, so changes can be expected in some of these areas. Unsettling rumors that have been circulating on the job could be officially refuted, giving you an increased sense of security.

3. THURSDAY. Opportune. A much more relaxing day is likely, although you will be inclined to put extra effort in the career and professional arena. A business meeting can be informative and productive, with a number of nagging issues discussed and resolved. Valuable data could be received from a mentor, which may be the encouragement you need to look for a better paying position that also increases job satisfaction. Singles should not object if a friend wants to play matchmaker; a romantic opportunity could develop through such an introduction. Lucky Libras will be given lots of love and warmth and encouragement at home.

4. FRIDAY. Positive. Your ruler Venus happily connects with serious Saturn, bringing a practical, structured, realistic tone to romance and to fiscal management. During the next few days Libra shoppers will be determined to get value for money and will be more discerning with all purchases. In a discussion with an older relative, listen carefully. You could hear information that is transforming, setting you on a more positive path. The ties of love are strong. Libras who are in a new relationship should not be surprised if it takes on a more serious tone. This is a good time to consider beginning a family or adding a pet to your household.

5. SATURDAY. Buoyant. Love and blessings continue to surround you. Enrolling in a short course can increase your knowledge and expertise. In addition, it might be the meeting place for the unattached to find a romantic potential. Formulating plans for a child's education could keep Libra parents positively occupied. A major purchase can bring loads of enjoyment for the whole family. Mercury, planet of information, slips into Capricorn, your zone of home and family, which will focus attention on the domestic quarters. If you have plans to redecorate, look for inspirational ideas in magazines or on Internet sites catering in particular to homeowners.

6. SUNDAY. Enjoyable. You will enjoy a change of scenery. If you have been rushing around, socializing, shopping, and trying to keep on top of a heavy schedule, this is the time to do something that pleases you. Get out and about and you may even find a new haunt or store that you haven't noticed before. A friendship might be a little rocky, no longer delivering the companionship and comfort that it once did; don't feel guilty. People come in and out of your life for a reason, so just move on, cultivating new friends who fit into your current lifestyle. If you haven't brought out festive decorations for your home, now would be a good time to start. Take advantage of the party season and have fun.

7. MONDAY. Revealing. Your deep, penetrating mind combined with enhanced verbal skills will be of great assistance if you are giving a speech, delivering a lecture, or presenting a special honor. If you have a complaint that needs to be addressed, go right to the top person. Compassion could be hard to muster for someone you feel is not making the most of opportunities offered. However, you might need to put these thoughts aside and provide guidance and wisdom. Tact and diplomacy are in ample supply, helping to phrase your thoughts in the best way. This is a great time to visit a holistic healer or alternative therapist to obtain help with an ongoing ailment or to keep your body in top shape.

8. TUESDAY. Manageable. If a cloud descends on you today, rest and relaxation may be something you aim for but are unlikely to achieve. Although your Libra mental alertness remains accentuated, you might be inclined to ask awkward questions or suffer from foot-in-mouth disease. This could easily occur if anger or frustration overcomes you, so do your best to remain cool and detached. This should reduce the possibility of embarrassing yourself or someone else. Working on a project in secret can provide a great deal of satisfaction. A long soak in a warm bath before going to bed could be the perfect end to this tricky day.

9. WEDNESDAY. Vexing. Unhelpful cosmic influences prevail. The sensitive mood makes this a difficult day, at least until late in the afternoon. Escape from pent-up stress by going for a walk around the block, meditating, or finding a place where you can chill out for a little while. For most of the working day you will want to shun social activities and mixing with other people because the preference to work alone is strong. A change of plans could find you committed to finalizing a project that has been on the back burner for some time. An ongoing health condition could reappear, signaling that it is time to do something constructive about the problem now, not later.

10. THURSDAY. Vital. Although you could wake up feeling a little weary, a burst of vitality will fuel your motivation and drive. You could even help someone in bad humor become happy. Put this influx of energy into the right medium, which could include pursuing a personal ambition, achieving a cherished goal, or playing a competitive sport. Status improves as other people notice your achievements. Praise for your efforts from a superior could also include an incentive to keep up the good work or a bonus recognizing current accomplishments. Make evening plans that include getting together with friends.

11. FRIDAY. Bumpy. Imagination combined with insecurity could get the better of you. With tricky Mercury rubbing Neptune the wrong way, concentration and confidence are apt to take a plunge. The tendency to daydream rises. Instead of focusing on tasks at hand, your head may be in the clouds, which could bring the wrath of a superior. Be on guard for cheats, scammers, and double-dealers. If something looks too good to be true, it probably is. Whatever way a situation develops right now, someone is going to wind up disgruntled or disappointed. Although Libra intuition is enhanced, acting on a hunch would not be a bright move now.

12. SATURDAY. Fulfilling. The focus turns to ways to improve your financial situation and increase security. The urge to spend on loved ones could be the signal to begin or finish festive shopping. You have the intuitive ability to know what each of your nearest and dearest desires. An unusual purchase could turn out to be a collector's item, worth every cent you pay. There may be a chance to reignite a relationship with someone who has drifted away. Or ongoing difficulties with a friend could be resolved to everyone's satisfaction, with no more hard feelings standing in the way of an enduring friendship. Love and friendship are the perfect mix.

13. SUNDAY. Surprising. Breakfast in bed courtesy of your significant other would be a terrific beginning to this busy day. Tricky trends prevail, suggesting it would be wise to keep a low profile if possible. Decorating the house, writing out greeting cards, or preparing festive food may be the most productive way to keep busy and away from the firing line. A dispute about money could erupt when someone objects to what they consider an unfair distribution of household funds. Although this might not be a pleasant discussion, it would be better to bring the matter out into the open to reduce the chance of escalating resentment. Someone could give you a special treat or surprise gift.

14. MONDAY. Mixed. Ambiguous trends are in play as the Sun challenges erratic Uranus and smiles at abundant Jupiter. As a Libra you should thrive on the ensuing activity and disruptions that are likely throughout the day. However, there should be an equal amount of good luck, raising your spirits and adding pleasure to whatever you undertake. It could be all too easy to jump to conclusions based on biased or inaccurate information, so don't accept what you hear without first checking the facts. Remain optimistic, but beware becoming overly confident. A big ego will not serve you well.

15. TUESDAY. Creative. Take full advantage of current celestial trends which heighten insight, sensitivity, and understanding. Awareness of your own special talents can help you shine through in a magical way. With strong imagination and the ability to mentally visualize, any work that needs a special touch should progress well. Events should move in your favor. Success can come from converting people to your way of thinking. Your focus might not be strong, so minimize the possibility of errors by delaying filling out an application, sending important e-mails, or writing business letters. If you are considering resigning from your current position, postpone this action unless the decision was made some time ago.

16. WEDNESDAY. Exciting. You may receive good news, or someone may sing your praises. A long-awaited invitation can add excitement. You could finally acquire something desired for a long time. The New Moon in the sign of freedom-loving Sagittarius puts an extra spring in your step and a song in your heart. The way you communicate is in the spotlight. This is a time that messages can be conveyed in a powerful and positive way. Contact neighbors and relatives if you haven't been in a touch for a while. Finish writing cards, letters, and e-mails to the special people in your life.

17. THURSDAY. Fervent. Sexual energy is strong and focused as a romantic haze drifts pleasingly across the Libra landscape. Amorous Venus smiles at passionate Mars, signaling that this is the time to experience fun and enjoyment. It's the season to be merry, and although you may be in a frenzy with domestic chores and family demands, make time to strengthen loving bonds with your significant other. Roll up your sleeves and prepare for guests, finish small decorating chores, and discard clutter in your living quarters. If a new car is on your wish list, this is a good day to search for the perfect new set of wheels.

18. FRIDAY. Active. High spirits continue, although if you have thoughts of taking it easy these may be dashed. Even if a mountain of work is awaiting your attention, the industrious Capricorn Moon provides the energy to handle numerous tasks before festive celebrating gets under way. Listen to what a friend has to say; their words could have a very positive impact on your future plans. A sensitive family issue could be resolved during dinner, clearing the way for a happier remainder of the month. Home should be a haven. Don't feel guilty if you prefer family company instead of performing household chores.

19. SATURDAY. Intriguing. The sky is awash with planetary action. The indomitable duo of lover Venus and erotic Uranus is likely to wreak havoc on the love scene. This could further shake up an already rocky relationship. Beware thinking that the grass is greener, behavior that can lead to problems you would be better off without. Guard against impulsive action, and don't get carried away and spend more than you intended. A strange experience is possible, so be prepared for the unexpected. Singles should investigate a new venue or meet-and-greet method in an attempt to get to know interesting new romantic possibilities.

20. SUNDAY. Restrained. Look forward to an extremely pleasant day. Make time to socialize. Your outgoing personality will make you a star among family members and friends. People are counting on you, and it is unlikely that you will let anyone down. Beware overly benevolent gestures, however. Your generosity may know no bounds, which will not be good news for your budget if you need to finish holiday shopping. It will be easy to go overboard; the temptation to splurge on luxury items could be hard to resist. With your ruler Venus happily entwined with Jupiter, the planet of excess, luck is on your side. However, moderation is still essential.

Buy a lottery ticket, enter a raffle, or take some other small risk; you may be very glad you did.

21. MONDAY. Dreamy. A wistful atmosphere prevails, making this the sort of day that romantic Libras love. It is an especially good time to be with your nearest and dearest, so you might prefer to remain at home rather than venturing outside. With your creative imagination extremely high, you can complete tasks that need an artistic touch. You may tend to take on too many responsibilities which could cause stress, so remember to pace yourself. The Sun now visits the sign of Capricorn, shining the spotlight on your home and family sector. You will probably prefer to entertain in the comfort of your own home rather than socializing in a public place.

22. TUESDAY. Hectic. Duty calls. If you will be hosting a holiday meal, make final preparations, stock up the fridge and pantry, and be sure you have enough chairs for your guests. There is a danger of going overboard with lavish catering and expensive gifts, so ask yourself if you can really afford to be so generous and whether it is necessary to do so. A pet could be the perfect present for someone who is alone, lonely, or has hinted about getting one. Even a goldfish in a bowl will give pleasure and comfort to a special person. Allowing youngsters to have some say in planning the holiday period will increase their sense of responsibility and participation.

23. WEDNESDAY. Productive. Family members are probably relying on you, but try not to get too stressed. If are a large amount of tasks remain to be done, make a list of priorities and methodically work from the most important down. In that way essential chores will be completed. As a Libra you tend to prefer quality to quantity, and things should be looking up in that area. If you are in the mood to shop, unexpected bargains can be found, assisting the household budget and helping you to make the upcoming holidays a little bit more special. With the excitement of Christmas, baking traditional treats and wrapping presents can include the whole family. Be sure to include both young and old in your plans.

24. THURSDAY. Festive. A strong competitive nature is evident, so take action and seize opportunities that come your way. Libras who are on the job can make good headway. Your natural leadership qualities and assertiveness can assist your climb up the career ladder. Although this is a busy festive time, don't allow yourself to become a doormat to the demands and needs of other people. A frenetic atmosphere may prevail at home, and it might be difficult to avoid getting enmeshed in the power plays of others. Family traditions will come to the fore, adding a special touch to celebrations. Spiritual activities could appeal, and attending a candlelight service should delight family members of all ages.

25. FRIDAY. Happy Holiday! As with most planned events, not everything will flow exactly as you envisioned. There may be a few obstacles to overcome, but these can add to the collection of family memories and recollections. Don't attempt to do everything yourself if hosting guests. Your vim and vitality could be lower than usual, making everything seem just a little bit harder and more stressful. Pay special attention to elderly relatives to ensure they are included in all that's going on; otherwise complaints could be upsetting. Your ruler Venus spreads blessings over the day with her entrance into Capricorn, your family sector. So Libras should find that a mostly calm and peaceful atmosphere will prevail on this holiday.

26. SATURDAY. Useful. This day will be very much influenced by mischievous Mercury. From now until January 15 the messenger planet will be moving in retrograde motion through Capricorn, your sector of real estate and family activities. It would be wise to limit purchases to essential items only and nothing major. Signing property leases and legal documents can be risky unless you double-check them for errors and hidden clauses. The post-Christmas sales are likely to excite you, and there should be plenty of quality bargains to tempt the savvy Libra shopper. Consider your goals for 2010 and begin making a list.

27. SUNDAY. Chancy. Life can be a balancing act, and there is no one that understands that more than a Libra. Today you can begin to unwind after the recent hectic round of socializing. Tiredness and lack of energy could be the encouragement you need to take it easy and rest. Playing computer games, enjoying the last of the left-over festive fare, and relaxing with a good book may be preferred amusement for those without social plans. If tempers become frayed from being cooped up, take a walk to burn off stress. Someone may be in a hurry to receive a promised payment, so if you owe money either pay in full or set a definite time when you can do so.

28. MONDAY. Intense. Your ruler sets the tone of the day, merging with intense Pluto and glaring at warrior Mars. Passion and emotional intensity are in force, and it is essential to keep alert for the green eye of jealousy. It definitely is the day to make love, not war. Personal attachments are more meaningful now. Your significant other could feel threatened or might be uncharacteristically possessive and controlling. A public display of emotions could be embarrassing and awkward if the situation is allowed to get out of hand. Good news can bring happiness to the family. Libras who are trying to conceive or adopt may experience luck now.

29. TUESDAY. Subdued. A serious atmosphere pervades the air. Focus on necessary tasks. Be careful when dealing with women who are older than you. Love takes a backseat, which you will probably be unhappy about. The romantic energy in your current relationship could be blocked, or your mate or partner might not be as responsive as usual, but don't react negatively. These influences will pass in a few days, so be proactive and show by your actions how much you care. Studying in order to constructively use your spare time or to further career advancement can be productive, particularly if you are hoping to increase your income in the new year.

30. WEDNESDAY. Uncertain. Emotions could still be unclear now for Scales who are in a committed relationship. However, absence can make the heart grow fonder for those living apart from a significant other, and you could be intently experiencing these feelings now. If possible, get in touch via e-mail or phone so you can renew loving bonds. Making a decision as to how and where to celebrate New Year's Eve could be difficult for Libras, known as the procrastinators of the zodiac. It might be wiser to make up your mind tomorrow, when you have a clearer idea of what entertainment will offer the most fun.

31. THURSDAY. Disconcerting. The cosmic dance of the planets sends an interesting mix of influences to end the year, but most of these are unsupportive. If a work bonus is not as high as you expected, or a promised pay raise or promotion hasn't come through, don't approach the boss today because you'll only get the runaround. Libras on the job may be very pleased at the end of the day, after encountering more than a fair share of upsets. With an eclipsed Full Moon in Cancer, you can expect cranky, emotional people to be out in force. A get-together of family members and friends may be the best choice if you would prefer a sedate gathering this evening rather than a wild night on the town.

LIBRA
NOVEMBER–DECEMBER 2008

November 2008

1. SATURDAY. Good. The best way to handle morning influences is to stay with your usual routine as much as possible rather than trying anything new. An ongoing creative project or plan should be well worth the effort, however. Make the most of inspiring thoughts and ideas. Take your credit card along if heading to the mall because you are likely to get an urge to purchase a new communication product such as a cell phone or computer software. If there are a few expensive items you would like to add to your collection, perhaps dropping a holiday gift hint to family members would be a smart move.

2. SUNDAY. Constructive. Finances permitting, it may be time to consider hiring someone to help with domestic chores if juggling employment and household duties is becoming too much for you. If this does not fit in with your budget and you are the one continually expected to perform most tasks, drawing up a duty roster of shared chores could be the answer. Neptune, the planet of illusion, is now moving forward in Aquarius, your house of creative expression, pleasure, children, and romance. The courage needed to stand up and face problems regarding these matters can now be found. Libras involved in a new relationship could benefit from spending more quality time together.

3. MONDAY. Difficult. This is not a very easy day, and it could be made worse by a tendency to put yourself down or to think gloomy thoughts. Increased tension or clashes are foreseen, possibly involving issues underlying both love and money. Over the next couple of days emotional warmth may be missing from your romantic relationship as seductive Venus challenges structured Saturn and erratic Uranus. This is a passing phase, and now is not the time to make waves or cause disruptions. Financial action that you have been deferring might be required sooner rather than later, but think carefully before signing anything that would be legally binding.

231

4. TUESDAY. Balanced. Serious Saturn opposes disruptive Uranus, conveying a need to balance your drive and determination with enthusiasm and insight. Goals can be achieved if immediate action is taken. This is the time to make positive moves. Don't fear making changes in the workplace or around home base. The pen is mightier than the sword, so if you have something to say but are not sure how to adequately express your feelings out loud, write a letter to your lover, to the local newspaper editor, or to a sick friend. Libras employed in areas where communication is vital should experience increased productivity because insight, understanding, and expression are greater than usual.

5. WEDNESDAY. Fulfilling. Creative and romantic vibes are strong. Yesterday communicative Mercury entered Scorpio, joining the Sun and Mars there in your house of personal finances and possessions Thinking and talking about what you value most may give you added insight as well as the ability to make informed decisions regarding your current status. If doing some early festive shopping is on your agenda, finding perfect gifts and goodies is more than likely. If the kids have been cooped up, Libra parents might need to loosen the reins a little to give them more freedom and independence. An intimate setting at home might be the preferred choice of entertainment tonight.

6. THURSDAY. Disconcerting. Do your best to rearrange your schedule to add variety and light relief. In that way there is less chance of becoming bogged down by routine. An accident and careless mistakes could occur if your concentration is allowed to lapse. Confirm details and information before taking action because there is a tendency to jump to conclusions before asking relevant questions. Breakage or faults around the house will cause irritation, particularly when it comes to having to pay good money for replacements. If you take on too much, nervous tension and stress could spoil your day.

7. FRIDAY. Interesting. Remember to think positively. Negative thinking can lead to a negative outcome. Don't ignore small disputes that might be escalating behind the scenes. Follow up and do your best to quell these to the satisfaction of all. Seeing what's available in high-end stores could be a delightful experience, especially if a shopping expedition is combined with meeting friends or your partner for coffee, lunch, or dinner. You could cultivate new contacts and develop an important association through a business meeting, interview, or audition. Although you might be expected to turn up for a social event, other options could beckon.

8. SATURDAY. Hectic. With too many chores and errands on your agenda today, you could end up becoming scattered by trying to do everything and accomplishing very little. It might be wise to make a list, then start at the top and work through one chore at a time. If health and fitness require a boost, be on the lookout for secondhand gym equipment that will help you maintain a healthy body. Scour the newspaper or cyber space and you might pick up a number of quality bargains. Plan an occasion at home with your significant other, or arrange an elegant social gathering for favorite friends.

9. SUNDAY. Calm. Rest and relax. Catch up on reading or participate in some other relaxing pursuit that eases tension and wipes away stress. Leave household tasks and take the time to enjoy a leisurely day. There could be a tricky period this morning when it might be difficult to get along well with siblings or housemates. No matter what they do, you might become irritated by their antics. If you hide out in your bedroom or office until these feelings pass, an argument can be avoided. Libras eager to venture out and escape from reality for a short time could enjoy a leisurely lunch at a local restaurant and a few hours at the movies.

10. MONDAY. Surprising. Fair warning is given to Libra now. This is a day when life has plenty of surprises in store. One may be a feeling of restlessness that encourages crazy behavior that leads to doing something out of the ordinary. Be ready to work around problems and to find solutions to matters that have been left unresolved. A well-connected supporter might suddenly come up with assistance that can get a project moving in the right direction. A promotion, pay raise, or financial windfall could arrive unexpectedly, putting a happy smile on your face and solving a few of your current financial woes.

11. TUESDAY. Eventful. The golden light of the Sun happily entwines with stable Saturn, encouraging Libras to take action. Today you can make things happen in the way you want. This is a good time to sign or discuss a work agreement, a legal contract, or a public relations promotion. Spending time with people you care about, especially from the older generation such as a parent or elderly relative, can be emotionally fulfilling. It might be time to clean out and sort through clutter before the festive season arrives in full force.

Recycle clothes you no longer wear or want, sort through books and magazines, and dispose of out-of-date food.

12. WEDNESDAY. Lovely. A highly romantic frame of mind takes hold of you and can be enjoyed in true Libra style. Artful Venus rules your sign and also the main events of the day. Before dawn Venus merges with passionate Pluto, then slips into your Capricorn home and family sector to visit there until December 7. Spend time with someone you really care about, but guard against displaying possessive or jealous tendencies. Introducing a new color scheme, making alterations to free up more usable space, or totally revamping your home or office is an exciting endeavor into which you can put your whole heart and soul.

13. THURSDAY. Puzzling. Life is bound to be slightly suspenseful today. Sensitive emotional issues need to be handled with kid gloves. The Moon is full in the sign of Taurus, which introduces tension into intimate and professional partnerships. If joint finances are causing discord with a partner, it might be time to consult a financial expert or accountant to provide tips or investment advice. Get to the bottom of what has been going on. Do some research first so you have necessary information if you are considering making a major investment, switching banks, or applying for a larger line of credit. Instead of rushing around after work, relax and unwind.

14. FRIDAY. Uncertain. It could be difficult to keep your spirits high, but this depends on your personal values and beliefs. Stay alert. There is a good chance that you might hear of an opening that suits your present requirements. Libras who are on the job could find that a simple request turns into a big deal, with progress slow. Waiting for other people to take action could test your resolve, but be patient. Acting rashly could cause more harm than good. Plan a visit to catch up with a friend or relative, or you might even be able to reunite with a lost relative or a friend from your younger days.

15. SATURDAY. Bumpy. If life was a little tricky yesterday, it may be even more so today. On the positive side you should have energy to burn, making this a good day to tackle jobs that have been just waiting for action. However, proceed slowly to keep from having to correct errors or clean up a mess later on. Throwing yourself into community work or a school project could prove worthwhile as well as fun. Travel for pleasure may be on your mind. Unfortunately, if you set off now you might not experience an uneventful departure. Mix-ups, delays, or problems with important paperwork could hinder you and cause you to wish you had stayed home.

16. SUNDAY. Profitable. It would be a good idea to get up earlier than usual this morning in order to have a few extra moments just for you. With a multitude of celestial influences in force, take advantage of the unusual, the different, and the unexpected. There is the possibility of a surprising windfall. If this does happen, you will want to work out the best way to invest extra funds. Motivating Mars moves into Sagittarius, your house of daily environment, neighbors, close relatives, and all forms of communication. As a result, extra caution is advised from now until December 27 if you drive any type of vehicle or are involved in any part of the transportation industry.

17. MONDAY. Successful. Work interests and monetary concerns are to the fore. This is one of those days when making a decision will be difficult. However, your constructive frame of mind ensures that anything you undertake can be successfully completed and will meet your high standards. Your practical attitude also allows a pipedream to be turned into realistic plans for the future. You are apt to be busier than usual and expected to take on greater responsibility at work. If life appears to be getting too hectic or your workload is becoming too heavy, it might be time to start delegating what doesn't need your special touch.

18. TUESDAY. Deceptive. If money matters recently came between you and a loved one, this issue could come up again today. You might need to use all of your Libra charm and skills to find a compromise that keeps a battle of wills from developing all over again. Don't take anyone at face value; be alert for deceptive trends. There may be upsets with a friendship, a romantic affair, or a social event, so be prepared for delays or disappointment. Launching a new project should proceed smoothly, but be careful not to take on too much or you will end up overloaded and pressured.

19. WEDNESDAY. Challenging. Endeavoring to resolve problems could be frustrating. No matter what happens you may experience an overwhelming feeling that nothing is turning out as you envisioned. Have patience and this phase will pass. Do as much as you can, but don't feel guilty if you are unable to perform miracles. If you have not received a promised promotion or pay raise, it might not have anything to do with your work performance. Perhaps your company is not experiencing expected growth and cannot afford to give wage increases right now.

20. THURSDAY. Unsettling. This is one of those days when you may feel that you're just running around in circles. The workload could continue to pile up, and you may worry whether you can keep on top of it all. Pace yourself and take one step at a time. Your outlook is unlikely to improve if someone is in a nagging and critical mood, making it difficult for you to stay cool or to remain in good temper. Review situations from the past to ascertain where you now stand with an old problem. It may be time to try a totally different approach. This evening practice a form of meditation that reduces stress and attunes your inner being.

21. FRIDAY. Uplifting. Get set for a busy four weeks ahead. The Sun swings into Sagittarius, your sector of close companions, for a visit until December 21. You may spend more time running errands, visiting relatives, and getting together with neighbors. Entertaining, reestablishing contact with friends you haven't seen for a while, and attending community activities will be fun as you gear up for festive celebrations. In a spirited mood you will want to take sightseeing trips close to home and arrange short weekend adventures to explore your own locality. A period of expansion and striking out in a new direction is foreseen.

22. SATURDAY. Effervescent. The Moon enters your sign of Libra before dawn. If you are in the mood to party, this can be a fun day with lots of social activities to enjoy. Hurry through household duties that can't be put off, then head to the stores to purchase a new outfit or shoes that you have been yearning to buy. That may not suit your significant other, but you need to give yourself a treat every now and then. Get together with neighbors or close family members and begin making arrangements for a community holiday party. Purchasing real estate could provide a real sense of security and stability.

23. SUNDAY. Harmonious. This is another starred day to purchase a personal treat. You are apt to be in a very friendly and talkative mood as informative Mercury zips into your Sagittarius zone, meeting up with the Sun, Mars and Pluto. Mercury will accelerate your thought processes and verbal dexterity. Socializing and chatting will take precedence. You might spend more time than usual being involved in a local community event. This may be the cue to invite new people in the area to share your hospitality or just to get to know neighbors better. Attending a short educational course to broaden your knowledge is likely to appeal.

24. MONDAY. Fair. The slow rate of productivity on the job might be a concern as a new workweek begins. This could lead to the cancellation or postponement of a trip, meeting, or social activity. You may suffer foot-in-mouth disease today unless you watch what you say. Embarrassment could be the result of speaking up at the wrong time. Avoid gossiping as well. Otherwise you might blurt out a secret that was not supposed to be made public. Declare a truce with a loved one. Holding a grudge is a waste of time and energy, and is not the usual Libra mode of operation. Investigate advertised deals to consolidate debt and lower your monthly payments.

25. TUESDAY. Communicative. A happy and friendly atmosphere exists. You could be so extremely talkative that other people have a problem getting a word in edgewise. If you find it difficult to stop talking and listen for a while, or if you have a long list of chores to complete, it might be a good idea to go off on your own for a few hours until you are able to catch up. Money could be a topic of discussion. Unforeseen expenses might increase pressure on an already depleted bank balance. Even if your cash flow is not a problem, this is not a good day to splurge.

26. WEDNESDAY. Expansive. Things should continue to go reasonably well for Libra as the Sun and Mercury move together through Sagittarius, your communication zone. Take advantage of opportunities that suddenly arise and good ideas that flash into mind. If you are planning to buy a new car, begin the process now. Your ability to negotiate and to drive a hard bargain is enhanced at this time. Pluto reenters Capricorn, your family sector, which encourages you to begin a major transformation of living quarters or to consider moving to another location. This might even mean relocating overseas for business or employment purposes.

27. THURSDAY. Renewing. It is out with the old and in with the new today. A New Moon in Sagittarius offers a fresh chapter in your everyday communications. This is a great opportunity to enroll in a public speaking course or begin studying another language to improve your overall communication skills. It is also a good time to write personal greetings, issue special invitations, or make important phone calls. Selecting a new car or computer equipment to purchase should proceed without a hitch. Today erratic Uranus moves forward in Pisces, your house of health and working conditions. So interesting solutions to outstanding problems will come to mind, being a mix of rational thought and intuition.

28. FRIDAY. Opportune. Taking action can make your dreams come true. Libra people have the gift of gab today, with the ability to talk your way out of any tight situation. Any type of communication should go well. You might be inspired to begin a project that requires mental focus and great attention to detail. Drivers should be more wary on the road, especially guarding against a tendency to speed or to ignore warning signs. Public speakers, lecturers, or salespeople should experience a very productive phase. Introduce a little romance and delight into the evening, spending the night at home with your loved one.

29. SATURDAY. Satisfying. You are likely to be in a fix-it-up mood. A project that calls for both practical and artistic ideas can be a stimulating challenge. Or you may opt to purchase a map and become a tourist in your own city, which can open your eyes to what is new. You could also begin to realize how lucky you are to live in an area that provides such a diverse range of activities and options. If you are unattached, you might be romantically attracted to someone considerably younger or older than you are. This is a good day for neighborly social activities or to entertain in the comfort of your own home.

30. SUNDAY. Enjoyable. Catch up on your beauty sleep, getting up later than usual this morning. A very easygoing and affectionate mood prevails, with enjoyment coming from time spent in the company of some favorite people. It's fine to see the best in everyone providing you are realistic and not gullible. Family or real estate decisions can be made with ease. Put your imagination and creative expertise to good use. Making holiday gifts could be a pleasurable way to keep occupied and to save money, and your efforts are sure to be appreciated by the recipients of your talent.

December 2008

1. MONDAY. Pleasant. Look forward to a great day on the domestic front and a most pleasant way to start the last month of 2008. Your ruler Venus merges with abundant Jupiter, increasing harmony and love within your home and family life. This means that even focusing on daily chores will be both satisfying and productive. Luck is on your side in romance, providing the opportunity to deepen the emotion in your love affair. This is also a wonderful time to take off on a trip in the company of people you enjoy the most. Just be careful not to overindulge in the good things of life.

2. TUESDAY. Stimulating. This is a starred day for getting along well with other people. Enjoyment comes from being friendly and outgoing. Identify something lively to look forward to at the end of your working day so that motivation remains high. Don't hesitate to do things on the spur of the moment. Take loved ones by surprise if you don't have any prearranged plans for this evening. Big department stores may beckon, and you won't need much encouragement to venture out and check what is on sale or newly arrived. Be discerning if purchasing gifts because your generous streak could encourage overspending.

3. WEDNESDAY. Diverse. This is another day when you need plenty of amusement and distraction to keep boredom and restlessness from disrupting your focus. Create your own diversions by rearranging your schedule in order to generate more interest. The urge to splurge remains in full force, so try to be modest with your spending. An invitation to take part in an entertaining event or a neighborhood get-together could arouse a thrill of anticipation for the community-minded Libra. Later in the evening you might prefer to step back from the whirl of social life and spend quality time with your mate or with certain family members.

4. THURSDAY. Busy. As the countdown to the holidays begins, you are apt to feel snowed under with too much to do and not enough time to it all. This is not a day to exercise your normal procrastination mode. Nor should you worry about who is pulling their weight or shirking their responsibilities. Start at the top of your workload and move through as quickly and efficiently as you can. Speak to a trusted coworker if you have need a sounding board for problems or concerns. This person can honestly tell you whether you have a legitimate reason to complain. Keep to a good nutritional diet and drink plenty of water.

5. FRIDAY. Buoyant. You are likely to bounce into the day with a spring in your step even if the weather is a little overcast. Do all that you can to remain healthy. Avoid being exposed to cold winds or cool responses. Remain open to new ways of doing the same old chores in order to come up with more efficient processes. Health problems could disrupt your working day. A coworker might call in sick, forcing you to take over their tasks as well as your own. You can become frustrated or you can remain calm, jumping in doing the best that you can under the circumstances.

6. SATURDAY. Slow. The day is apt to be a little off-key, and you will need to exert extra effort to put matters right. Worries regarding a potential reshuffling of employees or duties at your place of business, or a promised promotion that hasn't been forthcoming, should begin to clear up now. A situation that has been upsetting is beginning to clear. You should enjoy the process of writing holiday cards, organizing your gift list, or deciding on a festive menu. Something you were hoping to keep a secret might become public knowledge if you do not guard what you say. Keep amusement low-key. Plan a romantic meal for two so that you can spend time alone with your significant other.

7. SUNDAY. Starred. Cuddle up with someone special and enjoy being together this morning. If you are attending a special event, you should be at your charming best, lapping up the limelight and social atmosphere. Your ruler Venus glides into your solar house of Aquarius, which promises plenty of romance and good fun throughout the festive period. Solo Libras attending a party or enjoying other social activities can expect to meet a number of potential love interests. There is an increased chance of encountering that special someone who will make your heart flutter wildly. As a Libra you are known for a sense of style and good taste, and settling for second best will not be an option now.

8. MONDAY. Smooth. Friendly and amicable trends prevail. Other people might be so talkative that it seems impossible to complete your long list of chores waiting for action. Projecting more energy outward and joining with people in ventures that you might otherwise tackle on your own should be productive. This is a good day for Libra parents to take children off to the mall to find out what they really want as their main gift. Imagination knows no bounds, and letting your creative juices flow can be a joyful experience. Your diplomatic skills might be put to the test early this afternoon, but with tact any tension should quickly pass and be forgotten.

9. TUESDAY. Problematic. Remain focused on the tasks right in front of you. Don't be swayed into beginning the next item on your to-do list until each chore is completed in turn. It is a definite case today of make love, not war. There may be an excess of tension between you and your mate or partner. Unless this is expressed in a positive manner, arguments are likely to erupt. A bill from a government authority could prove upsetting, but there may not be anything you can do about it other than pay up first and complain later. Make sure any legal or financial transaction is attended to promptly to reduce the possibility of a fine or other penalty.

10. WEDNESDAY. Uncertain. Leave home a little earlier than usual because you are apt to encounter delays and traffic snarls. Altering your everyday agenda should help reduce anxiety and the restlessness you are bound to experience today. Questions may be raised regarding the cost of socializing, so be prepared with satisfactory answers in the form of comparison prices. If your mate or partner is the one depleting the budget, it might not be easy to speak up or to put your foot down. However, cooperation can be achieved if your timing is right. Set the scene and wait until later this evening to broach the subject.

11. THURSDAY. Fair. The idea of breaking out of your routine may appeal on one level. However, you will probably be more than content to just think about doing so without taking drastic action. The desire to expand your present knowledge and to broaden your life experiences may be the encouragement you need to consider ways of exploring new cultures or of taking advanced classes. Handle the moods of other people with care. An in-law or relative could be a little disagreeable, or perhaps your tolerance level is lower than normal. A pending legal decision should be made first thing this morning rather than after lunch.

12. FRIDAY. Sensitive. The Gemini Full Moon could strain relations between friends of yours who live near you and those who live far away. Patience is needed if you are setting off on distant travels. There may be a number of irritations and annoyances to cope with. If you are booking an interstate or international flight, take time to avoid overlooking important details. Your popularity is about to rise within the family fold. Mercury, the messenger planet, enters Capricorn, your solar sector of close environment. This can bring a nostalgic and sentimental mood as your thoughts turn to family, home affairs, and childhood events from the past.

13. SATURDAY. Low-key. Although your enthusiasm may be high, your energy resources might be below par. If you have been putting off having a quiet word with a loved one, take them aside and do so today. Make sure they know you are there for them, offering support, even if you are unhappy with some facets of their behavior. Take a quick look around the house and decide if you need to make any changes. Perhaps all that is required is a thorough cleaning and sprucing up in time for the upcoming holidays. If you haven't gotten out festive decorations, gather the family and make this a fun activity for everyone to share.

14. SUNDAY. Active. The so-called lazy and leisure day of the week may be anything but relaxing for you. Self-employed Libras might have to choose between finishing urgent work or taking time out to socialize with family members or friends. If work wins out, make sure you also snatch some time to have fun. If not working or on call, break out of your Sunday routine and head off for an adventurous outing. Libras who haven't had much time or opportunity to get out and party should go to town or at least the shopping mall. Romance is high on the agenda, and singles could meet someone who sparks immediate interest.

15. MONDAY. Tricky. Take care to avoid communication mix-ups or breakdowns. Or your computer could misbehave, causing frustration. There should be good news regarding a salary increase, business negotiations, or a promotion. Spend time with friends, especially if you need to resolve a problem or disagreement that sprung up between you recently. A situation on the job might require more creative effort than you are able to give. Speak to those in authority if you feel that you are being disadvantaged in some way. Do your best to unwind in a gentle manner this evening rather than rushing around.

16. TUESDAY. Varied. Current celestial influences bring energized and inspired creativity to the fore. Complex issues are also likely to emerge when other people see things in a very different light from the way you do. Someone may try to impose views and opinions on you. Do all that you can to avoid mix-ups and misunderstandings with neighbors or your siblings. Crossed wires regarding arrangements for a social function could also cause confusion. Finish decorating the house or hanging festive decorations outside at home or at the office if this task has not already been completed. Dinner at a restaurant or going to the movies with friends could bring the day to a happy conclusion.

17. WEDNESDAY. Manageable. Facing up to strenuous or complicated chores is not your strong point today. If possible, wiggle out of these tasks and focus on simple, monotonous work that you hardly need to think about. There is the potential for steady progress as you advance toward a looming deadline. Keep your social calendar open for spur-of-the-moment invitations, which may have a positive impact on business or career advancement. Libras who are on the job should be ready to accept behind-the-scenes assistance. Put your feet up whenever the opportunity arises, and include frequent rest breaks to restore vitality and energy.

18. THURSDAY. Subdued. This is another day when pampering and withdrawing from the limelight are preferred options. Do some serious thinking about your future plans, and review how you are progressing toward current goals. You could be torn between making changes and sticking to the status quo. If you cannot decide what is best to do, ask someone you admire for advice. Unless constructive criticism is offered, refuse to worry about any negative comments that are directed at you. If a loved one is overly critical or in a nitpicking frame of mind, it might be wise to ignore their remarks and retreat. You probably won't be in the mood nor have the energy to retaliate.

19. FRIDAY. Empowering. By midmorning your energy should return in full, which could be the cue to head for the department stores. Partying continues over the next few weeks, and you will want to look your best at all times. If you seem to have nothing special to wear to upcoming social functions, this is the perfect time to change that by engaging in some serious retail therapy. A new hairstyle, scent, and accessories could complete the picture, giving both your appearance and confidence a big boost. If you are in the mood for romance, don't miss out; mix and mingle, and romance could blossom.

20. SATURDAY. Renewing. Libras are definitely in the mood for self-nurturing and pampering. A relaxing body massage or facial would be a great way to start the weekend. A mini treat consisting of your favorite magazines, chocolates, or designer perfume could be the perfect indulgence. Being a social butterfly and having a fun time will be a priority for young Libras. Ideally, you should choose a social setting where your charm, friendliness, and generous hospitality shine through. A friend could play matchmaker, or in some way be instrumental in introducing a new romantic acquaintance or friend into your social circle.

21. SUNDAY. Promising. A loved one might become obsessed about something you don't even find interesting. It may be better to let them sort it out without any interference. During the past four weeks running errands, chatting with neighbors, and venturing out have kept you on the go. Starting today, however, your preference may be to remain closer to home base and let other people come to visit you. With the Sun now visiting Capricorn, your sector of home and close environment, your mood becomes more family oriented. Being with your nearest and dearest will be most satisfying. Finding new ways to express your creative talents can give you enormous satisfaction.

22. MONDAY. Powerful. Financially, there may be an unfinished business matter or a home issue that stretches your patience. Good budgeting is the key to reducing financial stress during this potentially expensive period of the year. A loved one could throw their weight around, or there may be a contentious situation where you are expected to yield and to compromise. Don't worry. This may be a case of losing one battle but eventually winning the war. Inspiration encourages Libras to implement life changes and to plan a move in a new direction. Don't settle for minor goals. Aim for something big that will lead to positive transformation.

23. TUESDAY. Productive. Shrewd money management will help you get ahead and stay ahead. Pay more attention to a debt or some financial obligation that has been hanging around. Pay it off or write it off. Try to finish up holiday gift shopping. Buy some food and drink treats for your family and guests to share and enjoy. You are feeling generous, but be sure to keep a watchful eye on price tags so you don't get carried away and exceed your budget. Staying within your own four walls will appeal most this evening. Use this time to finalize festive preparations so that nothing is left till the last minute.

24. WEDNESDAY. Eventful. If you still have chores to attend to before the celebrating begins, you are in luck. This is a great day for running around town and finishing up all that you need to do. If you are in a hurry, avoid talkative neighbors or friends or you may not get very much accomplished. You could be more friendly and outgoing as well, so you will have trouble trying to cut discussions short. On this Christmas Eve a sentimental mood could find you sharing a meal with extended family members or friends before heading out to a special gathering. Enjoy the spirit.

25. THURSDAY. Merry Christmas! This will be a busy day whether you are visiting or catering to family members and guests at home. Even if you aren't celebrating the day you will be in the mood to share good cheer with your nearest and dearest as well as special family friends. Someone who is sometimes difficult to please is likely to put on a happy face, allowing everyone to have an enjoyable, relaxing day. Consider inviting a coworker who is far from home to share your festive cheer and hospitality. Make sure you have the guest room ready and the pantry well stocked so that the arrival of unexpected guests doesn't take you by surprise.

26. FRIDAY. Carefree. Relax and enjoy another happy day to celebrate the season. Pleasure comes from spending time with loved ones. You will prefer remaining among your home comforts as you recover from yesterday's activities. After the cleanup is finished and the house is back to normal, plan to sit back, snack on leftovers, and enjoy browsing through your Christmas gifts. Watching favorite television shows, chatting or playing on the computer, or reading a good book could also appeal. If venturing out of the house, a newly released movie or a live concert would be a good way to spend a few hours. Take extra care on the roads, whether driving or walking.

27. SATURDAY. Harmonious. Compassion, love, and understanding are strong emotions that you are apt to experience in full measure today. Loved ones are likely to benefit the most from these feelings because you are willing to forgive past transgressions. Trust your good Libra instincts when talking with other people. Avoid discussing subjects that you sense could be off limits. Enthusiastic Mars marches into your Capricorn sector of home and family, bringing positive energy into this area of your life. Relocating, building a new home, or renovating an existing property may be put on your agenda now.

28. SUNDAY. Intense. It is time for Libra to get physical even if the weather is not ideal for outdoor activities. You are blessed with energetic stars due to the combination of Mars and Pluto, making this a great time to investigate a fitness program that can enhance your overall health and well-being. Implementing major transformations around the house is also possible now. Do-it-yourself projects can successfully move forward. Someone within the family could be rather quick-tempered or overly bossy. Rather than going on the defensive, try to steer clear of conflict. If this is not possible, it will be better to express your views in a calm manner and then be ready to forgive and forget.

29. MONDAY. Fruitful. You could feel rather self-indulgent and rightfully so if you have been busy entertaining and catering to family members and guests over the last week. If you don't have to be on the job, put your feet up and enjoy quiet time at home. If you have energy to burn, perhaps the end-of-year sales will beckon instead. Libras who received unwanted gifts or an item that didn't work should receive a full refund even without the receipt. Just apply caution if you have a limited amount of money to spend on sale items. Whether your passion involves exploring your creativity, finding a romantic partner, or generating more income, energy exerted in any of these areas should bear fruit.

30. TUESDAY. Joyful. Being part of a loving family produces happiness and blessings, but having to deal with domestic problems is also a part of life's experiences. Your popularity remains high, and your social calendar might still be bulging with people to visit and places to see. If you have the time, do something out of the ordinary to add variety to your day. Even Libras who are looking forward to a big night out tomorrow are likely to go out socializing this evening. If expecting guests over the next few days take extra precautions when working in the kitchen.

31. WEDNESDAY. Fortunate. The final day of the year should find you relaxed and contented. Lucky trends greet Libras, promising that whatever you attempt will turn out exactly as you envision. Your social, outgoing mood ensures that you will enjoy mixing and mingling throughout the day. Spending time with family members, close friends, and those who are on the same wavelength as you can be especially memorable. If you are entertaining at home this evening expect everything to go smoothly, with all guests having a wonderful time as you welcome in 2009. Happy New Year!

WHAT DOES YOUR FUTURE HOLD?

DISCOVER IT IN *ASTROANALYSIS*—

**COMPLETELY REVISED THROUGH THE YEAR 2015,
THESE GUIDES INCLUDE COLOR-CODED CHARTS FOR
TOTAL ASTROLOGICAL EVALUATION,
PLANET TABLES AND CUSP CHARTS,
AND STREAMLINED INFORMATION.**

ARIES	0-425-17558-8
TAURUS	0-425-17559-6
GEMINI	0-425-17560-X
CANCER	0-425-17561-8
LEO	0-425-17562-6
VIRGO	0-425-17563-4
LIBRA	0-425-17564-2
SCORPIO	0-425-17565-0
SAGITTARIUS	0-425-17566-9
CAPRICORN	0-425-17567-7
AQUARIUS	0-425-17568-5
PISCES	0-425-17569-3

Available wherever books are sold or at penguin.com

#1 *New York Times* bestselling author
Sylvia Browne

Book of Dreams

Sylvia Browne takes us on an
unprecedented journey through the
world of dreams—and reveals how they
can influence everything from health
and careers to love and happiness.

#1 *New York Times* bestselling author
Sylvia Browne

Visits from the Afterlife

With her sixth sense, coupled with stirring true
encounters, Sylvia Browne describes visitations
with ghosts, in-transition spirits, and other
troubled souls seeking peace and closure.
Through these spiritual visits, Browne explains
the reasons behind many of the world's most
bizarre and mysterious hauntings.